EASTERN TURKEY
A Guide and History

EASTERN TURKEY

A Guide and History

GWYN WILLIAMS

FABER AND FABER

3 Queen Square

London

First published in 1972
by Faber and Faber Limited
3 Queen Square London WC1
Printed in Great Britain by
R. MacLehose and Company Limited Glasgow
All rights reserved

ISBN 0 571 09342 6

Contents

※※※

Preface   *page* 13

PART I BACKGROUND

Introduction   17

How to Get to Eastern Turkey and Some Reasons for Going   21

Topography and Products   28

Peoples and Cultures of Eastern Turkey   33
    Prehistory   33
    The Hittites   39
    The Urartians   42
    The Phrygians   47
    The Persians   48
    The Armenians   51
    Alexander the Great and Hellenisation   58
    The Galatians   59
    The Kurds   61
    The Nestorians   66
    The Romans   67
    The Byzantines   70
    The Seljuks   73
    The Crusaders   79
    The Mongols   80
    The Georgians   81
    The Laz   83
    The Danishmends   84

Contents

The Artuks   page 84
Beys and Emirs   86
The Arabs   87
The Ottomans   87

Moslem Architecture in Eastern Turkey   90

Common Words and Elements in Place-names   94

PART II ITINERARIES

The Van Region   99
    Lake Van   104
    Environs of Van   105
    Van Kalesi   106
    Toprak Kale   108
    Öğrenburc   112
    Aghtamar Island   115
    The Circuit of Lake Van   118
    Adilcevaz   120
    Ahlat   122
    Tatvan   124

Hakkari   127

Westwards from Tatvan through Bitlis   132

Siirt and Tillo   138

Siirt to Diyarbakır   142

Muş and Bingöl   144

Elazığ and Harput   147

The Keban Dam   151

Elazığ to Diyarbakır   154

Mardin   160

Urfa   163
    Sultantepe   168
    Sumatar   170
    Harran   170

Contents

Urfa to Gaziantep   *page* 176

Gaziantep to Malatya   179

Erzincan and Altıntepe   186

Divriği   190

Erzurum   193

Eastwards from Erzurum   201
    Ararat   203
    Doğubeyazit   206

Kars   208

Ani   211

To Artvin and the Black Sea   214

The Pontic Coast   217
    Ordu   218
    Giresun   218
    Trabzon   219
    Rize   224
    Hopa   226

Trabzon to Erzurum   227
    Sumela   227
    The Way Back   228

Appendix: Eastern Turkey for the Alpinist Traveller by
           Sidney E. P. Nowill   231

Bibliography   247

Index   251

Illustrations

PLATES

1. Bobek Tepesi (3,520 metres) on Sat Dağ, Hakkari   *facing page*   32
2. Zab River with Cilo Dağ   33
3. Van Kalesi: entrance to underground palace   48
4. Toprak Kale: entrance to underground palace   48
5. Urartian cuneiform recently uncovered at Cavuştepe   48
6. Tumbled head of Zeus on Nimrut Dağ   49
7. Nestorian church in Zab Valley   49
8. Kurdish women at Eleşkirt   64
9. Kurdish children at Öğrenburc   64
10. The Tahir Pass (2,400 metres) in early November   65
11. Near the Tahir Pass: house with cones of cowdung fuel   65
12. Sumela Monastery   80
13. Harput: castle and early Christian church   81
14. Aghtamar Island: Lake Van   81
15. Aghtamar Island: the church   112
16. Aghtamar Church: east end   112
17. Aghtamar Church: detail of south-east corner   112
18. Hoşap Castle   113
19. Seljuk cemetery: Gevaş   128
20. Seljuk tomb: Gevaş   128
21. Seljuk cemetery: Ahlat   129
22. Mardin   129
23. Mardin: Şehidiye Cami   144
24. Tombs near Eski Van   145
25. Siirt: repairs to Ulu Cami minaret   145
26. Tillo: Ibrahim Hakki's house   160

Illustrations

27. Tillo: pistachios growing   *facing page* 160
28. Urfa: Halil ur Rahman Mosque   161
29. Urfa: sacred carp   161
30. Houses at Harran   176
31. Tobacco drying at Eski Malatya   176
32. Diyarbakır: the walls   177
33. Diyarbakır: Deliler Han   177
34. Diyarbakır: the Tigris from the walls   192
35. Minaret at Diyarbakır   192
36. Erzurum: interior of Çifte Minare Medrese   193
37. Doğubeyazit: Ishak Paşa Saray and old village 193
38. Ararat from Doğubeyazit   208
39. Gümüşhane   208
40. Trabzon: Aya Sofya   209
41. Trabzon: Gülbahar Hatun Mosque   209
42. Murgul: copper works   224
43. Rize   225
44. Giresun   225

Gratitude is expressed to Mr. Sidney Nowill for Plate 1 and to the Turkish Tourist Bureau for Plates 6, 12, 18, 22, 23, 41, 42 and 44. The other photographs are by the author.

MAP   *pages 22 and 23*

Preface

Any book on Turkey has to face the spelling of place-names. Turkish orthography is more rational and consistent than most but the alphabet introduced by Ataturk, to the benefit of Turk and foreigner, has some traps for the newcomer to Turkey. Some of these are explained in the section on Common Words and Place-names. I have used the current spelling of place-names so that the traveller may recognise the destination he is seeking, on signpost, bus and railway station, as in Muş, Elazığ, Trabzon, Izmir and Irak. In Diyarbakır the first *i* is dotted and the second is not. Malazgirt also appears as Manzikert, which was its name when the battle was fought in 1071. I have used some non-Turkish forms where these have become familiar to the English reader, as in Soliman the Magnificent, Seljuk, Ottoman, Moslem.

I wish to thank the Turkish Government Tourist Bureau for information, for the supply of photographs and for financial help on one of my journeys in eastern Anatolia. To Mr. Sidney Nowill I am indebted not only for his *Appendix on Eastern Turkey for the Alpinist Traveller* but for his lovely photograph of Bobek Tepesi. I am grateful to Dr. Akşit Göktürk for help in translation from Turkish and for his cheerful and patient company on journeys we did together. Any errors in translation, in transliteration or in presentation of facts, as well as the views expressed on the country, its people and its history, are entirely my own, except where I quote a source. And once again I am indebted to Mr. Alan Pringle of Faber and Faber for his friendly patience and constructive helpfulness throughout my planning and writing of this book.

To the people of eastern Turkey, officials at all levels, journalists, teachers, professional men, bus and taxi drivers, particularly Haci Muhittin of Van, shopkeepers and the man in the street or the field, from all of whom I experienced an unfailing friendliness, I give my thanks and recommend the traveller.

❧ Part I ❧
BACKGROUND

Introduction

✶✶✶✶

This book completes a view of Turkey which I began in *Turkey: A Traveller's Guide and History*.[1] I plan to take in what I can of Anatolia east of roughly Longitude 36.5. The most satisfactory experience I had in writing the earlier book was the realisation of how much of our western culture came into existence in Aegean Turkey, of how immigrant Greeks in the fruitful landscape and agreeable climate of a lovely and varied stretch of coast (from present Kaş to Çanakkale but chiefly in the centre of that region) made for themselves the prosperity and leisure in which their restless minds were able to absorb and evaluate in the first millennium B.C. what had been slowly and intermittently achieved over the previous seven or eight millennia in the hinterland of Asia Minor and the Fertile Crescent. Science, philosophy, history, epic and lyrical poetry and town-planning all began on that Aegean coast.

This present book attempts to take us back to the beginnings. I see Anatolia, the home of the Great Mother, as our homeland, as a point of departure for us in the west. I think it is necessary for us to consider how the impulses of our civilisation began and it's surely salutary for us to look about us in our world today to see what we have done with the great impulses. I feel an excitement, an awe, a fear in approaching eastern Anatolia. Fear because I've been corrupted by town living, awe because I'm conscious of distant beginnings which in fact don't seem to be so far away in time. I often think I'm nearer to the Urartians than I am to people I meet in Ankara or London, and I'm glad to have Dr. Arnold Toynbee's support for my feeling that we are really contemporary.

Eastern Turkey is a nodal point, a stopping and starting place in the

[1] Faber and Faber, 1967.

Introduction

history of our civilisation. Much that we take for granted in our way of life started there, many formative and destructive influences have passed through it and it has been a protective bulwark against pressures which would have altered us to an incalculable degree. What would Europe be like today if the Arabs, who weren't very good at sea, had not been held there by the Byzantines and the Armenians, if they had swarmed westwards to destroy Byzantium and complete their pincer movement, the left flank of which established itself for centuries in Spain? We might have had Alhambras in Vienna, Rome and Paris but surely not a Renaissance.

Ten thousand years ago, and this is as far as we can safely go back at the moment, the southern part of eastern Anatolia was already inhabited by a Mediterranean type of man, people very like us. (I may here be speaking as a Welshman. The English may not take so kindly to being likened to Italians, Berbers and Armenians and may in fact have sound ethnological reasons for their objection.) As in Europe, the last Ice Age was over. Here it had only ice-capped the Armenian plateau of the north-east and by this time the ice had mostly melted away. The upper reaches of the Euphrates and the Tigris, and the mountain ranges through which these great rivers cut their way to the south, enjoyed a temperate and rain-moistened climate. The southern slopes of this region formed the nucleus or central area of what Breasted named the Fertile Crescent, a belt of early habitation running northwards from the Dead Sea, along the mountains into Asia Minor, across the Euphrates and Tigris, then curving down along what are today the western mountains of Iran. It was along this belt that early agriculture and the first domestication of animals took place. South-eastern Anatolia and nearby north-western Persia were the home of the wild sheep and of wild wheat and barley. Eastern Anatolia is also the home of the grape. A late Hittite rock sculpture at Ivriz shows a king doing homage to a weather god who holds a sheaf of barley in one hand and a bunch of grapes in the other. A relief sculpture from the Lion Gate at Malatya shows the weather god arriving in an ox-drawn chariot and receiving a libation from a local king. The libation is being carefully poured from a jug into a great jar and I don't suppose the liquid was water.[1] It is reasonable therefore to suppose that knowledge of these basic things originated in the area under discussion and from there spread along both arms of the Crescent eventually to reach Egypt and Sumeria. Animals tamed during

[1] Seton Lloyd, *Highland Peoples of Anatolia*, illustration no. 103.

this Neolithic stage of Anatolian development were also the pig, goat and dog, animals native to the region but of wider provenance as well. Animals hunted here at this early stage were wild sheep and cattle, the wild ass, several sorts of deer, ibex, wild boar, hare and leopard. Archaeological evidence shows that Çatal Hüyük in the seventh millennium B.C. had the most varied diet of any known Near Eastern Neolithic site.[1] Still further west there had already been Hacılar, which about the year 7000 B.C. had mud-brick buildings on stone foundations, plastered floors and walls, agriculture and a domesticated dog, but no other domesticated animals and no pottery. Çatal Hüyük, from about 6700 B.C., is much more advanced and according to Mellaart a south-eastern cultural movement is indicated, for the Neolithic cultures of Mersin and the Amuq plain of north Syria are offshoots of Çatal Hüyük.[2] The prerequisites of civilisation had been evolved, architecture, a dependence on production rather than on hunting for food and a widening domestication of animals. The great southward-flowing rivers were the pathway for the knowledge of these things[3] and the bearers of the alluvium and water which were to make possible more intensive cultivation in lower Mesopotamia. Obsidian for tools and weapons was exported from the volcanic regions of central and eastern Anatolia from about 8000 B.C. and the knowledge of the Neolithic Revolution, as Gordon Childe has called this momentous change of direction in human living, might have been carried by this trade.

Prehistoric Anatolia has not so far been so well served by archaeology as Syria, Irak and Palestine but recent excavations encourage a growing certainty that here we have an important, perhaps the most important place of origin. Enquiry into the prehistoric habitation of eastern Anatolia is now being systematically stepped up and the evidence already garnered foreshadows a rapid and considerable expansion of our knowledge of early man in this part of the world.

So to the fascination of eastern Anatolia for the traveller jaded with developed holiday places, the unspoilt Turkish towns and villages, the

[1] James Mellaart, *Anatolia before c. 4000 B.C.*, Cambridge Ancient History Fascicle. 1967, p. 8. Çatal Hüyük is near enough to our area for its evidence to be valid here.

[2] ibid., p. 12.

[3] The rivers are still used for smuggling and Herodotus gives an interesting description of how wine was carried down from Armenia to Babylon in huge coracles which were broken up when the wine had been sold. See p. 52.

wonderful mountain scenery, the very vastness (this book covers roughly three hundred thousand square kilometres of sparsely populated country), to all this will be added the interest of a cultural pilgrimage to the beginnings of our civilisation.

How to Get to Eastern Turkey
and Some Reasons for Going

The area I am attempting to cover is bounded to the north by the
Black Sea, to the east by the U.S.S.R. republics of Georgia and Armenia
and by Iran, and to the south by Irak and Syria. The western boundary
is a line I have drawn on the map from just east of Antakya up to east
of Samsun. It is an upland region, mostly over 900 metres and rising
to over 5,000. There is much to attract the traveller who is not in too
great a hurry, mountain climbing with as yet unclimbed peaks and
uncharted glaciers, facilities for winter sports and places where the
horse-drawn sledge is the only means of conveyance in winter, many
kinds of game and wild animals for observation or shooting, trout-
fishing in unfished lakes and streams, many kinds of plants and trees,
some rare and even unrecorded, for the botanist, Hittite and Urartian
sites, relics of north Syrian planet-worship, Georgian and Armenian
churches, castles and irrigation systems, lovely Seljuk architecture,
strange monuments, the vast Lake Van, 1,500 metres above sea level,
with its silk-soft water and ancient riparian vestiges, Mount Ararat,
the probing modernisation of our present age, a new oilfield, new
roads, hydro-electric projects, new industries. And incomparable
scenery. There are interesting people to be met, settled, semi-nomadic
and nomadic, the tough, colourful Kurds, the charming Lazes and
Turkish officials tackling the problems of road-building, electrification,
re-afforestation, food production and education.

Eastern Turkey is not difficult to get to or to travel about. You can
do most of it in a good car if you take time where there are potholes
and rocks. From town to town, that is. Some of the most interesting
sites have as yet no good road to them and involve long walks or rides

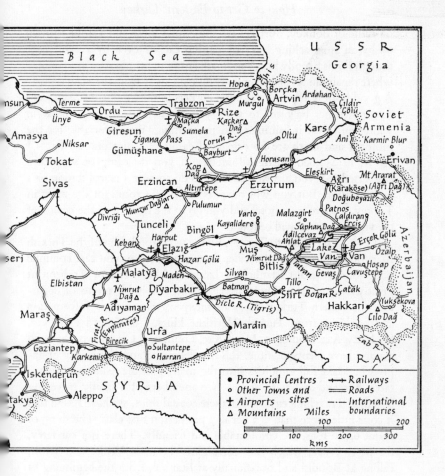

Black Sea

U S S R
Georgia

nsun   Terme   Ordu   Trabzon   Hopa   Borçka   Ardahan
Ünye   Maçka   Rize   Murgul   Artvin   Çıldır
Amasya   Niksar   Giresun   Sumela   Kaçkar   Oltu   Gölü   Soviet
           Zigana Pass   Dağ   Kars   Armenia
Tokat   Gümüşhane   Bayburt   Çoruh R.   Ani   Karmir Blur
                              Horasan   Erivan
Sivas   Erzincan   Kop   Eleşkirt   Ağrı   Mt Ararat
                           Dağ   Erzurum   (Karaköse) (Ağrı Dağ)
                 Altıntepe   Doğubeyazit
           Munzur Dağları   Varto   Malazgirt   Patnos
Divriği   Pulumur   Kayalidere   Süphan Dağ   Çaldıran
        Tunceli   Bingöl   Adilcevaz   Erciş
           Harput   Muş   Ahlat   Erçek Gölü
Keban   Elazığ   Nimrut Dağ   Lake   Van   Özalp
seri   Hazar Gölü   Silvan   Bitlis   Tatvan Gevaş   Hoşap
        Malatya   Maden   Batman   Tillo   Çavuştepe
Elbistan   Nimrut   Diyarbakır   Dicle R. (Tigris)   Siirt   Botan R.   Çatak
           Dağ   Hakkari   Yüksekova
Maraş   Adıyaman   Mardin   Cılo Dağ
                    Fırat R.   Zab R.
Gaziantep   (Euphrates)   Urfa   I R A K
        Birecik   Sultantepe
İskenderun   Karkemiş   Harran
           S Y R I A   Azerbaijan
takya   Aleppo

● Provincial Centres	—+— Railways
○ Other Towns and sites	=== Roads
✝ Airports	— · — International
△ Mountains	boundaries

Miles
0   100   200
0   100   200   300
kms

on mule or donkey. Surfaces are sometimes loose and a stone thrown up by an approaching lorry or passing car, or even by a small boy, though this is happily rare, can smash lamps or windscreen in a country where repairs and replacements are difficult away from the main centres. A good horn is a comfort at blind corners in the mountains. And jeeps can sometimes be hired to spare you the trickiest driving. Snow in winter and dust in summer can make things uncomfortable for the motorist and there are no organised camp sites, not one, so far as I know, in 250,000 square kilometres. If you do camp or sleep in a converted van you are well advised to do so near a petrol station or a police station. But you will never be short of a room for the night in Turkey. If there is no hotel and you go to the head man, the *muhtar* of the village, a room will be found for you.

If you come by sea to Turkey, by the very good ships of the Turkish Maritime Lines from Marseille, Genoa or Venice, you can continue your journey from Istanbul or Izmir to Iskenderun or Trabzon at greatly reduced rates. These latter ports are admirable points of departure for eastern Turkey. Cars are inexpensively carried. (Information and bookings from Turkish Maritime Lines, c/o Walford Lines Ltd, St. Mary Axe House, St. Mary Axe, London, E.C.3.) If you have no car and have plenty of time, this is a delightful and cheap way of approach. Make full enquiries into the many possible reductions, return fares, husband and wife or just two members of a family travelling together. Travelling *en famille* in these coastal ships, we have found that it costs little more than £2 per day per person first class. The ships, of about 6,000 tons, are comfortable and friendly. There is a car ferry, the M/F *Truva*, which runs fortnightly between Venice and Izmir, calling at Brindisi and occasionally at Istanbul, from the beginning of April to the end of October. It offers cabins, dormitories or Pullman seats in which you can sleep. You eat at a cafeteria. It takes three days from Venice. Rates are from 1,260 Turkish liras (1st de luxe) to 279 Tl for a Pullman seat. Car freight according to size, about £10 for a family car. And all this, except for food in the cafeteria, you can pay for in sterling in London.

If you land at Istanbul or Izmir and you are going to drive, it will take you two days to get to eastern Turkey, either through Ankara and Samsun to the north coast or through Konya and Adana to the south. If you land at Iskenderun you can see a good deal of eastern Anatolia by driving to Trabzon, following the route Gaziantep-Urfa-Diyarbakır-

Bitlis-Van-Ağrı-Erzurum-Gümüşhane-Trabzon.[1] From Trabzon you could return by ship or drive along the coast road to Samsun and then to Ankara.

The easiest way to get to eastern Turkey is by air. Turkish Airlines (Turk Hava Yolları) run an excellent and not expensive service from Istanbul and Ankara to Malatya, Elazığ, Diyarbakır, Van, Sivas, Erzurum and Trabzon and from these centres there is usually a bus, minibus or *dolmuş* (shared taxi) to smaller places. Cheap and comfortable long-distance buses run from Istanbul and Ankara to almost everywhere in the east. There is a daily train, with sleepers, from Istanbul to Ankara, Kayseri, Sivas, Erzincan, Erzurum, Kars and on to Russia.

Circumspection is advisable anywhere near the Russian frontier, about which both Turks and Russians display a certain nervousness. Permission must be obtained from the Governor of Kars to visit the ancient Armenian capital of Ani, which is very near the frontier. A party of British V.I.P.s recently came close to serious trouble through slightly flamboyant behaviour, in spite of being officially vouched for and conducted. Don't wander far from the conducted party in a place like Ani. Even if you have the highest-level introductions and permits you can be held up. Local officials do not always act immediately on instructions from Ankara. In Turkey every official goes through all your travel documents, whether they concern him or not, in the hope of finding something out of order, presumably in order to triumph over the issuing authorities and acquire a name for vigilance. Again a couple of summers ago a British climbing party, including a well-known travel writer, was held in virtual imprisonment for a week in eastern Turkey, even though its members had the highest credentials and authority from Ankara. There are no longer any prohibited areas in Turkey but permits are needed for some places. Ani is one, and the eastern side of Kars, and the spectacular road along the fringe of Ararat from Kars to Doğubeyazit. Don't attempt these places unless you have permission and, preferably, are accompanied by a soldier or an official. And even though introductions and permits from Ankara are sometimes queried, you should have them for these few tricky places. Turkish winter sports and hunting clubs and the Highways Administration will advise. Fishing licences are not necessary in Turkey. When

---

[1] Or via Malatya, Elazığ, Bingöl, Muş, Tatvan, which at the moment of writing is the better road. The Bitlis valley is more spectacular and the road is being widened.

I enquired I was told I could do anything I liked but dynamite them. Even this I have seen done openly and with apparent impunity.

According to the Turkish Game Law some animals and birds may be shot at any time of the year. They are crows, the wolf, jackal, lynx, wild boar, leopard, hyaena and tiger. The following are amongst the birds and animals which may not be shot from April 1st to August 1st: wild cat, marten, polecat, squirrel, otter, gazelle, weasel, porcupine, beaver, hare, fox, roe deer, mountain goat, bear; blackcock, cock pheasant, peacock, red-legged and grey partridges, quail, all kinds of wild duck, golden oriole, cuckoo, crane, great bustard, raven and all marsh birds. It is forbidden to shoot the following at any time: deer (except roe deer in season), young roe deer, mountain sheep, young mountain goats, hedgehog, bat, the francolin, the domesticated dove, kestrels and hawks, the golden-crested wren, woodpecker, goatsucker, hen pheasant, the nightingale family, the swallow and swift, the stork, the starling and the owls. Travellers intending to shoot should contact the Hunting Clubs in Istanbul or Ankara unless they have knowledge-able friends in the country.

It cannot be too strongly stressed that only experienced and well-equipped climbers should attempt the mountains of eastern Turkey and only in organised parties. You are not likely to be rescued, as you might be if you got into difficulties on Snowdon or the Matterhorn. When I went to Doğubeyazit my friends at Erzurum University begged me to promise not to attempt Ararat. Nothing was further from my mind, but an Oxford man did completely disappear on the mountain not so long ago. D. C. Hills's *My Travels in Turkey* will give you some idea of the difficulties involved in climbing Ararat and other mountains in eastern Turkey.[1]

The time to be taken by a road journey should not be estimated by map-reading, for distances are made longer by variations in road sur-face, but eastern Anatolia is fairly well covered with petrol stations. It is as well to carry the freely issued road maps of B.P., Shell and Mobil-oil, all three, as well as the road map issued free by the General Direc-torate of Highways, Karayolları Haritası. The Automobile Club of Turkey also issues road maps. The latest of these will reflect fairly accurately the state of the roads and they usually mark the important archaeological sites. The B.P. map will also indicate that company's excellent camp sites, known in Turkey as Mocamps, which will be

[1] See also Appendix on Eastern Turkey for Alpinist Travellers, pp. 231–45.

and Some Reasons for Going

useful to the motorist driving to eastern Anatolia, but so far the company has none in the area covered by this book.

There are still bandits in eastern Anatolia, in the Bingöl, Siirt and Hakkari areas. It is therefore wise to introduce oneself to the responsible authorities and to take advice if one intends to leave the main roads. Don't travel by night. Make every use of contacts with Turks and, if necessary, make them by introducing yourself. Turks will put themselves to endless trouble to help visitors, especially in the more remote districts. I found the correspondents of Ankara newspapers in places like Van, Tatvan and Siirt not only genuinely friendly and helpful but glad to get a story for their papers. Express a general and, if possible, some particular interest in Turkey. Amateur archaeologists will be suspected of treasure-hunting, but an interest in birds or flowers will be regarded as a harmless aberration. Remember to pretend at least to be interested in new developments, industry, schools, new hotels and so on. For the Turk, these are the important things in eastern Anatolia and it is polite to recognise this. Apart from the attention paid to it by the scholars of Istanbul and Ankara, antiquity is a tourist attraction for most Turks, though it can be a source of wealth to the clandestine peasant digger. It will be some years before the beauty of Lake Van will be widely enough known to attract motels and camping sites. It is now one of the unspoilt wonders of the world. Ararat too remains grim and little approached.

But you will be disappointed if you hope to take away a Van cat. I certainly never saw one there. I was told that they have all been taken away to become Ankara cats and that they were no more fond of swimming than other cats are.

Topography and Products

❧✦❧

Eastern Turkey is vast, over much of its area denuded of the trees of 10,000 years ago, the giant bones of our earth bared by erosion, its agonies petrified in extinct volcanoes. Rivers cut clean through rock but leave alluvial patches that make the blurred green of oases. There are three dominant colours, the green of spring, the tawniness of summer, the whiteness of winter. Habitations merge into the colour and form of the landscape and are hardly discernible. This is no country for fauns and dryads. The playful drunken Pan has gone, if he ever in some prototypic form inhabited the departed forests. It's the land of the thunder-god, of a mother-goddess on elephantine lines who never smiled till she reached the Carian coast, of the bull, the lion and the leopard. The stag too, to stand for hunting grounds. The country still has an untamed ferocity, a feral nearness to the bone, more poignant now and perhaps more daunting than it has ever been in human experience.

The pastoral way of life has been followed here since animals were first tamed but agriculture has had its ups and downs. The departure and elimination of Greeks, Armenians and Nestorians in this century has meant a decline in agriculture which the government is now attempting to restore by persuasion, education and experiment. Road-building —and the roads of eastern Turkey are many and surprisingly good— has been the greatest social influence. It has carried men away to work in the wealthier west, so that much of the hard manual work in Istanbul today is done by Kurds. The roads have brought benefits too, apart from the money brought back by these workers, electricity, water, new buildings, schools, a university at Erzurum, easier access to minerals and oil wells and markets for products.

On a contour map eastern Turkey looks like, and it is often spoken of as a high plateau surrounded by mountain ranges and cut through by great rivers. In fact one is hardly ever conscious of being on a plateau but rather of being in very mountainous country. Wherever one is, the horizon is always rimmed with mountains and not just flat mountains but agreeably broken outlines with satisfying peaks. The rivers are fierce and turbulent and cut through wild country where it is often impossible for road and railway to follow them.

On the north coast the mountains rise steeply from the Black Sea, from which they appear as a forbidding wall, to the peaks of the Pontic Mountains, up to such heights as the 4,000 metres of Kaçkar Dağ. South of this great barrier, mountain ranges run roughly west–east, one of them culminating in the 5,165 metre Mount Ararat, Ağrı Dağ to the Turks. South from Ararat to the Syrian border and around Lake Van is the greatest average height, most of the land in this area being over 2,000 metres and a good deal of it over 3,000. Lake Van is a little inland sea over one hundred and thirty kilometres long from south-west to north-east and very deep. Its formation is due to volcanic action, it has no visible outlet but is fed by a number of streams and rivers. Its water is heavy with soluble minerals. The Euphrates drains the centre of eastern Anatolia whilst the Tigris is partly fed from the permanent glaciers and eternal snow of the Cilo and Sat Mountains of Hakkari.

West of Hakkari the mountains of the eastern Taurus drop towards the plains of Mesopotamia, but there is very little land below 300 metres within the Turkish frontier.

Apart from Ararat and Little Ararat there are other extinct volcanoes. Süphan Dağ, about 4,400 metres, towers over the northern shore of Van, with Nimrut Dağ, not to be confused with the other Nimrut Dağ near Adıyaman, rising from its western shore. These, and another extinct volcano in the Bingöl mountains south of Erzurum, are marked as centres of recent eruption in the Istanbul University Atlas of Turkey. The earthquake belt runs from east to west through the middle of this area.

The variation of temperature is very great in eastern Anatolia. At Kars the maximum and minimum temperatures recorded are 35 centigrade above and 37 below. Erzurum, Erzincan, Sivas, Malatya and Gaziantep show a similar pattern without quite the same extreme cold in the case of the southern towns. Kars, Karaköse (Ağrı) and Erzurum have frost on about half the days of the year and these towns are in an area that has one hundred and twenty days snow cover annually. The Pontic Mountains and the northern coastal belt have a heavy and fairly consistent precipitation of snow and rain, but south of a line drawn through Sivas and Erzurum it is very dry in July and August.

PRODUCTS

The consistent rainfall and the warmth of the north-eastern, Black Sea, coast give it a sub-tropical luxuriance when seen by the traveller along the coast in early or mid summer. Trabzon and Rize are roughly on the same latitude as Naples and Barcelona and they have much more rain than the Mediterranean cities. Rize is the centre of tea-growing and production has risen rapidly during the last twenty years to satisfy the country's needs. Export of tea is now becoming a possibility. Lemons do not grow well here but the tangerines are the best in Turkey. Maize, a fairly recent introduction, is grown all along the northern coast. As we move westwards along the coast the rainfall diminishes gradually and other crops flourish. From Trabzon to Ordu excellent hazelnuts grow, are harvested and packed. Fine tobacco comes from this area and barley and rye are grown for local consumption. Good butter is sent to Ankara and Istanbul. It does not surprise us to hear that this richly productive coastal belt from Samsun to Hopa is the most densely populated part of Turkey, except of course for the big cities. The northern slopes of the Pontic Mountains are thickly forested with a great variety of immense trees but once they fall away southwards to the central plateau the story is very different. Over most of the interior rainfall is less in quantity but more erratic, causing occasional floods.

Only about one-tenth of the land of eastern Anatolia is cultivated. Erosion has followed forest destruction and the soil is generally poor, with pockets of alluvium in valley bottoms making oases of cultivation. Wheat is the principal food and money-maker but only about one year in three is really suitable for subsistence farming. In the absence of firewood, animal dung is made into neat round cakes for winter fuel, to the detriment of the fields. New varieties of grain are being introduced and irrigation and fertilizers will improve matters. In the Kars-Erzurum-Erzincan area there is good soil in the depressions but the long winter makes cultivation difficult. Wheat is sown in May and harvested in October unless it is caught by early snow. Cabbages, radishes, potatoes and turnips can stand the cold. A good deal of barley is grown but no fruit. One meets great herds of beef and milk cattle in this area. Sheep too but few goats. The meat and butter are excellent.

The Aras valley, which runs from east of Erzurum to the junction of the Turkish, Soviet and Iranian frontiers,[1] is much warmer than the upland areas. Rainfall is low but in a series of depressions between Kağızman and Iğdir irrigation from the river makes possible the production of grapes, rice and cotton. Near Lake Van an ancient irrigation system of canals, tunnels and regulators laid down by the kings of Urartu creates oases, and fruit, vegetables and grain are grown. The great area west of Van, the Bingöl-Tunceli region, is chiefly pasture for sheep and goats and there is little cultivation, though some barley, wheat and millet are grown. Sugar-beet is a very important new crop for this central area and there are big sugar refineries near Erzurum, at Erzincan, Elazığ and Malatya. As we move southwards there are more grapes and Maraş, Gaziantep and Diyarbakır are important vineyard centres. Rice is grown near Diyarbakır and beans, chickpeas and lentils mostly between the Euphrates and the Tigris in the southern part of our area. Pistachio nuts, more than half the world's production, are grown near Gaziantep and Siirt.

Cattle, buffaloes, sheep, goats, horses and donkeys are widely distributed, but camels occur chiefly in the Gaziantep-Urfa region and Angora goats only in the extreme north-east, around Artvin. Urfa is famous for its sheep, and the resulting butter, and for breeding good horses. Much of the smuggling into Syria from this region is of animals. In Ottoman times, before the establishment of the present Turkish frontier, there was a regular and natural movement of flocks and herds between the plains of Mesopotamia and the foothills of the eastern Taurus.

Eastern Turkey is, and has always been, rich in minerals and it is probable that copper and iron were first worked here by man. Silver was obtained from the Pontic Mountains in antiquity. Lead is mined there today and copper at Murgul near Artvin and Maden near Elazığ. There is a big chromium area east of Elazığ. Divriği is the great iron ore centre and mountains of it may be seen near the railway line awaiting transportation to the iron and steel works further west. Manganese is mined near Artvin and Gaziantep. Petroleum is being obtained in growing quantities in the Diyarbakır-Siirt area and valuable

[1] This river, the ancient Araxes, eventually runs into the Caspian Sea.

phosphates are being drawn from the smaller lakes in the Van area.

The planned electrification of eastern Turkey is proceeding and there are important hydro-electric power plants on the Ceyhan, Euphrates, Tigris, Çoruh and other rivers.

. *Bobek Tepesi (3,520 metres) on Sat Dağ, Hakkari*

2. *Zab River with Cilo Dağ*

Peoples and Cultures of Eastern Turkey

꧁ꕥ꧂

PREHISTORY

Until recent years the Jordan Valley, the Lebanon, northern Syria, Kurdish Irak and the Zagros Mountains of Iran have all been much more widely and systematically examined at the prehistoric levels than has south-eastern Turkey, north of the Fertile Crescent. Reasons for this have been accessibility and the subservient state of these countries until well into the present century, as well as the belief that prehistory began at Jericho and civilisation in lower Mesopotamia and Egypt. An arc of hilly country runs northwards along the Jordan, through the Lebanon and across the foothills of middle Mesopotamia to the Zagros Mountains which, like the rest of this crescent, have enough seasonal rainfall to sustain pasture and wild grain. Eastern Anatolia lies across the centre of this arc and with the increasing attention now being given to prehistoric sites by Turkish scholars it becomes more likely that the impulses towards the early cultures of this arc, the beginnings of what we know as civilisation, actually sprang from Anatolia. As Professor R. J. Braidwood considered the sites excavated in northern Syria and Irak, not far from the Turkish frontier, he became progressively more aware of the importance of Anatolia to the north and west.[1] This was the home of wild animals which were to be domesticated and of wild plants which would first of all be reaped and then cultivated. From here too would come the highly prized obsidian for the making of fine tools.

Until about 10,000 years B.C. much of eastern Anatolia was under glaciation and as the ice melted Late Palaeolithic man appeared in the well wooded and watered hills, living in caves, rock shelters and in

[1] Preface to the third printing of *The Near East and the Foundations of Civilisation*.

open places. According to James Mellaart[1] civilisation began at about this time in three areas, the Zagros Mountains of Persia, the hill country of Turkish Mesopotamia and the south Anatolian plateau. Flint was used for tools and arrow-heads. There were no houses and no luxury objects were produced. Grain may not yet have been gathered for food, or at least was not yet in any way processed, for no querns or grinding tools have been found of this period. Shanidar, just south of the Turkish frontier, is the richest site of this early period to be discovered so far. Radio-carbon dating has recently shown 'that man had begun to practise an elementary type of farming as long ago as 8900 B.C.'[2] The Natufian culture of Palestine, contemporary with Shanidar and reaching its climax in the seventh millennium, is linked by archaeologists with the Beldibi Cave near Antalya and seems to have acquired its knowledge of agriculture from the north.[3] Ideas about agriculture may in fact have come to this important culture with the obsidian imported from Anatolia. There was a factory for the processing of obsidian at Tilki Tepe on the eastern shore of Lake Van and obsidian from that area was exported to Palestine about the year 6500 B.C.[4]

In the meantime a highly organised Neolithic urban centre had developed at Çatalhüyük by the seventh millennium, and Mr. James Mellaart has revealed there 'the earliest paintings yet found on man-made walls'.[5] The qualification man-made is necessary of course to remind us of the 20,000-year-old paintings on the cave walls of Lascaux. It is impossible to treat one area of the Near East in isolation at any stage in its history or prehistory and one has to remember urban Jericho, the domed houses of isolated early Neolithic Cyprus and the rectangular houses of seventh millennium Byblos in northern Syria. Pottery too was developing all round the Fertile Crescent, the earliest painted pottery in Luristan, seventh millennium pottery in the Zagros Mountains.[6] Mellaart believes that the Hassuna type of pottery originated in the Diyarbakır-Mardin area.

It was from Anatolia that these interchanging influences and dis-

---

[1] *Earliest Civilisations of the Near East.*
[2] D. A. E. Garrod and J. G. D. Clark, *Primitive Man in Egypt, Western Asia and Europe*, Camb. Anc. Hist. Fascicle no. 30 (1965), p. 53.
[3] ibid., p. 54.
[4] Wright and Gordus, 'Distribution and Utility of Obsidian from Lake Van sources between 7500 and 3500 B.C.', *American Journal of Archaeology*, vol. 73., no. 1.
[5] *Anatolia before c. 4000*, Camb. Anc. Hist. Fascicle no. 20 (1967), p. 12.
[6] *Earliest Civilisations of the Near East*, p. 52.

coveries came to Europe. To quote Mellaart once more, 'The neolithic cultures of Anatolia introduced the first beginnings of agriculture and stock-breeding and a cult of the mother goddess, the basis of our civilisation.'[1]

The Halaf culture, named after Tel Halaf, the site just south of the Turkish border with Syria, seems to have been nodal, bringing together, as one might expect from its geographical position, the influences of both eastern Anatolia and lower Mesopotamia. It had domed rooms, at Karkemiş, up to six metres high and pottery that already suggests the influence of early metal-working.[2] Halaf culture grew after the collapse of Çatalhüyük and Hacılar and was itself destroyed in the fifth millennium by the growing Ubaid culture from which the Sumerian civilisation evolved. The centres of culture now move southwards, partly because of the invasion of eastern Anatolia by culturally inferior people from the north, partly because the use of flooded land and the discovery of irrigation enabled the Neolithic advances of the northern mountain fringes to be more fully exploited along the great rivers.

All this indicates eastern Anatolia as a likely place of origin of cultural experiment but until recently there was little actual evidence to establish this. Now, with intensified enquiry into these earliest stirrings of our western civilisation the blank spaces on the map of prehistoric Asia Minor are gradually being filled in. Rock drawings of wild mountain goats found at Adiyaman in 1938 were taken by Professor Sevket Aziz Kansu to be palaeolithic[3] but other rock drawings in the Saç Mountains of Hakkari are still undated. The reports of two Turkish scholars, Dr. Muvaffak Uyanik and Dr. Mehmet Özdoğan, show some of the Hakkari rock engravings, though certainly primitive, to be of a much later date than palaeolithic.[4] There have been palaeolithic finds in the Kars area and plentiful surface objects of the early Palaeolithic and Acheulian periods in the Maraş-Gaziantep area. The first important early Palaeolithic find was a Chellean type hand-axe found by J. E. Gautier at Birecik in 1884. Stone implements of the middle Palaeolithic have been found in the Direkli Cave near Sivas and implements of the Mesolithic and early Neolithic ages, not so finely made as those from sites further south, have been found in rock shelters and on open sites at Tekkeköy near Samsun on the Black Sea coast.

[1] ibid., p. 77.   [2] ibid., p. 119.
[3] 'Stone Age Cultures in Turkey', *A.J.A.* no. 51 (1947), pp. 227ff.
[4] *Belleten* (1968), p. 125.

The enforced and hurried investigation of many Neolithic sites in the valley to be drowned by the Keban Dam has not turned up anything startling, but the early and middle Bronze Age sites in this same area have given painted pottery similar to that found at Malatya. (Bronze Age sites in this valley will be referred to later.) And not far from here the very term Bronze Age has been called into question by the discovery of worked copper, a borer and needles, at Çayönü, near Ergani and between Elazığ and Diyarbakır. Carbon tests gave the astonishing date of 6700 B.C. for a huge courtyard where these were found. Excavation is still going on there and an interesting architectural feature uncovered is a free-standing stone support to a roof at this early date and the grill plan of the foundations.[1] The absence of pottery, and other tests, have established this as a preceramic village of about 7000 B.C. Tests applied to obsidian found here indicate that it came from the Bingöl area and also give the date 7000 B.C.[2] Stone implements and some malachite objects have been found. There may well be more sites like this to be unearthed on the fringes of the great mountain mass of eastern Anatolia.

One may therefore think of this area from about 10000 B.C., when the ice retreated, to the coming of the Hittites and the beginning of history, as a region where men lived as hunters in the rich forests that grew in the changed climate, trapping and killing in other ways a wide variety of birds and beasts, including many still shot there today. They learnt to gather wild wheat and barley, wild peas and lentils, apples, acorns and pistachios and then to cultivate them. The wild grape too. Wheat and barley were first of all steeped in water for eating, long before they were ground to make flour, and in this way it is possible that beer was discovered before bread was ever baked. A refreshing thought. These men used stone and obsidian, which is a vitreous lava or very hard volcanic glass. They learnt to carve wood and weave baskets, began to experiment with metals, copper and lead first of all, then gold, silver and eventually iron. They lived in caves and rock shelters, then learnt to make huts of wood. Houses of stone followed and then mud brick, an invention of southern Mesopotamia. During this time more sophisticated centres were developing outside

[1] Joint expedition of the Universities of Istanbul and Chicago under Professors H. Çambel and R. J. Braidwood. Report in *A.J.A.*, vol. 73, no. 2. Also verbal communications from Professors Ufuk Esin and Halet Çambel.
[2] *A.J.A.*, vol. 73, no. 1, p. 76.

our present area, at Çatalhüyük, Mersin, Tarsus, Byblos and Jericho, to flourish and fall, often to be destroyed by the fire of barbarian invaders. But this eastern Anatolian highland region was of a wildness to discourage urban development. The shrinking glaciers, the perpetual snow of the heights, the teeming forests, the extremes of summer and winter, all these induced migration and transhumance, instrumental agents in the diffusion of discoveries, so that this vast mountain area shows an astonishing uniformity of culture at this early stage. There was a stimulating and sometimes terrifying violence in nature, active volcanoes, rushing rivers, fierce animals, but the basic requirements of civilisation were here, plentiful wood and stone, metals, domesticable animals and the most precious of cultivable plants. The rivers made pockets of silt, still green oases today, in a barren landscape. Cultivation was first tried out here and there was fuel for the smelting of metal. The first pottery is of the simplest kind but attractive in shape, with simple, sometimes spiral decoration. Fires and cooking were important in such a climate and a good deal of care was given to the design of hearths and portable terracotta fireplaces.[1]

Bronze Age houses so far discovered vary in shape from round to rectangular. At Pulur in the Keban Dam area Dr. Hamit Kosay has found remains of early Bronze Age houses of mud brick on low stone foundations, portable and stationary hearths of terracotta, fire-guards and fire-dogs, clay basins for pounding and grinding food as well as portable altars about half a metre long, with relief decoration and idols.[2] Burials vary too from earth graves to stone cist graves within the walls of the house. Such a grave has been excavated at Erciş on the north shore of Lake Van. Karaz, near Erzurum, is already known as a Chalcolithic or early Bronze Age site and portable hearths, flint and obsidian blades and metal objects, daggers and bracelets, have been found there.[3] Further investigation at ground level of the Arslantepe mound near Malatya, excavations proceeding in the Erzurum plain and the final reports before the Keban flooding will tell us more about the Bronze Age and the earlier cultures in eastern Turkey.

Round about 2000 B.C., when a new kind of painted pottery, known as Cappadocian ware, flourished in central Anatolia, similar pottery, as well as black burnished and incised pots, was being made in the

[1] Mellaart, Camb. Anc. Hist. Fascicle 20, p. 41.
[2] M. J. Mellink, 'Archaeology in Asia Minor', *A.J.A.*, vol. 72 (1968).
[3] W. Lamb, *The Culture of North-East Anatolia, Anat. St.* IV, pp. 21–32.

western part of eastern Anatolia. About this time too there came incursions of Indo-European people from the direction of the Caucasus, bringing destruction to settlements in eastern and central Anatolia.

Along the Black Sea coast an independent Pontic culture had developed from the sparse Mesolithic and Neolithic beginnings into the splendid Bronze Age civilisation which spread southwards and is exemplified by the lovely objects found in the Alaca Hüyük tombs. Professor Seton Lloyd stresses the essentially Anatolian, un-Mesopotamian nature of this pre-Hittite culture which was clearly to influence the Hittites when they arrived in Asia Minor.[1] The Hattians, or people of Hatti, from whom the Hittites learnt so much, are thought to have been an originally Anatolian race. At Horoztepe and Mahmatlar, near Tokat, a fascinating variety of metal objects of high craftsmanship has been found, dating from about 2100 B.C. The metal most commonly used was bronze, but the source of the tin which went to make this alloy is not yet known. There is an eight-inch-high nude female figure suckling a spreadeagled child, a ceremonial rattle with typical mountain animals of Anatolia silhouetted along the edge and a fine horned bull. There are all kinds of domestic utensils and arms, and bronze fittings for tables and chairs. Here seems to have originated the to me not very happy practice of giving the legs of tables or cauldron stands human or animal feet.[2] Here was a culture which had mastered the processing of metal, without yet discovering the use of iron, and in which the aristocracy at least could afford many luxuries. And it seems to be a native Anatolian culture, even though it absorbed notions from north and south, from the Caucasus and from Mesopotamia.

During the early Bronze Age an important culture had arisen at Kanesh (Kültepe), near present-day Kayseri. At the beginning of the second millennium B.C. this attracted Assyrian merchants who were allowed to establish a trading centre of their own alongside the growing city. Access to this important centre was by way of Karkemiş, or Harran, to Birecik, Maraş and Elbistan and this became a great corridor for the exchange of goods and ideas. The goods were carried by the famous black donkeys of Cappadocia and the continuance of this trade over centuries is evidence of a period of peaceful conditions. This is perhaps the most ancient and important route of cultural exchange in the world, either following the Euphrates up into the heart of eastern Anatolia or breaking westwards along tributaries and

[1] *Early Highland Peoples of Anatolia*, pp. 28–9.   [2] See p. 46.

into further valleys to find a way through the Taurus Mountains to central Anatolia and the west. The records of these Assyrian merchants during the first two centuries of the second millennium constitute the beginnings of written history in Anatolia.

THE HITTITES

At the beginning of the second millennium a people speaking an Indo-European language infiltrated into north-eastern and central Anatolia, probably from the direction of the Caucasus. These people, whom we know today as the Hittites, took over the government of much of central and eastern Anatolia but since they also adopted the religious ideas and the crafts of the Hattian people, whom they found established in this area, the suggestion is that the occupation was slow and peaceful rather than sudden and violent. The first capital of the Hittite empire was Kussara, which has not yet been identified, but within a few generations they had established themselves at Hattusa, modern Boğazköy, two hundred kilometres east of Ankara. In the first flush of power the Hittites attempted to extend their dominion into Mesopotamia and successfully attacked Aleppo and Babylon, but they failed to hold on to these conquests and they retired into their natural fortress north of the Taurus. During the middle centuries of the second millennium an offshoot of the Hurrian people, who came from the mountains of north-west Persia, had established the kingdom of Mitanni to control the routes between Anatolia and Mesopotamia, but this kingdom was overthrown by the Hittite King Shuppilulnimash in the fourteenth century B.C. It is from the Mitanni that the Hittites are thought to have learnt the skill of horse-breeding.[1]

The Hittite Empire collapsed about the year 1200, the time of the fall of Troy, harassed by tribes to its north and reeling from the impact of the Phrygian invasion, probably from the west. The Hittites now retreated to the south-east and for five centuries more they carried on their civilisation in small kingdoms centred on Maraş, Malatya, Sakçegözü and Karkemiş, places which had long been centres of culture before their arrival. This is the Neo-Hittite period and the monuments which remain from it show a growing acceptance of Syrian and Aramaic elements into their culture. Evidence of the great period of the Hittite civilisation occurs outside and slightly to the west

[1] See O. R. Gurney, *The Hittites*, p. 105.

of the country dealt with in this book, at Boğazköy, Alaca Hüyük, Tokat, Kültepe and near Konya and there is nothing elsewhere to compare with the splendid carvings of the open-air temple of Yazılkaya, near Boğazköy. But the art of the late Hittites is not entirely one of decline and change. Its importance in the history of art may be that it was a channel through which Anatolian and so-called oriental influences permeated into Greek art of the seventh century B.C.[1] Ninth-century statuary found at Malatya and Maraş and Karkemiş is in the pure and traditional Hittite style. There is a fine eighth-century head of a goddess, much larger than human size, splendidly hatted and carrying a pomegranate in a hand which has been lost, found at Karkemiş, and there are typical Hittite lions, powerful and benign, from Karkemiş, Malatya and Maraş. Basalt rock occurs along the Sajur River, a tributary of the Euphrates, to the west of Karkemiş and the Hittites probably quarried there.[2] Many Hittite objects have been found at the village of Tel Bahram, about twenty-five kilometres south-east of Antep. A pottery drinking vessel which stood on a splendid ram's head, found at Karahüyük, Elbistan, suggests the origin of the Greek rhyton and a painted terracotta cup made in the form of a pointed shoe in another prototype.[3] (The gold and pottery wine-pouring vessels of third-millennium Anatolia, with their upward-pointing pouring lips, equally foreshadow the Greek *oinochoe*.) The civilisation of Europe owes a good deal to this enforced movement of the Hittites towards the north-eastern corner of the Mediterranean. At Kültepe in the nineteenth century B.C. they drank from the mouth of a charming though unrealistic terracotta animal which was filled halfway along its back.[4] The Hittites delighted in animals and used them widely and sensitively in decoration.

The Hittites had inherited a pictographic way of writing which was first of all cut in raised relief on the stone of monuments and then later incised more freely. This writing is now being deciphered. It employs common animals, birds and fishes, human heads in profile, hands holding daggers, shoes, wheels and parts of buildings. The lines follow an order known by the Greek word *boustrophedon*, that is turning at

[1] A bronze figurine, sixteenth century B.C., of a god, found near Tokat, looks like the archetype of all Greek chariot drivers. Plate 174, Catalogue of the Arts Council Exhibition of Hittite Art, 1964.

[2] D. G. Hogarth, *Accidents of an Antiquary's Life*, p. 167.

[3] O. R. Gurney, *The Hittites*, Plates 23 & 24, and Hittite Art, op. cit., p. 90. See also p. 46.

[4] ibid., p. 89.

the end of the line, as an ox turns in ploughing, and coming back in the other direction, with the symbols now facing the other way. Cuneiform writing was introduced in the sixteenth century, during the reign of King Hattusilis, and probably reached the Hittites by way of the Assyrian colony at Kültepe, where it had been in use for some centuries. The first Hittite texts in cuneiform that have come to light are royal pronouncements which embody narrative passages intended as warnings and solemn examples, parables one might call them, as well as a good deal of contemporary history.[1] Dr. Gurney finds this style of composition to be a Hittite creation which preceded the better-known Assyrian annals.[2] There are Hittite texts which give versions of Hittite and Hurrian myths and legends as well as Hittite and Hurrian versions of the Babylonian epic *Gilgamesh*. The discovery of the Akkadian version of this great poem at Sultantepe, south of Urfa,[3] indicates a route along which it might have passed on its way to Boğazköy. For the Hittites *Gilgamesh* was not just a foreign poem translated into their language but a work which touched them closely in its awareness of Anatolia, of the sources of water, wine and timber for Mesopotamia and of the living volcanoes from near which their great rivers came. Dr. Gurney gives an interesting account of the Hittite myth of the Slaying of the Dragon, of which fragmentary versions remain on tablets, and illustrates it with a sketch of a relief carving on stone, found at Malatya, of a god or king attacking a flaming coiled serpent.[4] He also gives an account of the stories of the Missing God, of the mission of the magical bee and of a myth of the birth of gods and the creation of the Earth, thought to be of Hurrian origin and closely resembling the view set out in the much later *Theogony* of the Greek poet Hesiod. We await fuller accounts of Hittite literature and its fascinating blend of Anatolian and other Near and Far Eastern elements.

The enforced movement southwards of the Hittites also brought with it the Hittite skill in military architecture demonstrated at Boğazköy. The fortifications of Karkemiş[5] cannot have been very different from the later Armenian, Byzantine and Crusader castles, the line of development which led from central Anatolia to Windsor and Caernarfon. Half-timbering was used in the construction of houses in

---

[1] Gurney, op. cit., p. 170 ff.   [2] ibid., p. 177.
[3] See p. 168.   [4] op. cit., p. 189. See also Seton Lloyd, op. cit., Plate 104.
[5] ibid., pp. 90–91.

these late Hittite cities, at Sincerli and Sakçagözü especially, not only because timber was plentiful but because such houses stood up better to earthquakes, a reason for the continued use of this plan in Anatolia today. At Karkemiş, outside both the earthquake zone and the timbered area, stone and brick were used.

The gradual infiltration of Aramaean and Assyrian elements into late Hittite art has been studied and classified by Professor Ekrem Akurgal.[1] Egyptian influence can also be detected at Karatepe, north-east of Adana and just outside the scope of this book.

THE URARTIANS

The civilisation of Urartu arose in the mountainous part of eastern Anatolia and in the highlands which are today within the frontiers of Soviet Armenia, Iran and Irak. Lake Van is at the heart of this country and it was from here that conquest extended Urartian power to the region of Erivan, where the famous Karmir Blur site is, and to the Rowanduz area in the Kurdish country of northern Irak.

Soviet archaeologists have recently unearthed, to the north-east of Erivan, traces of an extremely interesting pre-Urartian civilisation which dates from 3000 to 1200 B.C. At the end of the twelfth century B.C. something caused the level of Lake Sevan to rise and flood a fertile plain where these people lived. They had a town with broad straight streets and a fortress on a rock which was saved when the rock became an island and which was in existence until the twelfth century A.D. Implements and weapons of a Hittite type have been found as well as a number of funerary covered waggons with wooden disk wheels like those still in use in eastern Anatolia. These people worked gold, used bronze and gems, produced ceramics in clear white, red and black and in the fourteenth century B.C. were making bronze standards and copper cauldrons of the pre-Hittite Alaca Hüyük type.[2]

Urartu is first heard of in Assyrian inscriptions of the thirteenth century B.C. The name is probably another form of Ararat and even of Etruria, for there is a strong possiblity that the Etruscans originally came from eastern Anatolia. The great period of the Urartian civilisation, the ninth to the seventh century, was also the time of Assyrian

---

[1] *Art of the Hittites*, London, 1962.
[2] A. Mnatsakanyan, 'Treasures from an Armenian lake', *Illustrated London News*, 15 Apr. 1967. Arch. Sect. 2265.

ascendancy in this part of the Near East and much of our knowledge of
the Urartians comes from Assyrian records of wars fought against
them. In the year 860 B.C. Shalmaneser III began a series of campaigns
against this tough enemy in the north who threatened to move south
and east to cut important Assyrian trade routes. In the British Museum
there are bronze sheets which once lined wooden gates at the palace of
Shalmaneser. These were discovered at the mound of Balawat in Irak
and the reliefs and inscriptions record the siege of fortified places in the
mountains, some of them near Lake Van. Shalmaneser is depicted
celebrating with sacrifice at the shore of the great lake, whose cleansing
waters ritually and usefully washed his sword.[1] From these bronze
sheets we get a very clear picture of the dress and armour of Urartian
warriors and are able to observe their similarity to those of the Hittites
from which they presumably derive. They wore a shirt or tunic with
a broad belt. The spearmen carried a small round shield and the bowmen
a quiver at their belts. They wore a crested or conical helmet with a
long flap to protect the back of the neck. Royal helmets of elongated
cone shape with fine repoussé decoration depicting warriors, animals,
monsters and ritual ceremonies have been recovered from Karmir
Blur and Van.[2] The shield of the eighth-century Urartu King Sarduri II
has processions of fine bulls and lions.

Like the Hittites before them, the Urartians had their own hieroglyphic script, but in the ninth century they found it convenient to
adopt the Assyrian cuneiform alphabet and to adapt it to their own
purposes. This they cut on polished black stone blocks or on cleaned
surfaces of rocks on which they built their fortifications and palaces to
produce perhaps the most beautiful writing ever done on stone. In
these inscriptions they refer to their country as the Land of Biaini,
which is thought to be the origin of the name Van. Temples, palaces
and fortifications were built at Tuspa, present-day Van, in the ninth
century by Sarduri and his son Ishpuini. Inder Ishpuini's son Menua the
kingdom was consolidated and enlarged and inscriptions record his
great works, palaces, temples, towns, fortresses, gardens and the canals
to irrigate them. The great canal cleverly engineered to bring water to
Van still exists and the exactitude of its descending level is still a wonder.
The eighth century brought elegance and sophistication, with lovely
murals on palace walls at Erebuni, near Erivan. This fortress was built
in the eighth century B.C. by Argishti I, son of Menua, who extended

[1] B. B. Piotrovskii, *Urartu*, p. 3.   [2] ibid., Plates 16–20.

Urartian power into Transcaucasia. Lovely bowls and jewels were found there too. Penetration by Urartu to the Mediterranean checked Assyrian power and opened a route for Urartian objects, mainly through Tarsus, to influence the art and architecture of the Aegean Islands, Greece and Italy.[1] But the Assyrians returned in 735 B.C. to attack Tuspa itself and to ravage the heart of Urartu. The fortress of Van, Van Kalesi today, successfully resisted attack but the country suffered gravely in loss of possessions and prestige. Sennacherib destroyed Tarsus in 696 and cut the Urartian link with the west. The most damaging Assyrian campaign against Urartu was that of Sargon in 714 B.C., a war whose preparation and conduct are exceptionally well documented in Assyrian records. Sargon took the unusual step, for the Assyrians, of attacking through the mountains of south-east Turkey, the Hakkari region. The Assyrian annals give a detailed account of the vast treasure taken at the temple of the god Haldi at Musasir, an unidentified place somewhere in the extreme south-western corner of Anatolia, listing, amongst all kinds of booty, thirty-three silver chariots, six shining gold shields and three hundred and ninety-three silver cups.[2] A relief from Sargon's palace, lost in the Tigris when it was being transported to France but known from a sketch published by Botta and Flandin in 1850, shows the attack on Musasir, a city in the mountains, and on its temple, a pedimented building with typical Urartian cauldrons in front of it and the statue of a cow and calf said to have been cast by Sarduri II. But the Kingdom of Van recovered once more and there was much rebuilding in the devastated parts. In the seventh century the huge citadel of Teishebaini was built at Karmir Blur. Urartu lived on after the destruction of Niniveh and the collapse of Assyria but suffered the same fate at the hands of the same enemy, the Medes and their allies, at the beginning of the sixth century. Urartu, the Kingdom of Ararat, is still mentioned as a power and as an enemy of Babylon in the Book of Jeremiah (51: 27), but the end came about 590 B.C.

What shining places the Urartian hilltop cities and citadels must have been in their heyday! The Urartians liked to live in fortified places near good agricultural land. They chose long narrow spurs of hill with steep sides to discourage attack. These sides they topped with beautifully cut and carefully jointed masonry, often cutting shallow steps in the rock face to support blocks of stone which gave a sheer facing to the

[1] ibid., p. 6.   [2] ibid., p. 9.

rock. Such steps cut in the rock are an infallible sign of an Urartian site. Within these walls they put up great buildings of mud-brick on stone foundations and hilltop mounds of crumbled brickwork are another feature of Urartian sites. The Turks named a citadel near Van Toprak Kale, Earth Castle, for this reason.

No complete above-ground Urartian building remains but some idea may be formed of their architectural styles from records in bronze, stone and ivory. The three-storeyed castellated building depicted in the bronze at the British Museum, the series of doors and the number of windows suggesting great town houses rather than an external city wall, could well have been of brick on a stone foundation. The temple at Musasir, depicted on the lost Khorsabad relief, could have been of stone and wood. This building, probably of the ninth century and destroyed by the Assyrians in 714 B.C., had a filled-in frontage with six columns supporting a triangular pediment, the earliest record in art of a style which was later to become typical of Greek and Roman temple construction.[1] The Urartians also cut into rock to make great underground chambers, sometimes a complex of rooms with tunnelled passages and secret exits. The approach to some of these underground palaces is a rock-cut exterior or interior stairway so narrow as to be easily defensible. Surfaces of granite or blocks of basalt or whatever rock was at hand were finely polished to take the lovely cuneiform inscriptions at palace and temple entrances and on pedestals for statues. The Urartians were sensitive to the colour of stone and loved the contrast of basalt and a lighter-coloured stone. Floors in the citadel of Toprak Kale were decorated with tessellations of concentric circles of different coloured marble, specimens of which may be seen at the British Museum and the Van Museum. There was much mural decoration on plastered walls and some has survived at Adilcevaz, Karmir Blur and Arebuni.[2] The ground plans of Urartian sites show a rectangular design which was to be elaborated centuries later by Hippodamus of Miletus into a universally accepted town plan.

Urartian sites have now been examined at Van Kalesi, Toprak Kale, Cavuştepe, Adilcevaz, Patnos, Kayalidere near Varto[3] and Altıntepe, as well as in Soviet Armenia and Iran. The objects found in these excavations show a very high standard of taste and craftsmanship and constitute a link between the achievements of Alaca Hüyük and

[1] ibid, Figure 2, p. 10.   [2] See Piotrovskii, pp. 93 and 95.
[3] *A.J.A.*, vol. 71, no. 2. Mellink's digest.

Boğazköy and the art and architecture of Armenia. The animals on the church wall on Aghtamar Island are the lineal descendants of the bulls, horses and winged animals of Urartu. In delicacy and strength there are few things in art to equal the god or king standing on a bull, five fragments of which were found at Adilcevaz.[1] Fantastic beasts were used in the decoration of armour, cauldrons, thrones and other furniture and show great skill in the casting of bronze. The cauldron on a tripod stand, often with goat or bull feet, which became a commonplace of expensive European house decoration from the Roman villa onwards, finds at once its archetype and most perfect form in the lucky discovery at Altıntepe. As early as the eighth century B.C. cauldrons of this type were being exported from Urartu and some have been found in graves of that century at Phrygian Gordion. The Altıntepe cauldron has four bull's-head handles. Bulls' heads are treated sensitively and respectfully in Urartian art, as befits an ancient holy animal of eastern Anatolia, and specimens of these fine bronze heads are to be found in museums and private collections all over the world. There are some in the British Museum.

Typical Urartian pottery is undecorated, of simple, often elegant shape which seems to reflect forms in bronze[2] and with a reddish brown glaze giving a highly polished surface, very pleasant to look at and handle. Pottery bowls and cups were in common use and huge terracotta jars were made to store grain. Some beakers found at Karmir Blur are in the form of leather boots and must record the stitched, laced, pointed, unsoled leather boot worn in Urartu. It is amusing to think that the absurd Edwardian, or was it Victorian, man-about-town custom of drinking champagne from a dancer's slipper should hark back to this Urartian way of drinking. Another Urartian archetype imitated with not entirely happy results in Europe is the tall bronze standing candelabrum now in Hamburg.[3]

Seals were much used in Urartu and were usually of the stamp rather than the cylinder type. They are of different shapes, cone, bell and upright cylinder, pierced with a hole for carrying on a string and cut from rock crystal and steatite, or made of clay. One discovered at Karmir Blur has a divine figure standing on a bull in much the same attitude as the splendid figure of Adilcevaz. They were used to seal store-rooms and as royal signatures on cuneiform-inscribed clay tablets.

[1] See p. 104.   [2] Piotrovskii, op. cit., p. 75.
[3] ibid., p. 35.

Large numbers of these have been found and are still coming to light, often to disappear as rapidly.

Travelling in the mountains of eastern Turkey and finding and climbing up to these Urartian citadels, one forms the impression of a fully developed culture, of a people with a good eye for a fortifiable ridge of rock near fruitful land, a people who inherited the achievements of earlier Anatolian cultures and who were able to incorporate into this inheritance some of the discoveries of the civilisations which had sprung up in lower Mesopotamia. As masons they were as good as any the world has seen, as architects and builders they showed intelligent use of a variety of available materials and inventive daring in design. They showed a sure sense of balance and beauty and an admirable control of fantasy in decoration. Nowhere will you find such a strange, complete and yet agreeable contrast as a panel of their fine cuneiform inscription cut on to a polished surface in a setting of natural, unworked rock. They were great engineers and craftsmen and it may have been the very smallness of their highly organised centres, set in wild country and in a fierce climate, which made it possible for them to exploit at the same time the virtues of metal, ivory, wood, clay and script and the more obvious gifts of nature in stone, earth and water. The tendency of their rulers to live in underground rock-cut chambers suggests depths and complexes which further excavation may help to elucidate. But apart from the uniqueness of their civilisation and the interest and beauty of its remains they are important to us as a source and a channel of elements in our western civilisation whose provenance has till now been an unsolved mystery.

THE PHRYGIANS

Roughly contemporary with Urartu was the Phrygian civilisation of western and west central Anatolia, with its capital at Gordion. Having for some time a common frontier with Urartu the Phrygians exchanged ideas and products and possibly blows, for some archaeologists claim to have detected signs of Phrygian occupation of Urartian citadels and even of Phrygian colonisation of east central Anatolia. Probably of eastern European origin, not far removed from the early Greeks, the Phrygians were a means of bringing Anatolian ideas and impulses in music, architecture, art and religion to the early Greek civilisation. They declined rapidly in power and culture as a result of the Cimmerian incursion of the seventh century B.C. and the Persian conquest of the following century.

THE PERSIANS

Urartu fell and its cities were destroyed by the Medes and their allies during the early years of the sixth century B.C. Medes and Persians, with the help of Babylonians and Scythians, swept across Anatolia to the western limits of Asia in a conquest of imperial domination rather than of settlement or colonisation. The Phrygian power, weakened by the destructive Cimmerian invasion from which Urartu also suffered, gave way to the Lydian dynasty. In 546 B.C. Croesus, the Lydian king, was captured by the Persians and carried in triumph to Ecbatana.

The Greek expedition to Persia at the beginning of the fourth century B.C. and Xenophon's organisation of the retreat of the Ten Thousand are part of the story of eastern European resistance to the extension of Persian power, a resistance which was to culminate in the victories of Alexander of Macedon. The famous Ten Thousand were Greeks, mostly from the Peloponnese, who had been induced by Cyrus, brother to the Persian king and son of Darius, to take part in his attempt to seize the Persian throne. Cyrus marched, gathering troops, from Sardis eastwards, benefited from the generosity of the Queen of Cilicia, with whom he slept *en passant*, and took his time through Tarsus and the Syrian Gates, south-east of present-day Iskenderun, on to the Euphrates and down the river towards Babylon. North of Babylon, in an unexpected battle, Cyrus was killed whilst attacking his brother the king, and although the Greeks succeeded in their part of the encounter the insurrection collapsed. Persian guile and treachery led to the loss of the five Greek generals and a number of captains and, with the Greek army confused and uncertain what to do, Xenophon took charge and organised the march back, though he himself claims that he did not join the expedition as a soldier. Until the Greek army reached the mountainous region of the present boundary between Turkey and Irak it was constantly harassed by the Persians. Now the Greeks had to fight their way through the mountain passes of the land of the Carduchi, the Kurds, tough fighters and good bowmen, until they reached the confines of Armenia on the River Centrites, present-day Botan, crossing it somewhere to the east of Siirt. So far they had fed well off the land and found plenty of wine. They had

3. *Van Kalesi: entrance to underground palace*   4. *Toprak Kale: entrance to underground palace*

5. *Urartian cuneiform recently uncovered at Çavuştepe*

6. *Tumbled head of Zeus on Nimrut Dağ*

7. *Nestorian church in Zab Valley*

discarded the slaves they had captured, except for women the men wouldn't let go, and all unnecessary baggage in order to travel lighter and faster and to release guards for fighting. They crossed the Bitlis valley and met their first snow, which became deeper once they had crossed the Murat branch of the Euphrates, east of Kayalidere. Lack of food and the extreme cold now made many of the soldiers ill. Some were snow-blinded and the ones who lost their toes from frostbite were left behind. But they were well received in western Armenia, where they fed and drank well. Xenophon reports that the people of this part retired underground with their animals for the winter. The Greeks crossed the Çoruh river, ancient Phasis which gave its name to the pheasant, *phasianas*, said to have been brought to Greece from this valley, though not by Xenophon.

They now had to face the opposition of the Pontic tribes, the Chalybes and the Taochi, but courage and guile triumphed and once more there was plenty of food in the villages. A great moment was when the advance guard sighted the sea and gave the memorable cry 'Thalassa!', a cry that was taken up excitedly right through the army. They still had to use further guile and fortitude to deal with more tribes before reaching the sea at Trapezos, now Trabzon, an old Greek colony. A point vividly exemplified by Xenophon's narrative is the tribal variety and the absence of a central authority in eastern Anatolia in the fourth century B.C.

Two days' march from Trapezos many of the Ten Thousand had their stomachs upset by the local honey. It gave them vomiting and diarrhoea and seemed to make them mad, as though with drink. After a few days they all recovered. Xenophon reports seeing great numbers of beehives in this part and one still sees them today, often tied up in trees to keep the honey from the bears.[1] The Turks still recognise a type of honey which makes men mad, 'deli balı' they call it. The now dwindling Ten Thousand remained at Trapezos amongst the colonists, waiting for ships that had been sent for to take them home. Not to be a burden on their hosts and to perform a service, they plundered the enemies of Trapezos until there was nothing in the region left to plunder. They then began to march westwards along the coast and when they reached Kerasos, now Giresun, there were still eight thousand six hundred left of the force that had turned back from Babylon. Some were already travelling by sea. After defeating some

[1] See p. 215.

enemies of the Mossynoici the land army found plentiful bread and coarse wheat, jars of pickled dolphin, chestnuts and a rather bitter wine. Xenophon tells us of the curious and public sexual habits of the pampered aristocracy of the Mossynoici of this region of the Pontic coast. A strange and interesting people. 'When they were in a crowd they acted as men would act when in private, and when they were by themselves, they used to behave as they might do when they were in company; they used to talk to themselves, and laugh to themselves, and stop and dance wherever they happened to be, just as if they were giving a display to others.'[1]

After some trouble at Cotyora, modern Ordu, they marched on westwards, plundering, placating, entertaining the people they met with sports and dances, and making for Sinope and the Bosphorus. Most of them took ship before they left our present area. Xenophon's story is not only good reading and an important piece of military history but a lively source of information on conditions of living and difficulties of travel in the Asia Minor of the fourth century B.C. The ready inclination of Xenophon and his men to settle down where they found a desirable spot rather than return home, once they were in an area which had links with Greece, their eye for something better than their own barren land, especially with the flourishing example of the Greek colonists along the Black Sea coast before them, all this shows how the already varied racial mixture of Anatolia was to be further modified. Sir William Ramsay says, 'Hardly any of these great armies has failed to leave behind it some part of its numbers, and occasionally one finds a single isolated village in some secluded position which seems to contain a fragment of lost population.'[2] Ramsay gives as an example of the persistence of an old un-Asiatic Anatolian type the resemblance between the guide you hire and the sculptured god of the civilisation whose relics you are searching for. He thinks the Tahtaci, an Anatolian tribe that specialises in wood-cutting for fuel, may be survivors of an ancient pagan sect, perhaps the woodland servants of Cybele.[3]

It has been said that the Persians of the middle of the first millennium B.C. were imperialists rather than colonisers. They set up satraps, provincial governors, to rule the conquered peoples and often allowed these local rulers considerable autonomy. Like all empires, they drained

[1] Rex Warner, *The Persian Expedition*, p. 189.
[2] *The Intermixture of Races in Asia Minor*, p. 2.   [3] ibid., p. 17.

the conquered land to enrich the homeland, and craftsmen from Anatolia were drafted to decorate palaces at Susa and Persepolis. And like most empires they created a peace which enabled men to travel fairly safely through the known world, except through high mountains and deserts unsuitable for commerce and campaigning. Herodotus visited Egypt and Babylon from southern Anatolia. The Persian Royal Road from Sardis through Harran to Susa, with its links with Europe and its well-regulated posting system, demonstrates the efficiency and importance of communications within the Persian Empire. It was the defeat of Darius III by Alexander the Great in 321 B.C. that put an end to this empire and its possible and intriguing threat to Europe. A Persification of Britain, tempered by Anatolian mother-goddess worship and Greek humanism, was denied us by these victories of Alexander in Anatolia which eventually opened the way for the heavy-weight Romans.

Although the Greeks first and then the Romans checked the Persian bid to extend their empire into Europe, and the effect of a Persian conquest of southern Europe is beyond speculation, Persian religious and philosophical ideas did not require a military conquest to spread to the west. There were converts to Mithraism amongst Pompey's soldiers in Cilicia and Commagene and Mithraism, in the early days of Christianity, became the Roman soldier's religion. Mithraic temples have been found in London and near Hadrian's Wall. The Persian Zoroastrian dualism in Mithraism, the constant battle against positive evil, still underlies much western faith and certainly reverberated through my own religious education in Wales. Anatolian elements merged into Mithraism and were passed on. The cleansing blood of the Lamb, a commonplace of Christian hymnology, has its prototype in the eastern Anatolian ritual slaughter of bulls and baptism in the blood that washed away all guilt.[1] An Iranian doctoral student of mine made an impressive case for Persia as the main fount of our western civilisation, whose roots are certainly widespread, varied and not yet fully revealed.

THE ARMENIANS

Xenophon has not much to tell us about Armenia except that it was a big and rich country with a hard winter which made travel difficult, as

[1] See Michael Gough, *The Early Christians.*

it still does, that men there took their drink through straws from great tubs and that the country was under Persian domination in his day. Classical writers make the wildest shots at the origin of the Armenian people. Herodotus simply refers to them as Phrygian colonists, perhaps because they were armed in Phrygian fashion.[1] (We remember the contacts between Urartu and Phrygia.) Strabo, another Anatolian, took them to be close to Arabs and Syrians, possibly because of the similarity between the names Armenia and Aramaios (Aramaean being equivalent to Syrian) or because the aristocracy of Babylon was Chaldean or Khaldian from Urartu, which was to become Armenia, and because of the close trade links, reported by Herodotus, between Armenia and Babylon. The Armenians in fact speak an Indo-European language and either they came into Anatolia from the direction of the Caucasus, the probable route of the Hurrians and the Hittites, or they are an original Anatolian people. They took over Urartu after its decline and they are first known to us in the annals of Persia, the dominating power of that time. They were known as good farmers, gardeners and cattle breeders, as were the Urartians before them, and they became famous traders. Herodotus reports with some astonishment a curious and profitable commercial practice of theirs in their dealings with Babylon, how the Armenians built long coracles of hide to carry goods, mostly wine in barrels, down the Euphrates to the great city. The boats, which were big enough to carry donkeys as well, were broken up on arrival and the skins loaded on to the donkeys for the long walk home.[2] Armenians today, two and a half millennia later, have shown themselves to be equally resourceful tradesmen.

Like the Urartians again, the Armenians lived in fortified towns and were masters of military architecture in the eastern Anatolian tradition. With the rest of Asia Minor, Armenia was set free from Persian domination by Alexander the Great in 331 B.C.; but the process of hellenisation which followed Alexander's campaigns never reached Armenia and even under Roman influence Armenia retained its Persian-type administration, with regional satraps who were practically tributary kings running their own armies. The opening up and pacifying of the eastern world by Alexander gave the Armenians the opportunity of extending their commerce beyond Mesopotamia to Egypt, India and Central Asia.

Under Tigranes the Great (95–54 B.C.) Armenia was a prosperous

---

[1] *The Histories*, VII, 72.　　　　[2] *Histories*, I, 194.

and extensive empire, but the invasion of the country by Lucullus in 69 B.C., during his campaign against the redoubtable Mithridates of Pontus, followed soon after by Pompey's conquest, marked the end of prosperous independence and the beginning of the country's history as a client and buffer state of Rome and afterwards of Byzantium. A fairly strong but subservient Armenia was a bulwark against Persia and Parthia.

The Parthians conquered the country in 54 B.C. and disputed control of it with Rome and it was the Parthians who established the Arsakid dynasty in Armenia in the first century A.D. During this century, in A.D. 66, Armenia came under the suzerainty of the Emperor Nero. The third-century Gregory the Illuminator, respected minister of the Armenian King Tiridates, had been brought up as a Christian and neither blandishments, persuasion nor thirteen years of foul imprisonment shook his zeal, with the result that he finally converted his master. Tiridates had previously upheld the gods of Persia, Aramazd, Anahid and Vahagu, in agreement with the Roman practice of recognising the gods of a place or of its rulers, but now, about the year 280, his conversion made Armenia the first country to adopt Christianity as a state religion. The king and Gregory set about the destruction of the pagan temples, that of Aramazd at Ani, that of Mithras at Tercan. They broke to pieces the golden figure of the goddess Anahid at Erzincan. All this led to wars with Persia and to massacres of Christians in that country. The Christian story of blood and intolerance had begun.

In the meantime Constantine had in A.D. 313 made Christianity an official Roman religion. Gregory was ordained at Caesarea (Kayseri) in Cappadocia and for a while the Armenian church was subservient to Caesarea. Armed with a parcel of the bones of St. John the Baptist, obtained at Caesarea, Gregory established the first Armenian church at a spot which Lynch identifies with the Monastery of Surb Karapet, about forty kilometres north of Muş.[1] It was a take-over, rather than a clear break with the past, for, as in Wales, Christian churches rose on pagan holy ground. Lynch remarks, 'Many Armenians practised Christianity as a mere matter of form, regarding it as an aberration of the human intelligence to which they had been compelled to subscribe.'[2] Gregory preached the new faith in the Armenian language and the national church soon developed its own characteristics. Under Persian encouragement, anything to create a rift with the west, an

[1] *Armenia*, vol. I, p. 296.   [2] ibid., p. 296.

Armenian alphabet was evolved, completed if not invented by the Bishop Mesrop, and a school of translators into Armenian was set up early in the fifth century. For some centuries after this beautiful manuscripts were produced with illuminations in a style which blends what had been inherited from Urartu with Persian and Syrian influences. Riveting the attention in Armenian representations of the human figure are the great pools of eyes. The Armenian Church refused to accept the findings of the Council of Chalcedon (A.D. 451) and, so far as I understand the matter, continued to hold that in Christ there was present only one person and one nature, a realistic and humanistic view which alienated the Armenians from other Christians, including their neighbours the Nestorians and the Georgians. What remains of the Armenian Church holds the same view today. Armenian houses have no ikons and Armenians do not accept the infallibility of the Pope. The links with Syria became stronger than those with Byzantium.

During the sixth century, Justinian, in his attempt to hold the eastern Roman Empire together, remodelled the Armenian legal system but the effect of this was not profound or far-reaching.[1]

The Arab explosion of the seventh century took in Armenia and the country was raided in 652 and taken in 693. It remained for centuries under Islamic control, from Damascus and from Baghdad, all without diminishing the Armenian consciousness and culture. In this new orientation the country still straddled important trade routes and prospered accordingly. About the middle of the seventh century upholders of the Paulician heresy escaped into the Byzantine Empire, and when the Arab conquest came at the end of the century there was an even greater flood of refugees, most of whom were aristocrats with their families, servants and retinues, leaving the poorer people behind.[2] These movements were not always voluntary and Anatolia has a long history of enforced transplantation. In A.D. 578, for instance, whilst Armenia was still under Byzantine control, ten thousand Armenians were taken from their homes to settle in Cyprus, to till the soil and provide soldiers.[3] Others were settled in Crete, Thrace and Calabria. The Armenian exodus had begun. Armenians became prominent in the Byzantine army, sometimes supplying not only a preponderance of good soldiers but commanders of the quality of the sixth-century

[1] See A. H. M. Jones, *Cities of the Eastern Roman Empire*, pp. 224 ff.
[2] P. Charanis, *The Armenians in the Byzantine Empire*, p. 14.   [3] ibid., p. 14.

Narses. In their exile they retained their nationality and insisted on their descent, and there were several emperors of Armenian blood. They were important too in the intellectual life of the Byzantine Empire and the revival of learning which took place in Constantinople in the ninth century was headed by scholars of Armenian descent and connections. The tenth-century success of the Byzantines against the Arabs in Cappadocia and Cilicia encouraged the movement of Armenians into this area and the setting up along the Cilician coast of an Armenian kingdom which lasted from 1080 to 1375. The castles of Korykos are a monument to this kingdom. During these centuries too the Armenians back in their homeland developed their remarkable style of church architecture. Their earliest churches were basilical in form, as were those of their Georgian neighbours to the north, but during the sixth century the characteristic drum and cone form was invented, either to be the central piece of a bigger building or to stand on its own in monumental isolation, as in some of the smaller churches at Ani.

In A.D. 885 kingship had returned to Armenia proper in the person of Ashot, a member of the Bagratid family, of Jewish origin, long established in the country. (A branch of this family continued to rule Georgia up to the eighteenth century.) Ashot I's accession was recognised by the Emperor Basil I of Byzantium, but he and his successors suffered harassment from the Moslem rulers of Azerbaijan and for years the Armenians had to put up with raids, persecution and torture. Rival claims to the throne by Armenian noblemen helped to weaken the country. It was one of these rivals, the Artsruni King Gagik, not the later Gagik I, who retired from war and administration to Aghtamar Island on Lake Van and built a palace and the astonishing church which still delights us with its stone sculpture.

During the reign of Sembat II (977–989) Ani became the capital city and the great defensive wall was built. He laid the foundations of the cathedral which was completed by his son, Gagik I (989–1019). He also built the Church of St. Gregory which still remains fairly intact to demonstrate the typical Armenian church style, circular in body with a drum having twelve blind arches and a conical top, the point of which has now gone.

Disruption in Armenia and the tendency to surrender their freedom to the Byzantine power rendered the Armenians little able to withstand the devastating inroads of the Turkoman tribes during the eleventh century. Kars was sacked and its inhabitants massacred in 1050 and Muş and Malatya suffered a similar fate within ten years. These sporadic attacks culminated in the defeat of the Byzantine Emperor Romanus at Malazgirt in 1071 and the end of any form of Armenian independence. Ani fell under Arab and Kurdish rule and then shuttled between Arab and Georgian hands until the Tartars under Genghiz Khan sacked it in 1239. The final blow to the Armenian capital was a fearful earthquake in 1319. The Armenians were henceforward to be ruled by Arabs, Kurds, Persians and Seljuks and eventually by the Ottoman sultans who took over their land in the sixteenth century. The kingdom of Lesser Armenia in Cilicia survived in the struggle between Byzantium and the encroaching Turks almost to the end of the fourteenth century. Other Armenians emigrated during these trying years to Russia and even to Poland. They are to be found everywhere in the Near East today and when I lived in Egypt the best shoemakers, shirtmakers and jewellers were Armenian. More recent emigration has swollen the numbers and many of them have prospered in America, in the arts as well as in commerce. For centuries there has been a large Armenian colony in Istanbul, which has long been associated with the arts and particularly the theatre. The appearance of Moslem women in public theatrical performances was frowned upon before Ataturk's revolution and Armenian women were usually the actresses. A pioneer modern theatre in Istanbul, the Gedikpaşa Theatre which opened in the 1860s, had a company of twenty-six actors, seven of them Turkish and nineteen Armenian, as well as eighteen actresses, all Armenian.[1] Plays were performed by them in Armenian and Turkish.

The Kurds have always been the enemies of the Armenians, exhibiting not only a difference of religion but the contempt of a pastoral and marauding people for more settled town-dwellers and farmers. But up to the late nineteenth century the official Turkish attitude to the Armenians was one of careless tolerance. In correspondence with the Sultan's government in 1862 over the constitutional position of the Armenians they were recognised on both Ottoman and Armenian sides as a separate people. Traditionally the Patriarch of the Armenian Church had been their representative to the sultan and had in turn been the sultan's agent for carrying out edicts amongst the Armenian people. This was confirmed in 1863 but, at the request of the Armenians,

[1] Metin And, *A History of Theatre and Popular Entertainment in Turkey*, pp. 68–9.

their General Assembly was now to consist of two bodies, one religious and one political, both under the presidency of the Patriarch. This new constitution of 1863 took in the position and responsibilities of the Armenian Patriarch of Jerusalem, a city then under Turkish rule. An educational council controlled education in Armenia. There were also councils for law, property, monastic and other buildings, hospitals and inheritance. It is to be noted that only forty members, two-sevenths of the General Assembly, came from the provinces in the 1860s, five-sevenths being elected in Istanbul.[1] Eastern Anatolia was clearly too remote and unprofitable for either the sultan's government or the well-established Armenian colony in Istanbul to bother much about it. This General Assembly of the Armenian nation met regularly in Istanbul until 1892, when relations between the government and the Armenians began to worsen towards the final disasters.

Since early in the nineteenth century Russia had adopted the role of protector of the Christian communities of Turkey, chiefly as an excuse for interference in that country with a view to controlling the Bosphorus and a southern sea outlet. Access to the Persian Gulf as well as to the Mediterranean was a reason for similar behaviour on Russia's part towards Persia. The Crimean War was a result of the struggle between the European powers for influence in Turkey and for the control of trade and military routes. The victory of the British and the French inclined some Armenians to turn to the west for support in a bid for independence and there is evidence that towards the end of the nineteenth century Britain gave some encouragement to a movement of Armenian revolutionaries in Istanbul. Ever since the Turks established themselves in Anatolia the Armenians had enjoyed considerable cultural autonomy, but the natural if ill-judged movement of the Armenians towards complete freedom angered the Ottoman government, and this government's lack of interest and possible connivance in the terrible massacres of 1895 caused thousands of innocent and non-political Armenians to suffer for the mistake of depending upon an outside power for help when in fact they were only being used as pawns in an imperialist game. The mistake was repeated during World War I when Armenians and Nestorians joined forces with the Russians who pushed down from Kars, held by them since 1877, to take Erzurum and Van. But for Ataturk's rallying of Turkish resistance to the dismemberment of the country, an independent Armenia

[1] For a full text of the constitution see Lynch, vol. II, pp. 452 ff.

might well have come into being. The Armenians are now scattered and those remaining in Turkey are rapidly merging into the population of the country.

ALEXANDER THE GREAT AND HELLENISATION

As we have seen, Alexander's two great victories, at Issus in 333 and Gaugamela in 331, set Armenia free from Persian domination and extended its commercial range but did little otherwise to change its way of life. Paphlagonia, Cappadocia and Armenia, that is central and eastern Anatolia north of the Taurus Mountains, were left largely independent when Alexander died in 323 B.C. After his death, Seleucus Nicator, who had accompanied him in his campaigns, made Syria the centre of a vast empire which stretched to India and into Anatolia west of the Euphrates and up to the Taurus. Seleucus vigorously carried out Alexander's ideals of hellenisation linked with a sympathy for local cultures. Alexander himself had married the Bactrian princess Roxana and later Barsine, daughter of the Persian Darius, without abandoning Roxana, who was with child by him when he died. He allotted Asiatic wives to eighty of his generals, adopted Persian customs to placate his chief enemies and established cities in the Greek style from the Troad to Bucephala on the Indus and Alexandria in Egypt. Greek or Macedonian colonies were settled all over the empire and inter-marriage with local people was encouraged, but Alexander's ideal of racial fusion was not quite achieved, since Macedonian and Greek elements remained dominant in the colonies established. The way had been opened for the Roman Empire, Christianity and Byzantium. *Koine dialektos*, the common everyday form of Greek, became the lingua franca of this hellenised world, whilst classical Greek remained for literature and for the conduct of Byzantine government. Modern Greek has come from this *koine* and as a modern language dates from 1453, the year of the Turkish conquest of Constantinople. It was resistance to this language and culture, to hellenisation in general, which fostered the Armenian civilisation, its script, its literature and its version of Christianity.

Seleucus Nicator made Antioch his capital and built the city of Zeugma on the west bank of the Euphrates, at a point where Alexander had built a pontoon bridge and probably opposite present-day Birecik. At the age of seventy-eight, having crossed the Dardanelles with the intention of adding Thrace and Macedonia to his dominions, he was assassinated, after a reign of thirty-three years. He had already handed over to his son Antiochus the kingship of his lands east of the Euphrates, together with his young wife Stratonice, with whom Antiochus was in love. (The family lives of the Seleucid kings are interesting and sometimes tragic and the names of some of the queens, Laodice, Cleopatra, Berenice, are highly evocative.) This Antiochus, the First, was killed in battle against the Gauls, who were to settle down to become the Galatians. Another Antiochus, the Fourth, surnamed Epiphanes, was also a great hellenist and during his reign, 175–164 B.C., Antioch became a centre of Greek art. He was much hated because of his suppression of local religions in favour of the Greek gods. It was his attempt to do this in Palestine which provoked the Maccabee rebellion. For all this he was popularly known as Epimanes, the Madman, in mockery of Epiphanes.

After two centuries of reigns full of violence, war and tragic family stories, the Seleucid Empire was merged into Armenia in 83 B.C. but soon came under Roman control as a result of the campaigns of Lucullus in 69 and Pompey in 65. The kingdom of Commagene, the northern part of Syria between the Taurus Mountains and the Euphrates and north of the present Syrian frontier with Turkey, came into existence as a Roman buffer state and was for some years a Roman province. Its first king was yet another Antiochus of Seleucid descent and it was he who raised the impressive sanctuary on Nimrut Dağ in the year 30 B.C. and left a no doubt idealised representation of himself, in the company of his heterogeneous gods. It must be remembered that the Seleucids, true products of Alexander's idea of racial fusion, traced their descent from the Persian Achaemenids as well as from their Macedonian origin.

THE GALATIANS

As a result of the Roman drive into eastern Anatolia in the first century B.C. the kingdom of Galatia was extended eastwards and northwards to include the regions of Paphlagonia and Pontus, taking in present-day Trabzon and Batum. It pleases me to think that a Celtic language akin to Welsh has been spoken by rulers of Trebizond. The Galatians had in 279 B.C. entered Anatolia as a fighting and marauding band made up of sections of three Celtic tribes, after sacking Delphi. This was part of the outward explosion of the Celts from central Europe, their homeland, which took place during the middle centuries of the first millennium B.C. After rampaging through western Anatolia for some forty years, and preferring to exact tribute by the threat of destruction rather than to destroy, they were defeated by Attalus of Pergamon in 232 B.C. They were persuaded to settle down in a central Anatolian league with Ankara as its main centre. The extension of their power into eastern Anatolia was as a client state of Rome, as part of the consolidation of the Roman Empire in the east and as a reward for their help, under their king, Deiotaros,[1] against Mithridates VI of Pontus. After their involvement in the defeat of the Seleucid Antiochus and the desperate Hannibal at Magnesia in 190 B.C. the Galatians gradually came to terms with their natural and traditional enemies, the Romans. Amyntas, their third and last king—for up to the first century B.C. each of the three tribes had had its own chieftain—before his death in 25 B.C. bequeathed Galatia to Rome and Augustus. Amyntas had taken the side of Octavius in the war against Antony and Cleopatra and continued to serve Rome by clearing out bandits from the Taurus, in the south-eastern corner of his dominions. There is a lovely silver coin struck by Amyntas in the Antioch Museum. He had killed a bandit chief and then generously agreed to parley with the widow. He fell into an ambush on his way to her, was taken before her and put to death. Another Galatian, Adiatorix, took Antony's part, was taken prisoner after Antony's death and with his wife and three children graced the triumph of Augustus in Rome. Adiatorix and his eldest son were executed after the triumph. The youngest son tried to take the place of his brother, Dytentos, and when Augustus heard of this attempted self-sacrifice he made the two younger brothers high priests of the goddess Ma, known to classical writers as Artemis Taurica, at Comana Pontica, eight kilometres north of present-day Tokat. High-priesthood at this famous shrine ranked a man next to the king.[2]

The Galatians to whom St. Paul wrote his Epistle were mostly Jews of Celtic Ankara who were early converts to Christianity.

---

[1] *Duw Tarw* in modern Welsh, Bull-God or Bull of God.
[2] For information about these Galatians see Strabo, *Geographica*, Book XII. Strabo came from Amasia, near Comana. Also Ramsay, *Studies in the Roman Province of Galatia*.

THE KURDS

The Kurds have already been mentioned as a mountain people who opposed the passage of Xenophon's army and who have been ancient and traditional enemies of the Armenians. Like most of the peoples of the world the Kurds are a racial mixture. They are thought to be basically a blend of invading Medes and original inhabitants of what is known as Kurdistan, just as the modern Iranians are descended from a similar blend of Persians and natives. Both Kurds and Iranians are descended from Aryans who came into this part of the Near and Middle East from the north at an unknown time but possibly when the other Indo-European speaking people, the Hittites, came from the north into Anatolia about 2000 B.C. Today, although they are divided by the recently imposed frontiers of Turkey, Iran and Irak, the Kurds are as distinct and separate a people as the Japanese or the Welsh and are acutely aware of being Kurds. Kurdish is an Indo-European language and is close to Persian, rather as English is close to Dutch. There are three main dialects of Kurdish. The Zaza dialect is spoken in the central part of eastern Anatolia, from Diyarbakır and Malatya across past Muş and the region north of Lake Van to Doğubeyazit near the border and Azerbaijan in Iran. This form of Kurdish has not unnaturally acquired a number of Turkish words. The most important and the purest dialect is Kermanji, spoken in the Hakkari region of Turkey, in northern Irak and in the Kordestan province of Iran. Gurani is spoken in the Kermanshah province of Iran and is close to modern Persian, particularly in its Lori dialect form. Kermanji is the only form of Kurdish used officially, though not in Turkey. It is now the medium of instruction in the schools of the Kurdish area of northern Irak and poetry and prose, as well as school textbooks, are published in it, using the Arabic alphabet, as Persian does. Zaza and Kermanji speakers understand each other as well as a Yorkshireman does a Cockney, or since Kermanji is the language of literature, perhaps one should say a Yorkshire countryman and an Oxford don born in the south. Most Kurds accepted Islam during the Moslem advance northwards in the seventh century and most of them are Sunnis of the Shafei sect. But some fifty thousand of them are still today said to be Yazidi or Peacock-god worshippers, often unfairly known to the west as devil-worshippers and they seem to have been the Kurds most feared by Turks and

Armenians alike. According to Badger[1] the Yazidis or Yezidis are descendants of the ancient Assyrians though they resemble Kurds in appearance and use the Kurdish language. They worship the Sun and will not spit into a fire for fear of offending the holy principle. Water is sacred to them too. Out of fear and respect for the power of evil, a very Persian view of the duality of our universe, the eternal struggle between good and bad, they never refer to Satan by name, just as in Wales he is referred to as *y gwr drwg*, the bad man. They don't hold with fasting and many of them do not practise the Moslem rite of circumcision. The Reverend Badger concludes that there is little hope of their conversion to Christianity! That they were regarded as quite distinct from Kurds and much feared by law-abiding Turks is made clear in *Ayesha*, a novel by James Morier, author of *Hajji Baba*. An interesting account of them is given in Chapter XIX of that novel and Morier says, 'The Yezidies, as a race, are one of the most cruel and sanguinary that are known in Asia.'[2] And, 'Their name is synonymous with blasphemers, barbarians, and men of blood.'[3] Morier also tells us that the Yazidis believe that it is God who ordains, but that he delivers over the execution of his orders to the Devil. A colourful, violent race well exemplified by Morier's character, Cara Bey.

The Kurds are a mountain people and in Turkey today are referred to as Mountain Turks, since the existence of a Kurdish nation is denied by Turkish officialdom. They owe their continued persistence as a nation to the wildness of the mountains in which they live, for it has usually been their practice not to resist invaders, who are normally content to march through the mountains and on to richer and more attractive regions. In such a situation the Kurds have packed their tents and driven their animals to still higher mountains, away from the main passes, and have usually suffered little more than the loss of some beasts, since they are not people to store much in the way of crops. They put up no resistance to the Mongols, who cut their devastating way through Persia into eastern Anatolia in the thirteenth century, except at Miyafarikin,[4] where Kurdish rulers had taken to Arab ways and the city was taken and its people massacred. Only in this present century has the ancient and effective technique of withdrawing from invaders lost its validity; roads and railways are driven through the

[1] G. P. Badger, *The Nestorians and their Rituals*, vol. I, p. 112.
[2] *Ayesha*, p. 150.   [3] ibid., p. 148.
[4] See p. 143.

mountains for strategic as well as commercial reasons, difficult terrain can be patrolled from the air and tourism pushes further its corrupting tentacles.

A country known as Kardaka is mentioned in a Sumerian inscription of 2000 B.C.[1] The people seem to have been known to the Assyrians and Xenophon knew them as the Carduchi. Owing to their evasive tactics of non-resistance they have been nominally ruled by Arabs, Mongols, Seljuks, Ilhans and other rulers of Persia, Kara and Ak Koyun chieftains and Ottomans, up to the time of their division between three countries after the First World War. Rather like Armenia, Kurdistan has been a buffer region between Rome, Byzantium and the west and Persia, the Arabs and the east. The Treaty of Sèvres (1920) promised the Kurds autonomy within fixed frontiers and there would today be an independent Kurdistan but for Ataturk's drive to hang on to Anatolia for the Turks.

Though they practised a policy of evasion in the face of conquerors on the march, the Kurds have been far from unwarlike and have been ready to fight in other people's wars, away from their home ground. Acceptance of Islam gave enterprising Kurdish chieftains opportunities to benefit from the Arab outsurge. The Hasanwayh dynasty was established in eastern Kurdistan by Hasanwayh ben Hosayn Barzikani in the middle of the tenth century. Another Kurd, Abu Ali Marwan, in 990 established a dynasty to control the Diyarbakır—Mardin—Nusaybin region, under the nominal suzerainty of the Khalif. Both the Hasanwayhs and the Marwanids adopted Arabic as their language and are usually referred to as Arabs. They are not highly thought of by present-day Kurds, any more than the Tudor monarchs are in Wales today. But another Kurd, Saladin, is remembered with more honour and pride, probably because of his successes against the Crusaders. The Kurds are not unnaturally pleased to have produced one of the greatest heroes of Islam and certainly the Moslem leader most respected in the west.

Since the Seljuk and then the Ottoman conquests the Kurds have pursued their unchanging way of life in their mountainous homeland, but during the nineteenth century they began to be involved, as were their neighbours the Nestorians and the Armenians, in the interest the world powers were taking in Turkey. The Russians made use of the Kurds for their own purposes, as they did with the Armenians and

[1] Hassan Arfa, *The Kurds*, p. 3.

Nestorians, promising them some kind of autonomy and organising a Kurdish regiment with Russian officers during the Crimean War. In 1877, during the war which led to Russian occupation of much of north-eastern Anatolia, the Kurds revolted aginst the Ottoman government. Now for the first time they seem to have been inspired by the Russians to demand more than regional autonomy, rather the setting up of a free Kurdistan, to take in the Kurds of Persia and the Ottoman Empire.[1] Another plan, this time favoured by the Turkish government, was for the Kurds to invade Iran and to attach the Kurdish tribal lands there to an autonomous state under the suzerainty of the Ottoman power. Sultan Hamid II in the early 1890s, in an attempt to check Russian advances and to canalise the restless energy of the Kurds, their readiness to fight, formed Kurdish regiments of cavalry, this time officered by Kurds. Away from their mountains however, and denied the guerilla type of warfare in which they traditionally excel, the Kurds are said to lose some of their martial spirit.[2] But I have heard first-hand accounts of the complete fearlessness and fatalism of the Kurdish soldier in the Turkish army of today. During the 1914–18 War the Kurds remained loyal to the Turks and it was the Nestorians and Armenians who were this time seduced by the Russians into anti-Turkish activity which led to their destruction. The Kurds had for some twenty years, the early part of this century, been allowed by the central goverment to prey on the Armenians and now, after the Turkish collapse, the Armenian volunteers on the Russian side took their revenge. More than six hundred thousand Kurds are said to have been killed in eastern Anatolia between 1915 and 1918.[3] Corresponding slaughter and deportation of Nestorians and Armenians combined to reduce the population of this part of Turkey.

The Kurds are a conservative people and they were shocked by Ataturk's declaration of a republic and abolition of the Khalifate. The first Kurdish revolt against the new government of Turkey, in 1925, was on religious grounds. It was led by a Dervish named Sheikh Said and affected the area between Elazığ and Siverek in the west and Malazgirt and Lake Van in the east. The movement was marred by looting on the part of disreputable elements who had joined for the fun of it, but many Turks sympathised with it in their dislike of the revolutionary changes taking place in their country. I know someone whose Turkish grandfather was hanged for sympathising with this

[1] ibid., pp. 23–4.   [2] ibid., p. 25.   [3] ibid., p. 26.

8. *Kurdish women at Eleşkirt*

9. *Kurdish children at Öğrenburc*

10. *The Tahir Pass (2,400 metres) in early November*

11. *Near the Tahir Pass: house with cones of cowdung fuel*

revolt, which was suppressed after three months of fighting, during which the Turkish army succeeded in cutting off any Kurdish retreat east of Van or into the Hakkari Mountains. Sheikh Said and other leaders were hanged.

Another revolt occurred in 1930, this time politically motivated by the notion of Kurdish independence and affecting the area between Lake Van and Ararat. The main battle seems to have been fought on Ararat and Little Ararat and the Kurds, in spite of help from their brothers in Iran and Irak, were once more defeated by the better-organised Turkish army. It was during this fighting that the little township of Doğubeyazit was destroyed and vacated.[1] Yet another insurrection occurred in 1937, this time in the Tunceli region, where the Kurds hoped to hold out in this very mountainous part until other tribes were able to follow suit and join them. Once more the revolt was suppressed, the leaders executed and the rebellious tribes broken up and transferred to other regions. Detribalisation and stern discouragement of the use of the Kurdish language, together with better administration and commercial, industrial and agricultural advance, are the tactics now being used by the Turks to persuade the Kurds to accept government from Ankara as they did from Istanbul in Ottoman days. The Kurds today eagerly accept the educational opportunities provided for their children, imperfect though these may still be, and they are much more prepared for their daughters to be educated than are many Turks of central Anatolia. But it remains to be seen whether they have given up their hope of being united with other Kurds in a free Kurdistan. At the moment they are culturally frustrated in Turkey and the project of setting up an institute of Kurdish studies in Diyarbakır has so far come to nothing.

Educated Kurds today move quite naturally and almost indistinguishably, since the Turks are so varied ethnographically, in Turkish society, as lawyers, members of parliament, university professors and so on. Working-class Kurds become porters and building labourers in Istanbul, but speak their own language amongst themselves and keep their links with their eastern Anatolian homes.

[1] See p. 205.

THE NESTORIANS

The Nestorians are a religious sect rather than originally a separate people, but since they have until recently clung to their religion in the Hakkari region of Turkey through long centuries in which they have been surrounded by Moslems, they have become as distinct in race as they are in their faith. Syrians of northern Mesopotamia, still speaking a form of Syriac, they adopted the views of the nature of Christ put forward by Nestorius. It may be that the instinct to do this was similar to that of the Armenians in their religious apartness, that is resistance to Byzantine authority. Nestorius, who was Bishop of Constantinople from 428 to 431, was born at Germaniceia, present-day Maraş, towards the end of the fourth century. He is now generally thought to have been more orthodox than he appeared to the Pope in his day and to other church leaders from whom he received harsh treatment. His works were burnt by Papal order and he was persecuted by Cyril of Alexandria. He was carried off and mutilated by Nubians and died in the Egyptian desert in 451. A monastery he founded at Antioch became his centre and from there the teaching of his church, sometimes known as the Chaldean Church, and that of the closely allied Eastern Syrian Church, spread all over Asia in the fifth century.[1] He believed Christ to be two persons closely and inseparably linked and yet distinct, a view which stressed the humanity of Christ, as the Celtic heresy of Pelagius had already done. Nestorius was condemned for referring to Mary as Mother of Christ, not Mother of God. Most offensive to orthodox believers was his statement about Mary, 'No one can bring forth a son older than herself.'[2]

Heresies have often sprung from alternatives in grammar and in the interpretation of words, and in Nestorianism much seems to depend on the meaning of such words as *person* and *nature*, or the Syriac concepts which they attempt to translate. So the teaching of Antioch leant heavily on the human side of Christ whilst that of Alexandria, that capital of subtle hair-splitting, stressed the divine side. Antioch studied the Scriptures historically and analytically. Syria became Monophysite[3] in its faith and Persia Nestorian, but Edessa and Nisibis continued as

[1] *Oxford Dictionary of the Christian Church*, pp. 946–7.
[2] The Nestorians, *Catholic Encyclopedia*, vol. 10.
[3] For a clear account of these sects see E. M. Forster, *Alexandria: a History and Guide*.

Nestorian strongholds and up to the thirteenth century were centres of much learning. Since the Moslem take-over of those parts and the contraction of Nestorianism into mountain country there has been degeneration to ignorance. The Kurds have long been enemies of the Nestorians and in 1852 there was some British concern at reports of massacres of Nestorians by Kurds and the selling of women and children into slavery in the Arab parts of the Turkish Empire. Sir Stratford Canning intervened from the British Embassy at Istanbul at this time and rescued some of the intended slaves, buying them back with money raised by public subscription.[1] But the Nestorians hung on in the mountains of south-east Anatolia until this century, carefully tilling their little terraced fields in the wild Zab valley and the upland pastures. In 1915 the Nestorian patriarch committed his people to the Allied cause against the Turks, but the Russians failed them and they had to leave their little farms and neat stone houses to escape eastwards into Iran. Their homes were left untenanted for many years, until the Kurds moved into them. All that is left to remember them by in Turkey today are ruined farmhouses, still referred to as Nesturi, the occasional simple, dark, abandoned church,[2] the overgrown terraces of their fields, which you can spot as you drive down the Zab valley, and the designs of woollen socks still knitted by the Kurdish women, sometimes with a coloured cross on the toe.

THE ROMANS

The Romans seem to have been rather reluctant imperialists and the expansion of their power was usually the result of self-defence and of help given to allies. Only Trajan amongst their great leaders is comparable to Alexander and the extension of their empire was not through great purposeful campaigns like those of the Macedonian but rather by piecemeal annexations and pragmatic adventures. By the year 200 B.C. Carthage, Rome's early rival in the south, had been decisively beaten and its leader, Hannibal, reduced to desperate efforts to recruit other enemies to Rome. In the east the greatest danger to Rome at that time was Antiochus III of Syria, Seleucid inheritor of a large part of Alexander's empire, and it was to him at Antioch that Hannibal resorted in 193 B.C. He tried to persuade Antiochus to attack the Romans on their own ground in Italy, but the Seleucid was unwilling and

[1] G. P. Badger, *The Nestorians and their Rituals*, pp. 19–20.   [2] See Plate 7.

compromised by deciding to await the Romans in Greece. There he was defeated at Thermopylae in the year 191. He retreated into Anatolia, regrouped his forces and met the Romans, with their allies the Pergamese, at the Battle of Magnesia, one of the crucial days in the history of Europe. The toughness and training of the Roman soldiery under the Scipio brothers withstood the vast forces of Antiochus, his elephant corps, the advice of Hannibal and the skill of the Galatian cavalry. Antiochus was forced to retreat east of the Taurus Mountains whilst Hannibal escaped to Bithynia in north-west Anatolia to take his own life there when Roman pressure on his hosts became too strong.

The Seleucid hold on Anatolia now shrank to Commagene, a kingdom which was tolerated by Rome as a buffer state and which was for a time a Roman province.[1] In the meantime, during what remained of the second century and the first half of the first century B.C., Roman power was slowly consolidated by the reduction in strength of allies who had served their purpose, chiefly Pergamon, and the gradual commercial and administrative penetration of western and central Anatolia. During these years the most determined enemy of Rome was Mithridates VI of Pontus, a remarkable man, great linguist, administrator and soldier, who ruled over his country for fifty-seven years, from 120 to 63. A true western Asiatic, of Persian descent, he disliked the idea of Roman domination of the Near East and fought a number of wars against Rome. The first was quickly successful. Mithridates became master of the Roman province of Asia and in the winter of 88 ordered the massacre of all Romans and other Italians in Asia Minor. Eighty thousand are said to have died in one day. For twenty-two years war came and went between him and Rome. Towards the end he was helped by his son-in-law Tigranes of Armenia but was finally defeated by Pompey and Lucullus, escaped to the Crimea and took his own life there, in hopeless exile, at the age of sixty-nine.

With Pontus, Armenia, Paphlagonia, Cappadocia, Galatia, Cilicia and Commagene under some degree of Roman power, Rome ruled to the Euphrates and Augustus took over the inherited task of hellenisation. But once more eastern Anatolia was little affected, as we have seen in our glance at Armenian history, with the exception of the Black Sea coast, with its long established and prosperous Greek colonies past Trapezos to mythical Colchis. It was under Trajan that

[1] See p. 59.

Colchis, lying between the present Turkish frontier and the Caucasus Mountains, was added to the Roman Empire, and Trajan sent Pliny the Younger there with a special commission to look into administration and finance. Pliny was there in A.D. 113 referring back to the Emperor, as was his custom, problems mostly to do with money or referring to the *lex Pompeia*, which had served as constitution and law for north-eastern Anatolia for a hundred and fifty years. Trajan replied stressing the need for consideration of local law and customs. These were years of discontent in Roman Anatolia, with prosperous citizens unwilling to undertake public duties and with taxation biting more and more deeply into the purses of rich and poor. Bondmen and slaves welcomed the promise of equality offered by the new religion, Christianity, which Pliny, having examined and tortured some of the new believers on behalf of his emperor, reported as being 'a degenerate sort of cult carried to extravagant lengths'.[1] To the Romans all religions were equal and Gibbon sums up the Roman attitude thus, 'The various modes of worship, which prevailed in the Roman world, were all considered, by the people, as equally true; by the philosopher, as equally false; and by the magistrate, as equally useful.'[2] But Christianity with its special appeal to the underprivileged, was suspect and would be persecuted. The earliest churches are those we hear of from St. Paul and they were established in the southern part of western Anatolia, but the first Christian congregation was probably in the little cave outside Antioch and the first country to make Christianity its official religion was Armenia.

The Antioch-Euphrates corridor was not only the channel for the first outsurge of Christianity from Palestine but also a tempting door for ambitious drives to the east inspired by the memory of Alexander the Great and Antiochus the Great of Syria. It might be thought that the collapse of the Seleucids opened the way east for the Romans, but a ruthless and powerful enemy, the Parthians, still straddled the Silk Route, the old trade route from the Mediterranean to India and China. As a result, the considerable Roman trade with the Persian Gulf, India, China and the East Indies was by sea along the lines of the Greek merchants' handbook, the *Peryplus of the Erythrean Sea*,[3] that is the Persian Gulf. Darius of Persia had sent Scylax, a native of the south

[1] *Letters* of the Younger Pliny, trans. by B. Radice, p. 294.
[2] *Decline and Fall of the Roman Empire*, II, 1.
[3] See Sir Mortimer Wheeler, *Rome Beyond the Imperial Frontiers*, pp. 141 ff.

Anatolian coast, on a voyage of discovery from the Indus, round the Arabian coast to the Red Sea, and he may have been the author of this fourth century B.C. work which is attributed to him.

M. Licinius Crassus, consul with Pompey and triumvir with Pompey and Caesar, a man with a lust for wealth, became governor of the new province of Syria and was ill-advised enough to expose his Roman foot-soldiers to the heat and long marches of Mesopotamia. He was defeated at Carrhae, captured and put to death in 53 B.C. by the Parthians. Molten gold was poured into the mouth of his decapitated head as a comment on Roman ambitions in the Middle East.[1] When Trajan, in two campaigns of A.D. 115 and 116, broke the power of Persia, the land route to India had been forgotten and had to be explored anew.

Three centuries of the *pax Romana* induced a slackness in matters of fortification and a softer way of life along the Black Sea coast of Asia Minor and left the inhabitants as unprepared for self-defence against barbarian invaders as were the Britons in a similar situation. The Goths descended across central Europe in the middle of the third century, and in naval expeditions across the Euxine from the Crimea they sacked not only the great hellenised and romanised cities of western Anatolia but Trapezos as well. The Alani, a Scythian tribe, made a similar sweep of Anatolia in the year 276. They were later, in A.D. 406, to accompany the Vandals in attacks on the collapsing Roman Empire as far west as Gaul and Spain.

THE BYZANTINES

Byzantium became New Rome when Constantine made it the capital of the Roman Empire in the year 330, after considering Troy and cold-shouldering Antioch and Alexandria. But the Byzantine era may be more properly said to begin in the sixth century when, after the fall of Rome, a new culture emerged under Justinian with less that was Roman in it and more that was Greek and Anatolian, and with Greek, not Latin, as its official language.

Once more, eastern Anatolia was little affected by these momentous events in the west, but that most ancient corridor between Antioch and the Euphrates let in more than one Persian attack and then, in the seventh century, the Arab flood. The flood was checked in Anatolia and Europe saved from the right hand of a possible Arab pincer movement

[1] See p. 172.

upon Europe which might have linked up with the Moslem drive through North Africa to Spain. But a portent of the future was the passage through eastern Anatolia in the second half of the sixth century of the first Turkish ambassadors, who were received at Constantinople by Justin II, the more honourably because they offered trade with China by the Turkoman land route north of the Himalayas.

Throughout the centuries, until the coming of the Seljuks, Armenia acted as a buffer state for Byzantium, holding off Persia with varying effectiveness whilst pursuing its own cultural life. At the same time it supplied the Byzantine capital and empire with some of its most brilliant men. The attraction of Constantinople must have been great for ambitious craftsmen, scholars, soldiers, administrators and politicians. Armenians rose to the highest positions. The Emperors Basil I, Romanus Lecapenus, Nicephorus Phocas, John Tzimisces and Basil II were of Armenian stock. Famous generals were Petronas and John Curcuas. Nicephorus Phocas, a redoubtable warrior who knew the ardours of campaigning in eastern Anatolia but realised the necessity of vigilance to keep the Arab at bay, wrote a treatise on the tactics of war in such conditions. The exploits of a ninth-century general in the Byzantine army called Mleh or Melias were later attributed to Digenes Akritas, the hero of the Byzantine epic of frontier fighting.[1] In the ninth century too the scholars Caesar Bardas, Leo the Philosopher, Photius and John the Grammarian, all of entirely or partly Armenian stock, were prominent in the intellectual life of Constantinople, which had replaced Athens as a centre of learning. Armenian princely families were influential in the life of the capital from the sixth century on and there is no end to Armenian names in Byzantine history. Professor Charanis has given a detailed account of them in the book referred to in my footnotes.

The retreat of Byzantium from eastern Anatolia under the impact of the Turkoman probings of the eleventh century and the weakening and eventual conquest of Armenia by the Seljuks were relieved by two new ventures of considerable historical and cultural interest and importance. They were the establishment of an offshoot of Byzantium at Trebizond and the foundation of the Armenian kingdom in Cilicia.

Trebizond, ancient Trapezos,[2] had been an important Greek colony since the sixth century B.C. Easily fortifiable, it had over the centuries resisted many invasions, though not that of the Goths, who sacked it

[1] P. Charanis, op. cit., p. 44.   [2] See pp. 219–24.

in the third century A.D. It was not taken in the Seljuk sweep into Anatolia in the eleventh century. In 1204, when Constantinople was taken by the ruthless Crusaders, to be subjected to their unhappy rule for sixty years, two sons of the Emperor Andronicus escaped and set themselves up in Trebizond. Alexis Comnenos became emperor there and his successors ruled until the city was taken by Mehmet the Conqueror in 1461, eight years after his capture of Constantinople. So for two and a half centuries and for eight uneasy years after the fall of Byzantium, a brilliant civilisation flourished in this remote corner of north-east Anatolia. Trebizond was a natural seaport for land trade with Asia and it was this that attracted the Genoese, who muscled in on Black Sea trade in the thirteenth century and disputed control of the Asian trade routes with the Trapezuntines. Venetians followed in the fourteenth century. England too was not unaware of Trebizond's importance and a mission sent by Edward I under Geoffrey of Langley stayed there for two months in the summer of 1292 on its way to exchange gifts with the Mongol Ilhan ruler at Tabriz.[1] Like the Parthians of Roman times it was these Mongols who now controlled the profitable land trade route to Persia and the Far East. The Comnene princesses were famous for their beauty and were cleverly used to shore up the power and independence of Trebizond through arranged marriages with Christian and Moslem rulers. The walls of Trebizond still stand, as do many of its lovely churches and the extraordinary monastery of Sumela, built in 1375 by Alexios III.[2] Mehmet the Conqueror, to celebrate his capture of the city, said the first Friday prayers in the Church of St. Eugenios, which since then has been known as the Yeni Cuma Cami, the New Friday Mosque. So Trebizond became Trabzon, a Moslem town, but it kept a considerable Greek population well into our present century. Our hotel proprietor on the island of Thasos had been born there but had gone off as a boy to act as interpreter for the Russians and had been unable to return. Prominent Byzantines of Trebizond went over to the service of the sultan and became notable officials and scholars under the new régime of the Ottomans.

The late eleventh century saw the emigration to Cilicia[3] on the Mediterranean coast of Armenians who had suffered from the Seljuk

---

[1] A. Bryer, 'Edward I and the Mongols', *History Today*, October, 1964.
[2] See pp. 227–8.
[3] Already referred to in the section on The Armenians.

conquest and who now took advantage of Byzantine weakness to set up a kingdom there. This venture is outside the scope of this book except in so far as it shows how Anatolian experiments in military architecture were passed on to the west. The Armenians had inherited the expertise achieved in central and eastern Anatolia by the Hittites and Urartians, and their own refinements and modifications produced such castles as those of Silifke and Korykos, which taught the Crusaders a style of building that was to be further elaborated by the Normans in France and Britain. The Byzantines had acquired these skills much earlier but from the same source and the walls of Istanbul are not very different from those of Beğazköy put up two thousand years before them. Caernarfon, Windsor and the French châteaux therefore derive from eastern Turkey, through the walls of Constantinople and the castles of Armenian Cilicia.

Centuries before the fall of Constantinople, Byzantine power, never really dominant in eastern Anatolia, had completely faded away, except for the luxuriant Indian summer of Trebizond.

THE SELJUKS

The Seljuks were a branch of the western Ghuzz or Oghuz tribes, the most important eastern tribe of the Turkomans being the Uygur. By the eighth century the Seljuks were moving about the steppes of present-day Uzbekistan, mobile with their tents and ponies, good archers and worshippers of weather gods. In the tenth century they were reached by Moslem missionaries and converted to Islam. In the eleventh century there occurred to them the impulse to move which has affected many other peoples, motivated either by growing pressure from an encroaching enemy or by some mysterious internal combustion. In the eleventh century, under the leadership of different members of their royal family, they fanned out in a planned manner into India, Persia, Syria, Palestine and Anatolia. In 1063 Alp Arslan seized the leadership of the Seljuks and showed himself to be a king in the grand manner, a great general, a lover of hunting and a patron of the arts. Even before Alp Arslan came to power Seljuk raids had struck deep into eastern Turkey, benefiting from disruption in Armenia and demonstrating the inability of the Byzantine power to hold its eastern provinces. Ani and Kars were sacked in 1050 and their populations massacred. Muş, Malatya and Sivas fell in turn to the Seljuks, who also

73

took Antioch, Edessa, Kayseri and Konya before Romanos Diogenes attempted to cope with this new enemy and suffered his final defeat, and that of Byzantium in so far as the Seljuks were concerned, at the hands of Alp Arslan at Manzikert in 1071.

Eastern Anatolia was now Seljuk, except where the Byzantine offshoot held out at Trebizond and where the Danishmends, another Turkoman tribal dynasty which had invaded Anatolia late in the eleventh century, established an enclave around Sivas and Malatya until Kiliç Arslan II took over their lands in 1180. Malatya had five Danishmend kings between 1135 and 1175; Sivas six Danishmend rulers between 1095 and 1174.[1] Erzurum had Saltuk Oğullar rulers from 1071 to 1202. The Danishmends had intermarried with the Seljuk royal house but had remained their bitter rivals for the control of eastern Anatolia whilst showing less interest than the Seljuks in the western part of the country.

The Seljuks pressed on into central Anatolia after the Manzikert victory and Soliman, son of Kutulmuş, reached the Bosphorus, aided by a Byzantine rebel, and in 1078 made Iznik, as they called Nicaea, his capital. But some Byzantine successes, and some more effective Crusader forces than Walter the Penniless's pathetic horde, halted the westward drive of the Seljuks and under Kiliç Arslan they settled down to consolidate their hold on central and eastern Anatolia, after first of all making peace with the Danishmends. It was his grandson, Izzedin, who made himself Sultan Kiliç Arslan II, who finally eliminated the Danishmends towards the end of the twelfth century.

The thirteenth century saw the flowering of Seljuk culture. Konya, Alanya and Kayseri are outside the area dealt with in this book but at Sivas, Divriği and Erzurum we still have preserved the loveliest achievements of the Seljuks in architecture. These dashing warriors imposed a military aristocracy where they conquered and settled. On their passage through Persia they had picked up architectural and other cultural ideas which, once established in Anatolia as the Seljuks of Rum and independent of the Persian Seljuks, they put to the most varied use in their own unmistakable modifications. Through marriage their royal family received infusions of Danishmend, French, Byzantine and Trapezuntine blood, which may well have helped these intrepid tribesmen from central Asia to evolve their highly organised and civilised state. They founded all kinds of useful institutions—baths,

[1] For the Danishmends see p. 84.

hospitals, caravanserais, orphanages, poorhouses, mental homes, mosques and religious schools.

Under Keykubad I Sivas became a splendid town and a great commercial centre, whilst Konya became a glorious capital and Alanya, taken from the Armenians of Cilicia, a powerfully fortified winter residence and outlet into the Mediterranean. Keykubad's campaigns eastwards and his reduction of the power of Kwarazm, to the north-east of Persia, though perhaps necessary to him, had gravely weakened a buffer between Anatolia and forces of destruction that were on the move in Asia. Keykubad was poisoned in 1236 by his son, who became Keyhüsrev II. Unlike his father, who had been not only a great soldier and administrator but an architect, a craftsman in wood and a bow-maker, Keyhüsrev II pursued a life of pleasure and the link with the proud traditions of the past, symbolised in the most characteristic of Turkoman weapons, now seemed to be broken. The Mongols, already established in south Russia, now surged through Persia into Anatolia, took Erzurum in 1242 and defeated the Seljuk army west of Erzincan before continuing their onrush of plunder. Keyhüsrev accepted sub-mission to them and was strangled by dissident subjects. Seljuk independence and centralised government were gone for ever and the Seljuk state dissolved into internecine strife. The pitiful end came in 1308 with the murder of Mesud III, the last of the Seljuk dynasty. Hindsight lends significance to Mesud's honouring of Osman, leader of the Osmanli tribe, for his successes against Byzantium, but central and eastern Anatolia was to be split up between beys, emirs and tribal chieftains before the Osmanlis asserted their authority over the whole country after their conquest of Constantinople.

We are perhaps too apt to speak of the contributions of different civilisations to the sum of human achievement rather than to attempt to assess and enter into the fullness and balance of their separate cultures. So we tend to think of the Seljuks only as great architects, for their astonishingly beautiful buildings are what we are most aware of as we travel through eastern Turkey. Whatever influences might have given them ideas, Persian, Armenian or Byzantine, the Seljuks achieved a distinct way of using stone, one of the great styles in architecture. To me its most effective feature is the proportion and counterbalance of decorated and undecorated areas of building. Walls were made high and flat, of beautifully trimmed, light-coloured stone. Entrances, in contrast, would be fantastically and finely worked, in lofty, pointed recession, often descending in stalactite or honeycomb cutting to the doorway itself. It is this unfailing good taste in proportion between decoration and flat surface that makes these buildings so beautiful. Minarets were usually built of dark red brick, with blue tiles worked into a simple or intricate pattern. That of the Ulu Cami at Siirt is a fine example as are the Çifte Minare minarets of Sivas. Interiors were partly covered and partly open to the sky, the prayer room roofed or domed, the courtyard open and surrounded by rooms, sometimes with a gallery and another floor of rooms. The courtyard of the Ulu Cami at Eski Malatya had walls beautifully patterned with ceramic tiles. Plain tiles of a lovely blue were made in angular shapes for putting together into a plain, bold mosaic to wall the *mihrab* or the interior of a dome. The pointed arch was used to support galleries and for an entrance to a prayer room. The tracery of the stonework decoration is usually geometric and abstract, with occasional use of tall Kufic lettering and the suggestion of plant growth. Armenian influence is perhaps to be seen in the high relief sculpture round the entrance to the Ulu Cami and in other buildings at Divriği, as well as on the façade of the Çifte Minare at Erzurum and in the animal sculptures, unusual in Moslem art, on the city walls of Diyarbakır. Superb balance and a sure taste in the patterning of detail are what we find to delight us in Seljuk building.

The kind of Seljuk building the traveller in eastern Turkey will become most familiar with is the *türbe* or tomb. These are basically cylindrical buildings, the height of a small house, even when they are twelve-faced. They are often on a square base and are always of well-cut stone. They have conical tops roofed with stone slabs. Here again the proportions are admirable and the variety within this form is considerable both in the blind arches and decorated or undecorated panels with which the building is faced and in the stonework of the roof. Even if you are not able to make the comparison from the actual buildings, photographs of these tombs, which are mostly twelfth to fourteenth century, side by side with ninth- and tenth-century Armenian buildings will strongly suggest that the Armenian church is the source of the idea, especially since the tombs proliferate in the Armenian area. It has been pointed out that Seljuk tombs of this type exist at Mosul in Irak, in Persia and as far east as Urgench in Soviet Turkestan, but in no case do they come within centuries of pre-dating the Armenian drum and dome. Mrs. Talbot Rice relates the shape of these tombs to traditional Central Asian tents or to the pointed reed huts which Gertrude Bell saw still in use near Erzurum.[1] It may well have been the similarity to these tent shapes which gave this device of Armenian architecture its special appeal to the Seljuks and impelled them to build such stone tents for the dead at a time when they themselves were reluctantly giving up the mobile tents and settling down to stone and brick houses. Today one finds these tombs, isolated or in groups at the roadside, all round Lake Van and in the heart of Erzurum.

Carpet-weaving is the most important of the Seljuk crafts. Carpets are essentially tent furniture, easy to take up and transport in rolls, quick to create an atmosphere of home, of comfort and even luxury. A Turkish family out for a picnic today takes a carpet to unroll under trees. The Seljuks brought their knowledge of weaving with them from Central Asia where they are known to have been making carpets since before the third century A.D.[2] In the thirteenth century Seljuk carpets were exported from Anatolia and most of the rugs recovered at Fustat near Cairo have been Anatolian. Seljuk carpets show a great variety of geometric patterns and the use of lozenges of colour different from that of the background. Shades of red and blue are the commonest colours in Seljuk carpets, with an occasional light-green band or filling. Anatolian carpets became well known in Europe in the four-teenth and fifteenth centuries and figure as floor coverings in Dutch and Italian paintings from 1450 onwards.[3] They appeared so frequently in Holbein's pictures that they came to be known as Holbein carpets.

Although during the Ottoman era Turkish carpets became more floral and softer in design, the geometric elements of Seljuk design have persisted to this day and I have carpets recently made in the homes of central Anatolia which have some of the design patterns of the earliest Seljuk rugs.

The Seljuks were also expert wood-carvers and the fact that the great Keykubad I was a practised wood-worker indicates the honour in which the craft was held. Byzantium had had its wood and ivory carving and I have seen lovely wood-carving at St. Catherine's Monastery on Sinai and in the monasteries of the Wadi Natrun in the western desert of Egypt. But since the bevelled style of wood-carving is associated with Samarra, it may be accepted that the Seljuks

[1] T. Talbot Rice, *The Seljuks*, pp. 141–2.
[2] Oktay Aslanapa, *Turkish Arts*, pp. 14 ff.
[3] See Kurt Erdmann, *Der Türkische Teppich des 15 Jahrhunderts*.

brought this way of using wood with them from their passage through Mesopotamia, just as they did their carpet-weaving and expertise in bows and arrows from Central Asia. The lovely wooden *mimber* of the ruined Ulu Cami of Old Malatya, now in the Ethnographical Museum at Ankara, is the most perfect example of this Seljuk art. Bold, plain geometric interlacing of straight, flat or bevelled areas of wood create angled spaces to be filled in relief with complex palmette designs. There is a similarly decorated *mimber* in the Sare Hatun Cami at Harput, near Elazığ.[1]

The same fluency, tightness and good taste are observable in Seljuk calligraphy. This for them was a recently acquired art and the alphabet used was that of Arabic, which they had learnt in the tenth century, but the sense of design which we see in their weaving and in their stone and wood carving made the Kufic script a fitting element in abstract decoration. Closer to their Asiatic traditions is the *tuğra* which became the official emblem of the Ottoman state up to this century, a complex, bird-like form of signature, varying from one sultan to another, which Mrs. Talbot Rice believes to be derived from a brand mark used on cattle in the nomadic days of the Seljuks.

They loved music too and they would appear to have invented the military band. Music was played at regular times of the day by an official band in a Seljuk palace. Music accompanied songs and dancing and was even introduced into Moslem worship in the Mevlevi ritual, contrary to the usual practice in Islam. The Seljuk *kopuz*, a kind of guitar, and the *ney*, a flute, have always been popular Turkish folk instruments in the accompaniment of wandering minstrels known as *ozan*.[2]

As millennial travellers the Seljuks knew something of the rigours of wayfaring and they evolved a state system of hostels which has never been surpassed. Great rectangular buildings were erected for the convenience of travellers, strong enough for overnight security but with decorated entrances that rival those of the mosques and *medreses*. All the traveller's basic needs, and those of his animals, were met in these well-planned buildings. There was a fireplace for each party, for cooking and warmth, and a little mosque and ablution

[1] See illustrations and treatment by Dr. Semra Ögel in *Sanat Tarihi Yilliği*, 1964–5, pp. 110–115.
[2] Yetkin, Özgüc, Sümer, Ülken, Cağatay and Karamağaralı, *Turkish Architecture*, p. 10.

place for prayers. His boots were repaired free. Most of these *hans* or caravanserais were financed from foundations set up under wills. The most beautiful and impressive of these *hans* are between Kayseri and Konya, outside our present area, but versions of this Seljuk conception may be seen at Erzurum, Eski Malatya, Diyarbakır and, of course, at Istanbul, where the Ottomans perpetuated the idea.

That of the Seljuks was therefore a very complete civilisation, capable of a rare beauty in its public manifestations, but which went into administrative decline in the thirteenth century, to be shattered by the Mongol invasion.

THE CRUSADERS

It was the Seljuk capture of Jerusalem in 1071 that induced the mood in western Europe which was to build up to the Crusades. The First Crusade began with the undisciplined horde of Walter the Penniless, inspired by Peter the Hermit, getting as far as Anatolia to be wiped out by Kiliç Arslan I in 1096. But a more powerful army, led by Normans, took Nicaea from Kiliç Arslan in 1097 and stopped the extension of Seljuk power westwards. Bohemond of Antioch defeated Kiliç Arslan near Eskişehir but was himself captured by the Danishmend Amir Gazi of Sivas in 1100 and imprisoned in Niksar Castle, which resisted Lombard attempts to free him. Amir Gazi then allied himself with the Crusaders against the Seljuks and Byzantines, Jerusalem was taken by the Crusaders and Edessa (Urfa) was established as an independent Norman kingdom under Baldwin of Boulogne, in 1098.[1] The Counts of Edessa held the city and the region around it for close on fifty years.

The Second Crusade ran foul of the Kurdish Saladin and lost Jerusalem in 1187. Saladin's drive into eastern Anatolia weakened the Artuks of the Diyarbakır region and made them easier prey for the Ilhan Mongols of Persia. The Third Crusade, in which the Emperor Barbarossa was harassed by the Seljuks and was drowned in the Göksu, near Silifke, had little or no effect on eastern Anatolia. Nor had the Fourth Crusade, except that the sacking of Constantinople in 1204 by the Crusaders induced the escape of the Comnene brothers and the inauguration of the brilliant era of Trebizond.

[1] See pp. 163–4.

THE MONGOLS

The Mongols were nomadic eastern Asiatic tribes who seem to have lived by preying on others from the start. They became united and were brilliantly led by Timujin, afterwards known as Genghiz Khan, who, after a spartan childhood, became a great conqueror. He overcame China and then turned westwards through Turkestan to Russia, Persia and Turkey, massacring whole populations and disrupting cultures. The most ruthless of all conquerors, he died in 1227.

A great-grandson of Genghiz Khan, Hulagu by name, founded the Ilhan dynasty of Persia. Ilhan, or Il-khan, means local or tribal khan or ruler. *Il* is a Turkish word meaning province or region. The Ilhans of Persia were nominally vassals of the Great Khan of the east. Hulagu lived from 1217 to 1265 and married the daughter of a Byzantine. To Mongols and Turks she was known as Dokuz Hatun, the Eighth Lady. I cannot say whether she was Hulagu's eighth wife but her original name must surely have been Eudoxia. This marriage symbolises Hulagu's enmity towards the Khalifate and towards Egypt. Towards the Seljuks too, for Hulagu's army defeated that of Keyhüsrev II west of Erzincan in 1242 and thus added control of the Seljuk part of Anatolia to the Seljuk lands already taken over by the Mongols in Persia. Hulagu captured Baghdad and settled in Azerbaijan, just across the frontier from Turkey, making Tabriz his capital. His death was mourned with the last ritual slaughter of virgins to take place in Persia.

So the Seljuk state collapsed and central and eastern Anatolia broke up into small areas under beys and emirs. Hulagu's son, Abaqa, married the daughter of Michael Palaeologos and tried to establish relations with the Pope, France and England, using as agents the Nestorians, whom he favoured. The Mongols had already been familiar with Nestorian converts to Christianity in eastern Asia and had not yet adopted Islam. Abaqa sent a Nestorian priest, Rabban Bar Sauma, as ambassador to France and Rome, and this cleric met Richard I of England at Bordeaux. Islam was adopted by the Ilhan Ghazan (1295–1304) and persecution of Christians and Buddhists followed. Under him the Persian Ilhans became completely independent, after the death of Kublai Khan in 1294. These later Ilhans were great patrons of the arts and their culture was a blend of Chinese, Turkish, Islamic, Persian and Byzantine elements. Their miniature painting in

22. *Sumela Monastery*

13. *Harput: castle and early Christian church*

14. *Aghtamar Island: Lake Van*

the thirteenth and fourteenth centuries remained Chinese in character and the paintings of Siyah Kalem, whom the Turks claim but who could hardly be more Mongol in style and matter, may have been brought from Persia as part of the booty of Sultan Selim I.[1]

In 1307 Tabriz gave way to Soltaniyeh, near Kazvin, as the Ilhan capital and decline and disintegration set in. Abu Said was the first Ilhan to bear an Arab name and his death in 1335 marks the end of the Persian Ilhan Empire. But the Ottoman drive to establish dominion over the whole of Anatolia suffered a setback by the capture, humiliation and killing of Sultan Beyazit I by yet another Mongol and descendant of Genghiz Khan, Timur Lenk or Tamburlaine, in the opening year of the fifteenth century. Timur, who was not a Persian Ilhan, swept through Anatolia to sack Bursa and other cities, the strongholds of the new Ottoman power. Timur was born at Samarkand, was brought up a Moslem and was well educated, but he proved to be just as cruel and destructive as his great ancestor, though he greatly embellished his birthplace, Samarkand. There are lovely buildings remaining there from his day. To the Turks, his is a detested name; to the Indians too, for his sacking of Delhi was a most brutal, though to him profitable, exploit. The Persian Mongols had crushed a decaying Seljuk state and had made possible the eventual Ottoman domination of the whole of Turkey.

THE GEORGIANS

The Georgians have had little influence on the history of Turkey but since they occupied the extreme north-east corner of Anatolia, north of Erzurum, for so many centuries and left a number of buildings still little known because of the wildness of the country in which they were built, they require to be remembered in any book about eastern Turkey. Their country was known to classical writers as Iberia. The modern name comes from the Greek *georgos*, a husbandman, and reflects the fruitful nature of the Georgian plains. The Georgians speak an agglutinative non-Indo-European language which belongs, like Laz, to the Caucasian group. After the fifth-century Council of Chalcedon (Kadiköy), when the Armenian and Nestorian churches broke away, the Georgian Church, formed probably as a result of a mission by their King Mirian to Constantine about the year 325, sided with the Greek

[1] See *Turkey*, p. 34.

Church. They have an unauthenticated tradition that two Georgians won Christ's garment in the lottery after the crucifixion and took it to Georgia, where it remained until the seventh century.[1] There were close links between Byzantium and Georgia. Byzantine emperors endowed churches there and sent craftsmen, architects, masons and wood-carvers to build and decorate them.[2] The Georgians themselves contributed little towards architectural experiment but drew on Armenian and Byzantine models, but they may well have provided the channel through which the Byzantine influence passed into Russia.[3] Their earliest churches were circular or quadrangular and centralised, directing the worshipper's gaze upwards to the inside of the dome, where frescoes represented heaven. The dome rested on a very short drum or had no drum at all. This centralised church was probably an Armenian invention, though one must remember the Church of Sts. Sergius and Bacchus, now Küçük Aya Sofya Cami in Istanbul, which is practically circular and has a stubby dome on a short drum which in spite of this gives a magical effect of height inside. A similar design is followed in San Vitale at Ravenna and in the Cathedral at Aachen. Later Georgian churches incorporated the Byzantine basilical plan and are cruciform, with dome and long central body. The dome is higher and there is more drum in the churches of the tenth to the twelfth century. The Bagratid kings commissioned a number of beautiful churches in the Artvin-Kars area of Turkey, and though the plan may be Byzantine the decoration, intricate stone and wood carving of rich interlaced leaf patterns with animal forms, has a distinctly local flavour.

The pass northwards from Erzurum to Tortoni is known to the Turks as Gurgi Boğaz, the Georgian Throat, and Artvin, Ardahan and Ardanuki are Georgian names in Turkey today. The part of Georgia in present-day Turkey fell to the Seljuks before Manzikert but was restored to Georgia in 1205. The Ottoman campaigns of the early sixteenth century made it a part of Turkey but it has several times been occupied by the Russians, most recently from 1878 to 1920.

There are still some fifty thousand Georgians in Turkey and the language is still spoken in the mountains and valleys of the extreme north-east.

---

[1] Article in *Dictionnaire d'Archéologie Chrétienne*, vol. 6.
[2] Allen, *History of the Georgian People*, p. 271.   [3] ibid., p. 293.

THE LAZ

The home of the Laz people is the Black Sea coastline of the north-east of Turkey from Trabzon eastwards and the mountains and valleys behind, up to the watershed that faces the Black Sea. There are about sixty thousand people in Turkey today who claim to be Laz, about ten thousand of them living in their Pontic homeland, the others scattered along the Black Sea coast and in the towns of western Turkey. They are probably the original inhabitants of this part of Asia Minor, a people known in ancient times as the Channi or Chaneti and partly descended from the Colchians. In the early centuries of the first millennium B.C. the Greeks established coastal colonies in their country, Trapezos the most important, and they accepted government from Trebizond, in so far as their mountain way of life has been interfered with. The old story of resistance to new ways with the help of geography. They were Christian until the fifteenth century and Mehmet the Conqueror's capture of Trebizond, but they were then converted to Islam. They have a history of non-resistance. Their language, Laz, which they speak but do not write, is close to Georgian and is one of the Kartvelian group of Caucasian languages. Their way of life is largely pastoral and they cope with the extremes of their climate, and the rapid rise of the land from sea level to three thousand metres or more, by transhumance from permanent winter quarters to wooden built *yaylas*, their summer dwelling-places in the mountains. They are a proud and handsome people and Robin Fedden reports that they will not carry burdens but will lend their pack animals and offer the greatest hospitality. The men play bagpipes and they are fond of dancing. But they are not only mountain people. They build boats and are good sailors and in other parts of Turkey the Laz are famous as pastrycooks. They merge happily and easily into the population of Turkey when they are away from home and have never shown any wish for self-government or union with another power. A prominent Istanbul lawyer, a tall, fine-looking man, whom I met on a ship going to Trabzon, was very proud of being a Laz.[1]

[1] For a view of the Laz and excellent photographs see R. Fedden, 'In the Steps of the Argonauts', *Geog. Mag.*, Aug. 1969.

THE DANISHMENDS

As we have already seen, the Danishmends were a Turkoman dynasty which entered Anatolia and ruled in northern Cappadocia from the last quarter of the eleventh century till 1178. The origin of the founder of the dynasty, Amir Danishmend, is obscure. *Danishmend* is a Persian word for *teacher*, but the word may have entered Persian from Turkic, for the root, *danuş*, in Turkish means to consult, to ask advice. Amir Danishmend was involved in the events of the First Crusade, but historical fact is confused in the legend of which he became the epic hero. This epic, handed on by oral tradition, was first put in writing by Mawlana Ibn Ala in 1245 but that version is now lost. It was re-written in 1360 by Arif Ali. The romance links Danishmend with other eastern Turkish heroes, Abu Muslim and Sayyid Battal. Historically Amir Danishmend was ruler of a compact kingdom in central and eastern Anatolia, from Malatya to the Black Sea, with Niksar as his capital. Niksar, as Neacaesarea, had been a residence of the kings of Pontus and became an important Christian centre. A ruined *medrese* and a little mosque-tomb, both bearing the name of Yağ Basan, survive from the Danishmend period on a cliff top near the castle, which is the usual palimpsest of military architecture from ancient to Ottoman through Byzantine. The Danishmend Amir Mehmet Ibn Melik Gazi of Sivas captured Bohemond in the year 1100, imprisoned him in Niksar Castle, resisted all Lombard attempts to free him and then made him his ally. This amir extended Danishmend power by his success against Norman Edessa and Armenian Cilicia. On his death in 1132 he was followed by his son Mehmet. The dynasty then broke up in quarrels over succession and the resultant weakening allowed the Seljuk Kiliç Arslan to take over the Danishmend domains. Another Danishmend known to history is a renegade called Danish-mend-hajib. (*Hajib* is a Persian word for an official.) He presumably felt no Anatolian loyalties after the eclipse of his tribe and he served the Mongol Genghiz Khan.[1]

THE ARTUKS

The Artuks, also known as Urtukids and Ortakids, have a history similar to that of the Danishmends, but they enjoyed a much longer

[1] See W. Barthold, *Turkestan down to the Mongol Invasion.*

tenure of power in eastern Turkey. They governed the Diyarbakır region, either independently or under Mongol suzerainty, from the late eleventh century to the beginning of the fifteenth. The first Artuk, a chieftain of the Doğer Turkoman tribe, came to Anatolia in 1073, soon after the Seljuk victory of Manzikert, and served under the Persian Seljuk Malikshah, taking part in campaigns in Syria and Persia. His descendants settled in Diyarbakır and Mardin. One of them, Sukman, emulated the Danishmend exploit by capturing Count Baldwin of Edessa before Harran in 1104. The usual squabbling over inheritance led to the setting up of small Artukid kingdoms at Mardin, Ahlat, Amid (Diyarbakır), Arzan and then Miyafarikin, but Diyarbakır remained their main base, whilst different branches of the family lived and ruled separately during the twelfth and thirteenth centuries. They resisted Saladin's drive but he triumphed and occupied Miyafarikin. Then followed a decline of Artuk power, sandwiched as they were between the stronger Seljuks to the north and the Ayyubi successors of Saladin to the south and east. After 1234 only the Mardin branch remained. In 1260 Al Malik Al Said resisted the Mongols but his son, Al Muzaffer, capitulated, accepted their domination and thus saved the Mardin dynasty. They became loyal servants of the Ilhans of Persia.

Like the Seljuks, the Artuks were a military aristocracy and whilst they encouraged the arts they made little change in the basic economy of the land they governed, the traditional agriculture, stock-breeding, iron and copper mining and the control of the important north–south trade route between Mesopotamia and eastern Anatolia and Georgia. The earliest popular poetry in Anatolian Turkish comes from the Artuk region and the years of their power. They are also responsible for the interesting and un-Islamic use of animal motifs on coins and buildings, as on the walls of Diyarbakır. Danishmend and Artuk coins much resemble those of Byzantium, a fact which has not yet been explained, though it would seem natural for an originally more primitive people to take over a style together with the practice of minting money. There are Artuk coins in the British Museum.

The Artuks were great builders, again like the Seljuks, and their work may still be studied in a profusion of mosques, *medreses*, bridges, hans and fortifications. The splendid Urfa Gate at Diyarbakır is an example of their work but the most beautiful building remaining from their age is the Sultan Isa Medrese at Mardin, built in 1385. Their centres were on the verge of Kurdish country and they managed relationships with the Kurds as well as anyone has done. They were far from being the sitting pigeons the Kurds found elsewhere. The Artuks showed a great respect for Arab culture and were tolerant towards all kinds of sects, Moslem and Christian. The monasteries of Tur Abdin were within their domain and the Artuks allowed them to continue to function. The Sultan Salih connived at the Kara Koyun capture of Mardin in 1408, in exchange for Mosul, and Artuk rule, which had given peace and prosperity and much lovely building to Mardin, was over.[1]

BEYS AND EMIRS

The Mongols had broken the Seljuk power but after the death of the Ilhan Abu Said Bahadir in 1335 the Mongol state itself went through a period of dynastic struggle which undermined the central authority. Local beys and emirs, who had accepted Mongol domination from Persia as part of the Seljuk collapse, now took the opportunity to cut away and for the best part of two hundred years, up to the early decades of the sixteenth century, central and western Anatolia was divided into principalities with capitals in fifteen or more towns from Bursa and Balikesir eastwards to Maraş, where the Dulkaderoğullar ruled from 1339–1521. These dynasties were named after their founders, *oğullar* meaning *the sons of*.

In eastern Turkey two powerful tribes, the Karakoyunlu and then the Akkoyunlu, set up important states. They were named after their totem animals, black (*kara*) or white (*ak*) sheep (*koyun*). Stone versions of the black and white sheep they used in their burials are to be seen at Erzurum and Van today. While the most powerful and aggressive of the western beyliks, the Osmanoğulları, later to become the Osmanlis or Ottomans who united the Turkish Empire, were busy by-passing Constantinople, until they took it in 1453, and pressed on into Europe, the Karakoyunlu were extending their power south and east at the expense of Irak and Persia. Their first capital was at Erciş, at the northern end of Lake Van.

[1] I am indebted to the Fascicles of the uncompleted new edition of the *Encyclopaedia of Islam* for information about the Danishmends and Artuks.

THE ARABS

Arabs, or a Semitic people closely allied to them, were established in northern Mesopotamia and in the Urfa region during most of the active life of the Roman Empire. As part of the Islamic explosion and after their defeat of the Byzantine army under Heraclius in 636, the Arabs occupied Aleppo and Antioch and went on during the 640s to raid Armenia. A brief peace arranged in 659 between Byzantium and the Khalif Moawiya was soon broken and an Arab drive through Anatolia reached the Bosphorus. The Arab fleet for years besieged Constantinople but, disconcerted by the Byzantine secret weapon, Greek fire, retreated in 677 and was destroyed in a storm off the south coast of Anatolia. After a revival of Byzantine strength in Anatolia the Arabs conquered Armenia in 694. The struggle between Byzantium and the Arabs went on over the centuries in central and eastern Anatolia, Arabs raids countered by Byzantine campaigns to get ride of them. During these years, and up to the twelfth century, Ahlat on the west shore of Lake Van remained an Arab enclave in Christian territory, but apart from this Nicephoros Phocas in the tenth century succeeded in driving the Arabs from what is today Turkey. It was another Armenian, John Curcuas, top general of the Byzantine army, who cleared the Arabs out of Erzurum in the second quarter of the tenth century. The Arabs had been checked and completely eliminated as a power in Anatolia when the new Islamic menace of the Seljuks began to loom. But the Arabs remained as a firmly established element in the population in the Mardin–Urfa–Gaziantep region and about a quarter of a million people speak Arabic in Turkey today. Anywhere along the south coast from Antalya eastwards you will hear radios tuned in to Arab stations. Some old houses in Urfa are little Arab palaces.

THE OTTOMANS

Tamburlaine's destructive sweep into Anatolia and his capture and killing of Sultan Beyazit I in 1403 were a setback to the imposition of Ottoman authority over the beyliks and emirates of Anatolia, but the Osmanlis recovered from this, regathered their forces, conquered Greece, then Constantinople itself and eventually most of the Balkans.

The end of the fifteenth century saw a lull in the Ottoman outsurge towards the west but the early sixteenth century saw them turn eastwards to attach eastern Anatolia to their empire and to push on southwards from there. Selim I, known to the Turks as Yavuz, the Resolute, and to the west as the Grim, defeated the Persians, who had established themselves in eastern Anatolia, at the Battle of Çaldiran, north-east of Lake Van, in 1514, and the campaigns of his son, Soliman the Magnificent, confirmed Ottoman authority over the whole of what is today Turkey.

The Ottomans were originally an Oghuz tribe which entered Anatolia, with their spearhead of four hundred fighting horsemen, about the middle of the thirteenth century, the last of the Turkoman tribesmen to come to Asia Minor. They were welcomed by the Seljuks, then in desperate plight under growing Mongol power. They settled around Soğut in the province of Eskişehir and the original Othman, whose name is remembered in the terms Osmanli and Ottoman, was a tribal chieftain on the borderland between what was left of the Byzantine Empire and Seljuk Anatolia. This border then ran roughly from Antalya through Kutahya to Sinop on the Black Sea coast and was known to the Turks as the *Uc* (pronounced *uj*). We have seen that Othman was honoured by Mesud III, the last Seljuk ruler, for his work against the Byzantines. The chieftains of this border had much in common with the Byzantine *akritai* and on both sides the warriors were honoured as upholders of their faiths. This is the heroic age of Moslem-Christian confrontation in Anatolia and splendid poetry came out of it, both in Greek and Turkish.

Under distant and uninterested Ottoman administration from Istanbul, eastern Turkey seems to have slept for centuries, so far as the outside world was concerned, until the drive and vision of Ataturk made it as much a part of the new Turkey as Thrace or Ionia. The Armenians kept a kind of cultural autonomy and the Nestorians lived their secluded lives, making the best agriculturally of their wild corner of the Hakkari. Both communities were harassed by the Kurds, who occasionally supplied local rulers tolerated by Istanbul.

Ottoman lethargy was thrown off by Ataturk and as a result smouldering enmities have either burnt themselves out or been suppressed. The Nestorians and Armenians have gone from eastern Turkey and the Kurds have had to swallow their religious opposition to the post-Ottoman régime. A depopulated region is being opened up for agriculture, industry, education, health services and tourism but it has not even yet been freed from its millennial function as a buffer zone, for its eastern frontier is the only one the NATO powers share with Russia.

Moslem Architecture in Eastern Turkey

The mosque architecture of eastern Turkey is most varied and in its way sums up the history of the country, the movement of people, the ripening of cultures and the interchange of influences from the eleventh century onwards. Before the tenth century, when they moved into Persia, the Turkoman tribes had little knowledge of architecture, for they were tent-dwelling nomads. The splendid tent of the princely Asiatic nomad, with its circular body and pointed conical roof, may be the common origin of the centralised building with conical dome which is characteristic of Armenian, Georgian and Seljuk building, or at least inclined the Seljuks to adopt an Armenian plan which they found immediately appealing.[1] The Seljuks picked up ideas which suited them in their travels and conquests and developed them in their own assured way. Into Anatolia they brought not only modified Persian and Syrian ideas but architects and craftsmen to carry them out. The great Ala ad-Din Mosque at Konya was built by a Syrian architect. In much the same way Byzantine emperors had taken architects, masons and wood-carvers to build the churches they endowed in Georgia. There too the result was not a repetition of Byzantine achievement but something new into which elements of local design were incorporated.[2] The late Byzantine flowering at Trebizond provides another example of this with its evidence of work by Seljuk stone-masons, whether prisoners or refugees or on loan. Styles are in this way organic and change to suit the tastes and needs of the people who commission the buildings.

Georgian, Armenian and Trapezuntine churches were taken over as mosques by the Turkoman conquerors, as they were in Istanbul after 1453, and the style of the adopted building influenced future construc-

[1] See p. 77.   [2] W. E. D. Allen, *History of the Georgian People*, p. 271.

tion. A comparison of Sultan Ahmed Mosque with Aya Sofya exemplifies this.

The evolution in Anatolia of the *ulu cami*, or great mosque in its earliest form, which was introduced from Syria by the Seljuks, has not been fully worked out. The problem of roofing a great space had been met in the great mosque at Damascus by the use of large numbers of columns. Examples of this method of early mosque construction in eastern Anatolia are to be seen at Harput, Diyarbakır and Siirt. The great flat roofs of this type of mosque were sometimes covered with cupolas, as in the Ulu Cami at Bursa. In the thirteenth century, the plan of a full dome on a square base, which the Byzantines had achieved at least eight centuries earlier, was followed in the Ulu Cami at Eski Malatya and at Divriği. Squinches in the four corners of the rectangular space supported the dome and at Malatya these are of brick. The use of brick is typically Persian and the Ulu Cami at Malatya is a fascinating blend of styles, with Syrian stonework and interlaced tiles of Anatolian character.[1] The open courtyard at Malatya is unusual, since Seljuk mosques rarely had courtyards. The enclosed prayer room with projecting open courtyard such as one meets in mosques in Istanbul look like an evolution of a very ancient Anatolian invention, the *megaron*, and since experiments in this plan were made in the fourteenth century in the beyliks of south-central Anatolia, the intervening model may well have been great churches of the fifth century, like those which still remain at Korykos in Cilicia, with their walled courtyards balancing the domed basilica of the church itself, a plan which seems to extend and refine an Anatolian conception which predates Mycenae by a thousand years. After the Ottoman conquest of eastern Turkey in the first half of the sixteenth century, mosques were built there in the Ottoman manner in which the experiments tried out at Bursa, Edirne and Istanbul were carried to their lovely culmination by the great Sinan. A mosque in this style is the Lala Paşa Cami at Erzurum, built in 1563, with its central dome, numerous cupolas and narthex with columns and arches. The minaret of this mosque, however, is not one which Sinan would have designed. His minarets are taller and slimmer, beautifully balanced, with plain flat stonework sometimes relieved by a few well-placed blue tiles.

The evolution of the minaret too is a complex and interesting subject. The first minarets seem to have been the watch-towers at the

[1] Hill and Grabar, *Islamic Architecture and its Decoration*, p. 71.

corners of the quadrangular pagan *temenos* at Damascus, inside which a mosque was built. In the ninth century the Khalif Al-Mutasim built himself a splendid capital, with gardens, palaces, polo grounds and other requirements of the elegant life, at Samarra, on the east bank of the Tigris, one hundred and thirteen kilometres north-north-west of Baghdad, a place which had seen a Neolithic civilisation flourish in the fifth millennium B.C. Here in the same century his successor Al-Mutawakkil built a great mosque, which today looks like a ruined fort, with a free-standing spiral stone minaret thought to have been inspired by the Babylonian *ziggurat*. Later in the same century Ibn Tulun built a great rectangular mosque in Cairo on the same plan and with a similar minaret in one corner of the walls, thus combining the Damascus and Samarra conceptions. Since Ibn Tulun was born at Samarra there would appear to be no doubt about the influence here, though I think the Pharos of Alexandria, as depicted in a Cyrenaican mosaic of the sixth century at Castel Lebia, may also have encouraged and influenced Ibn Tulun. He is known to have converted what was left of the Pharos into a mosque after the earthquake of 796.

The Seljuks brought the square minaret from Syria, where, for all I know, they themselves may have evolved it. Compare the eleventh-century square minaret at Aleppo.[1] There are any number of these at Diyarbakır. The same influence is surely to be seen in the campanile of Aya Sofya at Trabzon and perhaps in the towers of San Gimignano. The Seljuks also brought into Anatolia the circular, decorated brick minaret which they had developed in Persia and they persisted in making their minarets of brick even after taking over the excellent stone of eastern Turkey for their main buildings. Seljuk minaret construction and decoration in Anatolia are in much better, more restrained taste than in Persia, Afghanistan and Turkestan, the occasional use of blue ceramic tiles in geometric composition producing effects of great beauty at Siirt, for instance, and Erzurum. A tradition of fine masonry which went back to Urartu restrained the tendency to overdecoration encouraged by the possibilities of brick. Compare the fine flatness of a Seljuk wall in Anatolia with the fiddling though balanced complexity of the tenth-century Samanid tomb at Bukhara, where brickwork is made to look like woven reeds. From Persia too the Seljuks brought the notion of twin minarets, erected at either side of a main entrance, as at Erzurum and Sivas.

[1] Hill and Grabar, op. cit., Plate 518.

Early mosques sometimes have a stubby, undecorated, purely functional minaret, like that of the Ulu Cami at Harput, remembering perhaps the original watch-towers or designed by a local architect with restricted means and little education in styles. Finally comes the slim, pointed post-Sinan minaret of the Ottoman régime. Turkey alone has the candle-snuffer topped Ottoman minaret.

The *medrese* or theological school was to provide similar opportunities to architects to those of the colleges of Oxford and Cambridge. This was another Seljuk innovation and an early builder was Nizam al-Mulk, wise counsellor to Alp Arslan at the end of the eleventh century, though the first known *medrese* is that built at Nishapur in 1027 under Mahmud of Ghazna. It was at Nishapur that Nizam al-Mulk built his first *medrese*. His purpose was to protect the Moslem faith from the many heterodoxies which had flourished in the ninth and tenth centuries. These complex buildings show a great variety in the disposition of living quarters for students and the highest architectural skill was lavished upon them. Two of the most beautiful buildings of this kind are the Çifte Minare and Yakutiye *medreses* at Erzurum. The Sultan Isa Medrese at Mardin seems almost to be carved out of the Citadel rock under which it stands.

The Seljuks seem to have evolved some elements of architectural decoration in Anatolia itself. The plain tile, usually blue, either square for outside use or cut into angled shapes to back a *mihrab*, is eastern Anatolian. Here also originated that very effective way of dealing with a recessed space, a doorway or a *mihrab* in a flat wall, the stalactite and honeycomb ways of cutting stone. One tends to think of this in a doorway or inside a cupola as a descending pattern, when it is in fact a kind of multiple squinch for the support of masonry above. The effect of this intricate cutting, in contrast with the purity of Seljuk walling, can be of great beauty.

The pointed arch of Seljuk architecture, another device for the support of masonry above a door or in galleries, is surely the source of an important element in Gothic building, taken back, like ideas for castle building, by Norman crusaders.

Common Words and Elements in Place-names

ayran—diluted yoğurt, a refreshing drink
bağ—vineyard
buz—ice
cami—mosque
çam—pine
çay—tea or a stream
dağ—mountain
dolmuş—shared vehicle
eski—old
göl—lake
han—caravanserai
hüyük—mound, often an ancient town site
imam—leader in worship at mosque
kale—castle
kara—black or land, as in *karayollar*, landways or roads
kaymakam—governor of a *kaza* or district
kilim—carpet without pile
mihrab—prayer niche
mimber—pulpit
muhtar—headman of village
orman—forest
ova—meadow or plain
şarap—wine
su—water; maden su—natural mineral water
taş—stone
tepe—hill
toprak—earth
türbe—tomb

vali—provincial governor
vilayet—province
yeni—new

Warning: C is pronounced as j, ç as ch, ş as sh. The undotted ı is like the
    i in shirt. Double dots over o and u transform them as in German.
    English travellers should attempt to pronounce vowels openly,
    not as diphthongs unless the spelling indicates a diphthong, as in
    ayran.

Part II

ITINERARIES

The Van Region

You can get to Van by road, rail or air. Both the roads, from Diyarbakır through Bitlis and from Elazığ through Bingöl and Muş, are possible for ordinary cars and, if you are approaching Van from the north, the road from Eleşkirt, on the Erzurum–Doğubeyazit road, through Patnos and Erciş, is good. If you go by train you will have the excitement, at the end of a two-day journey from Istanbul, of a 100-kilometre train ferry across Lake Van. A railway is now being constructed to take this train on to Persia. But of all these ways by far the most exciting is by plane. The T.H.Y. plane takes off from Diyarbakır, having arrived from Istanbul and Ankara, giving you that splendid view of the black-walled city from the south, swings over the cultivated plain of the Diyarbakır Basin and then abruptly attacks the mountains, which are often made more forbidding by towering storm clouds. Suddenly you look down into the deep blue crater lake of Nimrut Dağ.[1] To the north is Süphan Dağ, a snow-covered and splendid volcanic cone. Then you are over Lake Van, just north of the line the steamer takes from Tatvan to Van Iskelesi or Landing Stage. To the south is a line of grim mountains, which rise to a height of 3,500 metres, and the wild uplands of the Hakkari. The pilot takes you into Van from the north-west and curves daringly in between Van Kalesi, the ancient Urartian citadel, and the modern town, to reach the simple runway. From the airport, before driving into Van, you will wonder at the line of the ancient fortress running across the green fields and trees. This is a spectacular flight that should be done once. You'll be surprised too to observe the passengers on the plane: business people certainly and the odd lawyer and government official, the tall Englishman with his gun and clubland air, the unplaceable first generation American

[1] See p. 124.

(of Armenian origin?), but also people you'd never expect to be able to afford air travel and who certainly wouldn't be on planes in Europe, old women with great bundles, a modest, ill-dressed family with overawed children, except for the youngest, a squawking show-off. But then in this part of Turkey a bus, even the sophisticated long-distance one, is apt to be involved in tribal migration, a sudden invasion of women in wonderful costumes and of their men in shabby suits and cloth caps.

Van, ancient Tuspa or Biaini, from which the name Van is probably derived, became the capital of the land of Urartu in the ninth century B.C. when King Sarduri I established himself on the great rock near the lake, now known as Van Kalesi. His name is recorded on a wall at the western end of the fortress, the link with the harbour which then existed. For centuries this citadel resisted attack by the Assyrians though the latter slowly whittled away at the Urartian empire. From about 600 B.C. the Urartians are replaced in history, in circumstances of which we have no record, by the Armenians who, according to Xenophon, intermarried with them. As capital of a buffer state falling more under the power of Persia than of Rome Van dwindled in importance and the temples and palaces of Urartu were probably destroyed there well before the Christian era. Jews were settled there in considerable numbers in the first century B.C., and prospered and grew to number eighteen thousand families by the fourth century A.D. when they were moved to Persia by the Sasanian King Shapur. With the Arab outsurge and the collapse of Sasanian power, Van became capital of the new Armenian kingdom of Vaspurakan. In the face of Seljuk penetration of Anatolia in the eleventh century and of dissension among the Armenians themselves, Van turned to Byzantium for help but fell to the advancing Turkoman flood. The Turkish garrison resisted Tamburlaine but the city fell to this general destroyer. At the beginning of the sixteenth century the city was once again nominally under Persian domination but actually in the possession of a Kurdish chieftain. In 1534 it surrendered without a fight to Soliman the Magnificent and since then has been Turkish, except for some years in the forties of the last century, when Van was once more held by a Kurdish chief.

In spite of these changes in the government of the city the Armenians remained numerically in the majority up to almost the end of the nineteenth century. When Lynch visited Van in the mid 1890's he found that two-thirds of the population was Armenian. The old

walled medieval city, at the southern edge of Van Kalesi and containing
the bazaars and business houses, was then inhabited by Moslems and
Christians, whilst in the garden town in the east, the present site of
modern Van, there were mixed quarters and Armenian and Turkish
quarters. Well into the present century these two towns remained, one.
of them a centre of commerce and the crafts, with a garden suburb
separated from it by about a kilometre of open fields. The old town
was completely surrounded, except where the cliff face of Van Kalesi
made a natural wall, by a castellated, bastioned wall and had four
gates. Quite a considerable population was packed into this small area,
with its narrow streets and crowded bazaars. Although most of the
Christians probably lived in the suburb, many of them lived cheek by
jowl with Moslems within the walled city, and there were six churches
there for them to worship in. According to Lynch[1] these were built
largely of wood and burnt easily, so that there is no trace of them left
after the troubles of this century. Hardly anything is left of the old
city, Eski Van, Old Van, as it is called, except the shell of some mosques,
one of which is being restored.[2]

The present town of Van has a pioneer air today. Its churches have
disappeared and many of the old houses have been laid low by earthquakes. A fearful earthquake occurred twenty years ago. But there
are still some beautifully proportioned houses, some of which must
have belonged to well-to-do Armenian merchants. Many of these
went to Istanbul to make money but kept their homes going in their
ancient homeland.

Recent buildings in Van are mostly educational and administrative
but new hotels, modest enough in their pretensions, are now springing
up. Until a few years ago this was a military area and movement in and
out was restricted, to foreigners almost impossible. I have stayed at the
Bes Kardeş and found it adequate. The hotel will give you a simple
breakfast if you ask for it but no other meal. In eastern Turkey, however,
it is better to go out for breakfast to a place which specialises in the
meal and there is always one in the centre of the town. My breakfast
café in Van was at the corner of the Municipal Garden and one break-
fasted out under the trees in summer. They served a caky sort of bread,
flat, dry but not sweet, butter, honey and the local mountain cheese,
a Kurdish delicacy known in Turkish as *otlupeynir* or herb cheese. This
is a dry white cheese with two sorts of herb in it, a succulent sort of

[1] op. cit., vol. II, p. 102.   [2] See later, p. 108.

grass from the marshes and a dry thin herb from the upper slopes. With all this I drank hot boiled milk, the local custom, and finished up with glasses of tea served by a boy from another establishment deeper inside the garden. At seven o'clock in the morning this was already a meeting-place for people who had business or nothing to do in Van. Usually whilst I had my breakfast a horse-drawn farm cart turned up with a load of snow, roughly shaped lumps of about a cubic foot in size, each one covered with wood chippings and costing one lira, for use in chilling drinks and ice-cream in the teahouse. The snow is stored on the Erek mountain about three kilometres out of Van and lasts through the summer till autumn and the first snow showers. The boy who cleaned my shoes on questioning turned out to be from Gevaş Primary School at the south end of the lake. He was making an honest *kuruş* while waiting for the result of his examination, in the hope of being able to go on to a technical school.

The market street of Van runs parallel to the main street, on the lake side, and is interesting. One thing to look out for is the beautiful knitted woollen socks of the Kurds, mostly white, some black, done in an infinite variety of lovely patterns with coloured decoration, sometimes crosses which are relics of Nestorian design. Almost every one of these is a museum piece but they are very good inside Wellingtons, if you can bear to soil such lovely things. They wash well. Dried things, spices and minerals in open-mouthed sacks always attract me to finger and smell and a cheerful bearded ancient in Van market had four different kinds of salt in sacks. I'm fond of sea salt, believing its flavour to be superior to that of the additive-riddled powder that comes to our tables, and I asked the old merchant whether he had any. He pointed with contempt to a sack which he said contained Black Sea salt from Trabzon. All right for pickling fish, which they do in summer with lake fish in Van, but no one would think of using it for good cooking. He then made a funnel of paper and scooped into it some salt which he insisted on my taking as a gift. It was ground rock salt from Canık. He then asked me how old I was. He had fought at Kut and he wondered whether I had been there with Allenby, or was it Townsend? He was disappointed to find that we hadn't once been enemies, but we parted none the worse friends for that.

I've never been in a place more conscious of and keen on education than Van. Ataturk intended to establish a university here to serve eastern Turkey but after his death Erzurum was substituted, wrongly according to many intelligent people, and the present half-university was built there. Van has a big and well-run grammar school, the Ataturk Lisesi for boys and girls, with about one thousand pupils. There's a new and impressive Girls' Teacher Training School with six hundred boarders, two hundred day girls and fifty boys as well. This gives the pupils a secondary education as well as primary teacher training and practice in social studies. When I visited it the girls looked happy and keen under an intelligent and energetic Director and they will go out to the schools of eastern Turkey where they are most needed. There is no question here of a drain to the cities of the west. There are still primary schools in eastern Turkey where the teacher–pupil ratio is one to eighty or even ninety. Erniş, at the northern end of Lake Van, has the counterpart Boys' Teacher Training School, also a boarding school, set in a pleasant green promontory. Van also has a Commercial Training School for Boys, a Girls' Institute of Arts and Crafts and a Primary Boarding School. Another Primary Boarding School is being built at Gevaş, at the southern end of the lake. There is great competition for places in these schools and institutes and the country people, specially the Kurds, seem eager to have their children, even their daughters, educated, just like the people of the upland areas of Scotland and Wales and presumably for the same reasons.

Van has a museum which should not be missed, poor though its contents may be in comparison with the lovely things which have been removed, legally and illicitly, from this district. The present building is small and poky but a new building is under construction next to the nearby primary school. There is a considerable collection of prehistoric implements, Urartian pottery, Byzantine, Seljuk and Ottoman coins. It has an extremely interesting fragment of floor decoration from the Urartian citadel of Cavuştepe, a kind of *opus sectilis*, concentric rings of black and white marble set into circular sockets in a stone slab. (There is a similar fragment, presumably from Toprak Kale, in the British Museum.) But for me the greatest thing was the lovely basalt relief, in broken sections, of the divine King from Urartian Kefkalesi. These noble fragments, when I saw them, were tumbled together with some Urartian cuneiform-inscribed basalt blocks and a few black and white stone totem sheep of the two Turkoman tribes named after them, all lying in the school yard and awaiting erection in the new museum. The five pieces of the great relief were found by Peter Hulin in the wall of the Seljuk castle of Adilcevaz, tumbled down and re-used from the Urartian citadel above the village. Enough is left of the relief for a complete reconstruction to be made and this will stand three metres high. The splendid figure, which according to Piotrovskii is the god Teisheba,[1] stands on a fine bull, one foot on its back and one between its upcurved horns. In front of and behind the richly robed figure are either a sort of candelabra of spearheads or formalised sacred trees. The figure appears to hold a dish in its left hand and a spearhead or sacred branch rather like a trowel in its right hand. It is in low relief, with the head standing out a little more than the rest of the sculpture. When put together it will be one of the most beautiful things found in Turkey and it is to be hoped that it will remain in Van and not be swept into the already overcrowded Hittite Museum at Ankara.

LAKE VAN

This lake, anciently known as Thopitis, Thospites, Arsene, Arethusa, Arsippa, and to the Arabs as Lake Akhlat, is 1,650 metres or 5,400 feet above sea level and about three thousand square kilometres in extent, with a projection towards the north-east. It was probably formed by earthquake and volcanic eruption in the south-west corner of a great plain or hollow in the mountains, thus blocking the natural flow of water in a south-westerly direction. Today it has no visible outlet but a number of small rivers run into it. The level is preserved by summer evaporation and this accounts for the chemical composition of the water. In spite of its size, the lake is not big enough to minimise the grandeur of the surrounding mountains, from whichever point on the shore or on the water you may view them. The water is a soft blue in colour, changing subtly with the weather and the time of day. In summer the water is warm and soft to the skin, marvellous to swim in, buoyant. It's like gliding through silk to swim in it and your skin feels silken when you come out. It has a bleaching effect on hair and boat-men on the lake are said to trail their soiled linen in it for a painless wash. The water has several times been analysed and the results suggest that it must vary to some degree according to where it is collected, but all analyses I have seen give soda the highest percentage, followed

[1] *Urartu*, p. 64.

by chlorine, carbonates and sulphates.[1] Like most lake water it is better for swimming from an island or a boat than from the shore, where there is apt to be undesirable matter in suspension. I recommend Aghtamar Island. I made the mistake once of swimming at Van Iskelesi a hundred metres down current from where Kurdish women were beating carpets in the water. This cleans the carpets quickly and efficiently but doesn't improve the water. The water makes the eyes smart just about as much as sea water does. Nowhere have I so much enjoyed swimming.

Over the years unexplained and much debated fluctuations in the surface level of the lake have been reported and in the summer of 1969 the water was high enough to flood gardens near the Van landing-stage and the road south of Ahlat. There are tales of underground streams running into the lake and of a shepherd who dropped his stick into a hole, well to the east of the lake, and saw it floating on the surface of the lake a day or so later. Recent books have stated that owing to the alkalinity of the water there are no fish in Lake Van, but I have seen and eaten Lake Van fish. Lynch reports the presence in the lake of one kind of fish 'resembling a large bleak' and Strabo, though like all early geographers and historians rather vague about Lake Van, gives it one kind of fish.[2] There is a fish which looks to me like *coregonus* of the family of Salmonidae, a kind of whitefish more like the pollan than the gwyniad. They congregate near the river mouths in late spring and early summer (June is a good month for them) and swim up the rivers to breed, as do their cousins the sewin and the salmon. They are then easily caught in baskets or even by hand, without any tickling skill. They are very good to eat, fried or pickled in brine or grilled in a *tandır*, the recommended method.[3] It is said that they are not caught well out into the lake itself, perhaps because at other seasons they feed at very great depths, but I once saw a boat trailing a net a hundred metres out from the shore.

ENVIRONS OF VAN

All round Van it is green and the town itself has gardens, trees and avenues watered by streams and by the irrigation system inherited from Urartu. Once the land is released from the grip of snow and ice

[1] See analysis in Appendix II, Lynch, op. cit., vol. II, pp. 468–9.
[2] See also Pliny, *Natural History*, VI. 31.   [3] For the *tandır* see p. 125.

of half the year, the explosion of growth is amazing. An old Armenian proverb quoted by Lynch[1] says, 'Van in this world and paradise in the next.' Salads and vegetables are plentiful in summer and the grapes are good so long as they are not caught by early autumn frost. Wheat is grown in the neighbourhood and Van has two flour factories. Meat from the plentiful flocks and herds is good and restaurant meals are good and cheap.

VAN KALESI

This citadel of ancient Van, or Tuspa, as it was known to the Urartians, is the kind of site these people sought and felt secure in, a long narrow ridge of rock with precipitous sides. The rock reaches a height of about 100 metres and in profile looks, as Evliya Çelebi remarked, like a kneeling camel.

A motorable dirt road from the town divides to fork the huge outcrop of rock which rises from the fields and which once met the waters of the lake. Take the road to the right, running along the north side of the citadel. The visible walls that crest the ridge with their crenellations are of Seljuk construction and are best appreciated from this side. Halfway along this northern side a little Moslem cemetery has the tomb of a famous Islamic missionary. Go up past this tomb, on foot now of course, to a platform of rock which is an Urartian temple site, and you can rest on a typical Urartian bench cut, with curved back, out of the rock wall. The rock here is a very hard limestone which takes a considerable polish. There are two enormous arched niches here and the locals say that these were excavated by Americans who took away two huge gold statues of ancient goddesses. The Turks call the place the Temple of the Mother and Daughter but Lynch, who was here in the 1890's, describes it as it is today and says it was called 'Khayane-Kapasi or gate of treasure'.[2] So it's likely that someone at some time found something valuable here. The western niche has a statue base of black basalt with a cuneiform inscription which records the restoration of this temple by the good King Menuas, the great warrior and builder who round about 800 B.C. was responsible for the irrigation system which made possible the gardens of Van. The widespread inscriptions in the name of Menuas, near Lake Urmia in present-day Persia, in the Aras valley north and east of Ararat, at Hasan Kale near Erzurum and

[1] op. cit., vol. II, p. 38.   [2] op. cit., II, p. 110.

near the Murat river in the west, all go to show his power and the extent of the empire of Urartu in that day. This temple exactly faces the hilltop temple of Toprak Kale and I wonder whether this is of any significance.

From here continue westwards along the foot of the hill to a gushing spring of sweet water, excellent drinking. Just beyond observe the solid masonry of the Urartian jetty, for the lake once reached this point and this was the harbour of Tuspa. From the spring go up a steep path to the crest of the ridge and down a sudden descent, now guarded by an iron railing, to a little platform and a rectangular entrance into the rock face on the south side of the citadel. On the polished wall along the steps and all round the entrance are lovely Urartian cuneiform inscriptions in a marvellous state of preservation.[1] They record the conquests of King Argistis I, son of the great Menuas. The entrance leads into a big windowless room cut out of the rock, with smaller rooms leading off. Every room has rectangular niches cut into the rock wall about a metre above the floor. From the very dark room to the left from the entrance a twisting staircase leads down into darkness, presumably to other rooms or an escape postern. Such a tunnel comes out a little to the west of the entrance, in a flat place between rocks. Back in the main cave observe two holes high up on either side of the doorway, suggesting to me a wooden door to be slung inwards on to the ceiling, easy to let down quickly and peg sideways into position through holes that are still there. There would be no question of a battering ram being able to operate on the tiny platform outside and only two or three men could attack the door at one time. These underground chambers were surely impregnable.

Having mounted the outside stairway once more you can climb up to the highest level, the interior of the citadel. Here there is not much left standing—barracks occupied by the Turkish soldiery up to this century, some ancient temple sites and the ruins of a mosque built by Soliman the Magnificent in 1538.

Go back to near the landing-stage and by climbing over a mud-brick wall you can reach a path which follows a stream or canal along the foot of the south side of the rock. (The abundance of good water must have been one of the reasons for the choice of this site. I was not able to find the ill-smelling naphtha well inside the citadel reported by Lynch but not seen by him.) You can either follow this water, which

[1] Plate 5.

has watercress growing along it, to the ruins of Eski Van or cut across to a gap in a high mud wall and an easier dirt road.

Eski Van, Old Van, walled by the Ottomans after their sixteenth-century occupation, looks like an age-old ruin but actually lasted as a thriving town well into this present century. Lynch has a photograph of the walls and another of a crowded street with wooden balconied houses. The story they tell at Van today is that it was burnt down by the Armenians when the Turkish men were away fighting the Russians in 1914. It was in revenge for this that the Turks later drove the Armenians out of Van, the story goes. The Husrev Paşa Mosque near the south gate still has good decoration and the next mosque to the east of it is now being restored. The Ulu Cami, the Great Mosque, at the foot of the cliff at the western end of the town must have been a fine building but it was already a ruin when Lynch was here. Much of the damage to these buildings has been done by recent builders in Van using them as quarries of dressed stone. From this southern edge of the old town two partly underground Urartian palaces can be seen high on the cliff and halfway up, to the left of these palaces, there is a cuneiform inscription about the foundation of the fortress. Just outside the old town skeleton cone-topped Seljuk tombs look forlorn against the background of marsh, the lake and volcanic Süphan Dağ beyond.

TOPRAK KALE

This other Urartian fortress towers over Van town from the northeast. The Turkish name soon explains itself for the top of the hill is a great mound of earth (*toprak* earth; *kale* castle) which one discovers to be the remains of immensely thick mud-brick walls. The ascent to the castle, about four kilometres on foot from Van, cannot well be made by any other vehicle than a jeep or landrover but a car can get you to within a fifteen-minute walk to the summit. The fortress should be approached from the west and north, where a rough road goes to the top, not from the south. The southern side is not only very steep but is blocked by a Turkish army camp and firing range. The army has an unfortunate but understandable tendency to use these Urartian strongholds, with their high flanks of rock, as backgrounds for firing practice, so that one's visit is apt to be disturbed by the nasty noise of small arms fire and even by the whine of a ricochet overhead.

Having gone up the wide sweep of the mountain on the north side

of the fortress one first of all reaches the remains of a building constructed of huge blocks of well-cut masonry, some blocks with bossed
sides, the origin of the style ultimately much favoured in Renaissance
Italy. Only one course of masonry remains on the levelled rock foundations but others can be seen strewn down the hillside where the elements and marauding quarrymen have tumbled them. This must
surely be a temple, built thus of stone though flanked by the detritus
of less permanent mud-brick constructions. Huge steps have been cut
out of the hillside in front of it, surely too big for easy ascent. The
temple faces west to Lake Van, Van Kalesi and the setting sun. Are
there associations with death? A little channel cut across the front of
the building could have been a drain, or a channel for fresh water or
sacrificial blood. Could bulls have been slaughtered here for the
baptism in blood which washed away sin, a notion carried as far as
Britain by Mithraism, parallel with that of the blood of the lamb?
Speculation, however foolish or undocumented, is forced upon one in
such a mysterious and unexplained place. The temple is thought to be
that of the god Haldis, who may be the figure standing on the bull's
back in the splendid relief from Adilcevaz, now in Van Museum. In
this case the branch-like object in his right hand might be a sacrificial
knife, whilst his left hand holds a bowl for bull's blood.

From here I went on past the hilltop of earth to the southern side of
the ridge where there is a deep cleft in the rock bastion. Here most of
the almost perpendicular rock face has been cut into shallow steps,
receding as they rise. This is a characteristic of Urartian fortress
construction and almost every visible surface of rock on this hill is cut
into such steps. They are today explained as a means of supporting a
facing of sheer stonework which would be unclimbable. This covering of
masonry was either never added here or has tumbled away. Could
that have been a secret of attack, the prising away of the lowest course
and a dash for safety whilst the whole lot slid and bounced down to
the valley? Here I scrambled down to a square-cut entrance at the foot
of the stepped rock, trying not to notice the crackle and thump of
gunfire down to my left. From this entrance a wide, winding staircase
is cut out of the rock, rather like in the Welsh Castle of Carreg Cennen,
past circular holes cut through the rock face for light and to serve
as lookouts, to a huge cavern, again entirely chiselled out of the rock,
as at Van Kalesi. This is thought to have been part of the palace of the
Urartian King, possibly the great assembly room, for a bench with

curved back had been cut out of the rock on at least three sides of it and as far as I could see in the gloom. I had foolishly come without a torch, and matches and burnt paper failed to penetrate the dark recesses of this vast subterranean chamber, which is said to measure twenty-five by fifty metres. There was water and a regular drip, which suggested to me that a natural cave might originally have been enlarged and the water channelled off. The Urartians were expert at control of water. The ceiling of the great chamber, like the ceiling and sides of the approach staircase, had been cut in long scooped hollows about a foot wide, for no possible purpose but decoration, perhaps to simulate a wooden or bound reed ceiling. A weird silence filled the place, pointed by the drip of water to mark the slow passage of time. What magnificent torch-lit gatherings took place here, what light on gold and burnished bronze? What national complex drove these people back into these wombs of rock? No rational explanation of defence really fits, for these caverns could become death-traps as easily as impregnable hide-outs. We know little more about these people today than Lynch did when he described them, without even knowing what they were called and taking these caverns to be tombs, as '. . . not lacking in the instincts of imagination; and, year by year, they must have taken pleasure in gazing out upon the landscape from the grottos constructed to receive them when they died. A people of Cyclopean walls, embossed shields and chariots, they would almost seem to have belonged to the race of giants, preceding the evolution of fox-like man.'[1]

Once more back to the earth top of the ridge. I have never seen such huge and well-made bricks of baked mud, bound together as they are by a fine cement to make great thick walls. One room has been excavated, clearly a store-room for it has great earthenware jars set into its floor, similar to those found at other Urartian sites, at Kefkalesi and by the Russians at Karmir Blur near Erivan.

The view from the top of Toprak Kale is splendid, southwards over a fertile plain to Mount Varag and then eastward to other conical peaks. To the west is Lake Van. Down below is modern Van in its setting of trees, looking very new from this angle. This fortress became the capital of Urartu in the eighth century B.C., probably in the reign of Rusa I. It was sacked by the Cimmerians in 707.

Circling back to our original point of entry we passed a high earth-brick gateway into the central buildings of the citadel. The slopes

[1] op. cit., II, p. 111.

below the fortress were a mass of herbs in June. I recognised thyme and rosemary. There were many flowers, bushy white lupins, bright yellow and blue flowers that were strange to me and a 'bull-thistle', a little, many-branched thistle which the driver cut and, stripping off its spikes and the outer skin of the stalks, offered me to eat. It was sweet and refreshing, rather like cooked asparagus but crisper. I noticed afterwards that it was being sold in bunches in Van town and that it was correct to walk along biting at the succulent stalk. Thunder rolled down in the Hakkari and some huge drops of rain hurried us back to the jeep. There was thunder over Hakkari and the threat of rain in Van every afternoon for a week in mid June.

The site of Toprak Kale has been known, though not appreciated for what it is, for a century and it has been the scene of regular pot-hunting and ransacking by amateur and professional diggers. Layard first suggested an attack on the site and lovely things found there are now in museums in London, Paris, Berlin and Leningrad. There is a report that in the 1870's local people found a great gilded bronze throne here and broke it up for easier selling. Layard bought some of these fragments in 1877 and they are now in the British Museum. Several parts of this magnificent throne, decorated with ivory, coloured stones and a kind of enamel as well as gold, have been identified and it may become possible one day to reconstruct it. The animal figures, sphinxes and gryphons, and the solid, finely cast legs and joints, all stripped of their gold now, might be brought together again if such a throne or representation of a throne were to come to light in future excavation.[1] Beautifully cast bulls' heads, made to be handles of bronze cauldrons, are still coming to light at Toprak Kale, Karmir Blur, Gushchi and other sites, and a complete cauldron and stand were found at Altıntepe near Erzincan in 1938. I think there must be a good deal of faking now as well. I was offered some very dubious specimens in the market quarter of Van. Excavation at Toprak Kale has recently been organised by Istanbul University and under the direction of Dr. Afif Erzen.

There are other Urartian sites, of lesser importance, close to Van. A short distance to the east of Van and at the foot of the Varag Mountain is a remarkable detached crag known as Ak Köprü or White Bridge, near a village of this name. Round the corner of the hill from this point is a triple recessed niche above a shallow cave, carrying a cuneiform inscription with the names of Ishpuini and Menuas and

[1] See Piotrovskii, op. cit., pp. 26–30.

therefore probably put up by the latter. This deep niche is locally known as Çoban Kapısı, the Shepherd's Door, because a shepherd is said to have learnt the open sesame to it in a dream, entered it and then forgotten the secret, so that he never reappeared.

Another tremendous jutting rock, the western end of a ridge a few kilometres north of Van, marks the northern limit of the cultivable plain of Van. It is known as Kalecik, the Little Fortress, and there are traces of Urartian stonework at its summit. They could never have resisted such a rock. There was once an Armenian chapel at the top of the rock, since this was once an Armenian village, but the present villagers destroyed it 'because it was not good for their religion'. A mosque is now being built at the foot of the rock, the gift to the community of the head man, who entertained me and some Turkish friends of mine. The Kurds have built their village at the southern foot of the rock, round the corner from the destroyed Armenian village. I was taken there one evening by Bay Tayar Dabbaoğlu, the Director of the Girls' Teacher Training School, chiefly because three girls from the village, aged from fourteen to sixteen, were students of his. We were received by the Haci Hasan in a marvellously decorated room, walls and ceiling painted to imitate, unconsciously I am sure, a rich tent interior. The nostalgia of the nomad working out in a settled abode, just as frustrated Londoners have window-boxes in mews. The girl students were found, it was a holiday and they were at home, and they came in and kissed our hands. We sat and looked at some splendid kilims which had been woven in the house and at the infinitely varied Kurdish knitted stockings. Tayar Bey was borrowing some of these things for an exhibition he was getting together at his college. We then did a conducted tour round the village, admired the mosque under construction and the lovely view down to Lake Van. I took photographs of the village. Back in the colourful room one of the girls brought me a glass of fresh *ayran*, having heard that it was a favourite drink of mine, and then we all had glasses of tea. Touching and impressive was the pride they showed in the fact that their girls were going out to be teachers.

ÖĞRENBURC

I called one afternoon during this summer of 1969 to present my respects to the Vali of Van, the governor of the province, and found him a

15. *Aghtamar Island: the church*

16. *Aghtamar Church: east end*

17. *Aghtamar Church: detail of south-east corner*

18. Hoşap Castle

dignified, friendly and cultured person. He was pleased that I had already seen so much of Van and its surroundings and insisted on my having the use of his station-waggon for the following day so that I could visit some distant and remote mountain villages and see something of the crafts and village life. The station-waggon was roomy and by next morning the party had grown to include three teachers and eight of Tayar Bey's schoolgirls, who were making a sociological study, as well as Tayar Bey, Akşit and me. The party was split between the school jeep which followed us and our station-waggon, driven by a uniformed and armed policeman who, at the start of the day, obviously didn't think highly of the picnic. We made first of all for Özalp, past the Urartian sites of Anzaf, where there is little to see, and Lake Ercek. After the relatives I had met at Van it didn't surprise me that prominent citizens of Özalp, this remote town near the Persian frontier, were a cousin and uncle of Akşit's and the uncle took us for a walk to the eastern edge of the town to taste the famous water at a fountain that makes a little oasis with its overflow. At Özalp, where we called ceremonially on the mayor, another car joined us, carrying local government officials, and we struck south-eastwards along a good dirt road over rolling but unexciting upland country towards the Kotur valley, which runs into Iran. Again now striking southwards off this road on to a smaller one we climbed to the large, straggling village of Öğrenburc. This new name, Tower of Learning, I found to be amply justified by the interest its inhabitants took in the education of their children. When it was Armenian it was Satmanis, for which there are many explanations, the most popular being Village of 100 houses, or of the 100th house. A rich Armenian lady who settled here is involved in many of these explanatory stories. Here we were given a splendid Kurdish feast, roast kids torn to savoury chunks by the hands of our hosts and eaten pinched into pieces of tasty thin bread, with *otlupeynir*, rice and spring onions. The rice was the extravagance, since they produced everything else themselves, except the tea that followed, served in the usual glasses. We sat cross-legged, five or six at each great tray on the carpet down the middle of the room. The schoolgirls ate with us, though no village woman came near us, and after the meal I was impressed by the quiet patience of the *muhtar* in answering their questions about the village. They all had their notebooks for facts and statistics. Outside afterwards some of the men complained to me in halting Turkish of the shortage of teachers. I think the ratio at this village school was two teachers to one hundred and sixty children.

A place like this, high up in mountains remote from central administration, must always have been subject to brigandage. In Armenian days it was the Kurds who raided, and since then the settled Kurds themselves have suffered from cattle raids from over the nearby Persian border. Now, they tell me, cattle raids have diminished since the establishment of a military post here. While most of the party went over to visit the barracks, I sat in the village shop. The shopkeeper, a quiet, formal man, said that the village ballad singer was away with the flocks at their summer pastures on 3,550 metre Hirabit Dağ but he produced a tape-recorder and played some of the ballad singer's songs and other men came in quietly to stand or sit and listen to the high strong wavering subtle rhythm of their Kurdish music. All other sounds, not that there were many outside, were shut out by the thick mud walls and the atmosphere was perfect. The shop was dark and earth-floored, had some things in sacks, a few simple agricultural objects, mattocks and ploughshares, some sweets, biscuits and cigarettes. Later when the officials of the party came back from the barracks and approached the door of the shop a warning was given and the Kurdish music was switched off.

It was evening when we left and the cattle were streaming back uphill, hundreds of them together, to separate into their proper enclosures for the night, cows to be under cover, bulls together in little walled open places. Boys rode bareback and shouting through the plodding cattle, glad to be back after their day's cowherding. Girls were carrying water and women were washing dishes at a spring. Smoke from newly kindled dung-cake fires rose into the clear mountain air. The smells had a healthy tang and I was sorry to leave.

From near here the Kotur valley runs down into Iran and the earth road is being improved. It's the quietest frontier post I've ever seen, not a house or a café or an office except for the two little police posts with the usual stretch of no man's land in between. This quiet way into Iran is very little used since most motor traffic goes either south-east from Van or east from Erzurum to Doğubeyazit. Smugglers use even quieter ways through the mountains. One has a sense here of the vastness of Asia.

AGHTAMAR ISLAND

Aghtamar Island with its unique Armenian church is reached from a point on the south shore of Lake Van about forty kilometres from Van. You drive on a good road along the green shores of the lake, southwards, and then westwards to Gevaş, a pleasant little town famous for its orchards. A sign of your nearness to the landing-stage is a very beautiful *türbe* or Seljuk tomb to the south of the road. This is the burial place of a fourteenth-century lady, Halime Hatun, and her body lies in the crypt below. The tiling of the twelve-segmented cone roof is particularly lovely but needs to be cleared of moss and lichen. Tremendous mountains rise to the south and a few hundred yards away is a new primary boarding school for the mountain children. The school at Gevaş[1] has one teacher for ninety children. Near the tomb is an extensive Seljuk cemetery which has suffered from use as a quarry but which still has very beautiful tall tombstones carved mostly in fine abstract patterns, like those of the more numerous tombstones at Ahlat. I was taken here by Bay Erol Altay, the architect responsible for the new school, and he organised the boat and a picnic lunch for the island.

The jetty for departure for the island is opposite a large café which stands high above the road. Since military restrictions have only recently been relaxed in this area very few foreigners have been to Aghtamar during this century, but today the only formality expected of you is that you should ask at the café for permission to cross to the island and for the trip to be arranged for you with the owner of the motorboat. The charge is sixty liras per party[2] for the return trip, about four kilometres each way. For this the boatman will take you over to the island, leave you there and return for you at an agreed time. In the afternoon of holidays or at weekends in summer he runs it as a *dolmuş*, alarmingly overloaded at times, and then it's much cheaper, but your visit to the island won't be so pleasant. A Sunday afternoon or *bayram* picnic on the island has become a fashionable outing for residents of Van.

The church and palace of Aghtamar were built early in the tenth

---

[1] Gevaş was formerly Vestan and this is the name of its ruined fortress.
[2] I think the charge for tourists is higher than for Turks and residents in Turkey, so if you live in Turkey insist on the lower charge.

century by the Armenian King Gagik[1] and for a short time it was the capital of an Armenian state. But this was surely more of a hide-out than an administrative centre and probably safer than a castle, since overland invaders would hardly bring boats with them, or even know how to build them or have time to. I think Gagik must have been one of those disillusioned near-eastern rulers who, like Nabonidus, were impelled to retreat from their commitments into some kind of hermitage. There was already a little monastery on Aghtamar, dating from the sixth century, when Gagik came there, and the remains are still to be seen to the east of the church.

From the island landing-stage you climb up a rough path past earth terraces that were once the gardens of the early monastery and the tenth-century palace. Part of an earthenware storage jar protrudes from the side of the path. The church, quite staggering from the water and still impressive as you approach it, is somehow pathetic now amongst the almond trees and the thistles. It is built mostly of the pale chocolate coloured sandstone of this part of Turkey and its main body is tall and cruciform, with a huge twelve-sided cone-topped drum to cover its central area. The south porch, through which you will probably enter, is an eighteenth-century addition and though pleasant in itself it detracts from the unity of the whole structure, being so palpably stuck on. The glory and interest of the church lie in the sculptures in projecting relief on its outside walls. These are of two kinds. A series of continuous friezes runs round the whole of the exterior. The lowest is a fluent geometrical pattern based on the vine, then, much higher, lively animals, strange birds and hunters are held together by a swirling scroll of carved stone. Higher still there are more animals and a row of human heads. All this imposes a certain formality on the whole design, but the set pieces, which seem to rest on the lowest band of decoration, are all treated individually, with no attempt to link them together. They represent stories from the Bible, a lumpish and sexless Adam and Eve at a stylised apple-tree, with the serpent tempting Eve on the other side of a window, a David with a sly look in his eye as he prepares to sling a stone at Goliath. The dragon is there, this time with Saint Theodore. There are some very good animals, a lovely bear, some very sheepish sheep and a lively pair of cocks fighting. All these figures are roughly life size, or appear so from the points at which one views them, and look extraordinarily fresh and new. Aesthetically you may consider

[1] See also p. 55.

them degenerate descendants of the finer Urartian and Hittite traditions, but they have considerable human interest and in this unlikely situation they provide an uncommon experience.

Inside the church there is no decoration visible in the high dome but there are considerable remains of fresco painting on the walls. There are scenes from the life of Christ, the flight into Egypt, the slaughter of the innocents, with one very black sword raised over an infant, Christ washing the feet of the disciples and then a line of apostles or saints round the altar end. Archangel wings rise over the south entrance. The frescoes seem to have lost much of their colour and are mostly black and white, with light blue on some garments and traces of yellow, and there are signs that the walls have at some time been covered with blue lime wash, probably during Moslem use. The removal of lime wash or plaster, either by human or atmospheric agency, has gone down to the basic original drawing in many places. The paintings show a good deal of lively, realistic action, except in the posed figures.

Outside, to the north of the church, there are tumbled gravestones of intricate and lovely design, richly floral in comparison with the abstract Seljuk designs on the tombstones we saw near the mainland shore. A path leads from this little island cemetery across the low ridge and then to the left, down to the north shore. At the foot of the path and a metre or so above the lake there is a hand pump which yields sweet fresh drinking water, but it must first of all be primed with lake water. There were a few birds about. I saw gulls, rock doves and a pair of pochards which kept circling the island and landing on a rocky point. This was where I had the most enjoyable swim of my life, once into deep water past the rather troublesome stones. Then we picnicked in the shade off food ordered by Erol Altay at the shoreside café, cheese, tomatoes, spring onions, young cucumbers and a great bowl of yoğurt which had been carefully carried over by the island's watchman. He left us to our swimming and when we were eating came down again to the pump with three very cheerful chaps who turned out to be Van prison warders having a day out. We talked and, noticing that we were without bread, they insisted on our taking one of their loaves. (The watchman later brought us the loaf the café proprietor had forgotten to include in the picnic lunch.) One of them pulled out what looked like a fountain pen and passed it round, asking whether each one of us in turn could see Van across the water by peering through one end. It came last of all to me and on being held up to the light presented six propelling views of naked European girls, not at all gross or pornographic but rather natural, almost amateurish, shots of young women who didn't look like whores or even models, in a drawing-room or stepping into a bath. It had been smuggled in from Iran, they said, but it looked German to me. It gave a few moments' simple pleasure to us all except one puritanical jailer who refused to look through it.

Aghtamar has a tree known as *iğde*, the oleaster (*elaeagnus augustifolia*), with a delicate scented yellow flower. The Turks like to pick sprigs of it and carry it in their hands, sniffing it occasionally, as old women used to do with *hen wr* or lad's love when I was a boy in Wales.

We left Aghtamar Island as the Sunday afternoon crowd began to arrive. A whole bus-load of men swarmed on to the motor boat when we got off and I was glad not to be on it for that journey. As we left the island the boatman took us to the western end where the rock is high and precipitous and past the little ruined chapel on a tiny island of rock. What could it have been, a hermitage for someone for whom even Aghtamar Island wasn't sufficiently cut off from the world? A private chapel for King Gagik, builder of the church, who must have loved islands and solitude? I myself love both and I could take the visit of the jolly prison warders but not the Sunday afternoon swarm.

THE CIRCUIT OF LAKE VAN

The complete circuit of the lake today presents no difficulty to an ordinary car, except in winter or when summer floods have cut the road. It is well worth doing and in a leisurely manner. Westwards from Gevaş and the Aghtamar landing-stage the road goes in and out of the mountains to avoid following the inleted coastline and projections into the lake. There are splendid views of the lake and of the noble cone of Süphan Dağ to the north. You can by-pass the pleasant lakeside village of Reşadiye or go down into it, and this is the better road. From here westwards the road improves through Küçüksu, at the foot of the mountains, and on to Tatvan.

From the south-eastern corner of the lake, about thirteen kilometres east of Gevaş, a motorable road finds its way southwards, past the 3,575 metre Artos Dağ and on to an important tributary of the Tigris, variously named along its reaches. Here at Çatak, in the heart of the great mountains, there is excellent trout fishing.

The Circuit of Lake Van

If you go northwards round the lake from Van the road soon passes Kalecik and its little Kurdish village. The school is noticeable, a neat yellow building with corrugated roof, like all rural primary schools in this part of Turkey. The road crosses the considerable Marmed River, also known as Karasu, or Blackwater, before swinging once more towards the lake, the shore of which is flat and marshy here. From the north-eastern corner of the lake a road goes off up the Bendinahi valley to Muradiye and continues, much more roughly, up to Çaldıran. The castle of Muradiye was built in 1500 by the Persians and was taken in 1514 by Sultan Selim I. Its foundations are Urartian. There's another Urartian fortress at Koryat Kalesi to the south-east and yet another at Çaldıran. A cultivable valley with defensible positions appealed to these experienced mountain dwellers. At Çaldıran there is still living a very famous weather prophet. In the late summer he predicts the hardness and length of the coming winter by separating the wool on the back of a sheep and running his finger along the division. He is found to be dependable.

The white cone of Süphan Dağ continues to dominate the view as we swing westwards along the north shore of Lake Van. The land is well watered, a number of streams run into the lake and fish are caught in great numbers at their mouths in early summer. We pass Erniş, a green little place, with its Boys' Teacher Training College. A restored Seljuk tomb by the wayside announces the beginning of Erçis, a long straggling untidy town and an important agricultural centre. I had a glass of tea in the shady but fly-infested open-air café in the middle of the town whilst our taxi driver Haci Muhittin went to say his midday prayers, all the more important on a Friday. There was nothing of interest in the tiny shops and I saw no weaving. The fly-whisk I bought to drive off the flies, made of horribly coloured dried grass, came from Gaziantep, the man said.

From Erçis a good road goes off to join the Erzurum–Doğubeyazit road at Karaköse, newly named Ağrı. We went along it as far as Patnos. This road soon leaves the well-watered valley to climb to drier uplands, along a good hard earth surface with some rough patches between Patnos and Ağrı. In June the ochre landscape has great sheets of deep blue flowers to astonish the eye, branched things up to about a metre tall growing I think where the ground has once been ploughed. Haci Muhittin said they have roots like potatoes which are pulled, ground and made into cakes and a drink. I think it must be chicory (*Cichorium intybus*). Along this road there are frequent signs of terracing and abandoned cultivation, dating presumably from Armenian occupation.

The ancient fortress of Aznavur[1] at Patnos is another typically Urartian site, a long narrow defensible ridge dominating a cultivable plain. The citadel is best approached by landrover or jeep, or of course on foot if you leave your car on the main road or on the lower reaches of the track, which runs along the western edge of the new barracks. Here again there is a military firing range and it might be as well to ask the Kaymakam for advice on the visit. They were firing when I was there and one ricochet whined unpleasantly over my head as I went up the stony path. The military area is fenced and signed and no attempt should be made to enter it except by the main gate. On the summit a temple facing Süphan Dağ has been cleared, revealing worn basalt blocks with broken cuneiform inscriptions and mud-brick walls on a stone foundation. This is the least interesting Urartian site I have visited, remarkable for me only in yielding my one piece of obsidian, a flaked, pointed implement of some sort. That and the absolute solitude of the far side of the ridge in the cool sweet herb-tinctured air.

From Patnos again southwards the good Haci took a short cut along a good earth road past Sarian and the skirts of Süphan, with fine views of the volcano, back to Lake Van and the Erciş–Tatvan road, a very good surface except for occasional corrugation, which you either crawl over or risk everything and take at speed. Five miles north of Adilcevaz we passed a little oasis with a ruined *han*.

ADILCEVAZ

Adilcevaz is a little green town with running water and tall trees. It was here, in the ruined Seljuk castle which rises immediately above the town, that Peter Hulin found the five pieces of the magnificent relief of the Urartian god or king now in Van Museum.[2] These must have been carried or tumbled down from the Urartian fortress known to the Turks as Kefkalesi which towers over the valley to the west of the town. They were then re-used in the construction of the castle. Lynch reported a 'colossal site' at the citadel hilltop and C. A. Burney's

---

[1] See Burney and Lawson, *Anatolian Studies*, X, pp. 192–4.
[2] *Anatolian Studies*, VIII, pp. 211–16. C. A. Burney and G. R. J. Jackson.

suggestion that excavation at Kefkalesi 'should reveal many buildings' is being amply justified by Turkish archaeologists. The walled city has been mapped and inscribed stones and reliefs have been found. A huge basalt block, a pillar base which once formed part of a great pillared hall, with a representation in relief of an Urartian fortress, is now on show in the new Urartian room of the Ankara Hittite Museum. It measures 140 by 140 by 110 centimetres. Three long storage rooms have been revealed, with huge storage jars or *pithoi*, like those at Toprak Kale and Karmir Blur, sometimes in double rows.[1] Archaeologists have detected signs of plundering at Kefkalesi before the city was burnt. It's a stiff walk up to the citadel and only a jeep, landrover, horse or mule will carry you there. The caretaker can be found on enquiry in the village. Jars and inscribed stones are on exhibition at the Orta Okulu, the Intermediate School for children from twelve to fifteen.

We lunched at a very good little restaurant in the informal square, on grilled kebabs of kid, rice, with *ayran* to drink. After lunch, or at any other time, one takes tea under a tree on the edge of the clear rushing stream that comes down past Kefkalesi and is here on the point of plunging into Lake Van. On the previous day Akşit had explained the planetary system to Haci Muhittin and he was now expounding it to the respectful villagers. It was obviously as new to them as it had been to him a day before. Though obviously contrary to religion his exposition seemed to go down well with them all except a quiet, burly, white-haired man sitting slightly outside our circle. His comment, after a lull in the discussion, was, 'All nonsense. The world is in the belly of the Caucasus.' It was the day of the first American landing on the Moon and it seemed to me to put that exploit into a more human and mundane perspective. The Caucasus Mountains hold an important and mysterious place in eastern Anatolian folk poetry and that world view generally, a memory of the impact those mountains made on the first Hittites and Turkomans to cross them on their way south and west. They are the home of giants and monsters, and have strange fires burning in them, presumably the first volcanoes these invaders had ever seen.

[1] M. J. Mellink, 'Archaeology in Asia Minor', *A.J.A.*, vol. 71, no. 2.

AHLAT

Southwards from Adilcevaz the road rises high above the lake to give spectacular views. Between here and Ahlat there are long beaches with no house or human being in sight, so that it's easy to swim at leisure away from all villages. Ahlat made me think of Sartre's extraordinary view of Paris as a perpetual battleground against greenness, the grass, weeds, shrubs and trees always on the point of investing the city. Ahlat seems to have given up the struggle and interesting fragments of old buildings are almost swamped with green. The walnut trees here are especially big and leafy. The lived-in houses are well built of the fine chocolate-coloured sandstone of this region, a stone and style used as far as splendid Bitlis and, of course, Aghtamar Island. I am speaking of the modern township that one drives through and which is really the old suburban quarter, known as Erkizan, of the old city. Eski Ahlat, Old Ahlat, is over a kilometre inland from the lakeside castle, in a ravine at the junction of two valleys which run down towards the lake. There are trees and running water but very few traces of the ancient greatness of Ahlat. The churches and monasteries of the Armenian city have long ago disappeared. It was taken by the Arabs in the seventh century and remained the centre of an Arab enclave until swamped by the Seljuk advance into Anatolia in the eleventh century. It was held for some years by the Marwan Kurds and then for the whole of the twelfth century by a dynasty founded by a Turk, perhaps a Seljuk, named Sokman. These rulers called themselves the Shahs of Armenia. In the thirteenth century there came Eyubbi descendants of the Kurdish Saladin and then a period of Kwarazmian[1] rule before the city was restored to the Seljuks. It was overrun by the Mongols in 1245 and a new dynasty was set up by them through the marriage of a Sokman prince and a Georgian princess. It was taken by the Ak Koyun tribe of Turkomans and remained an important centre of theirs until seized by Soliman the Magnificent in 1533. It then declined rapidly in importance and dwindled to little more than a frontier post with its walled town and castle erected on the lake shore by Soliman II in 1554. The walls with their two gates, the citadel and the two sixteenth-century mosques remain.

But one goes to Ahlat to see the spacious cemetery which is its glory, a great expanse of otherwise waste ground marked by cone-topped

---

[1] Kwarazm was in north-eastern Persia.

tombs and lying between the castle and the valley of the old city. On the roadside half a mile north of the castle there are two fine tombs,[1] the eastern one that of Nugatay Agha and his wife, dating from 1279, and the western one that of Hasan Timur Agha, date 1281. Between them and the great cemetery, reached by an inner road that leaves the main road, is a stubbier and uglier tomb, its conical roof resting on short columns, with an inscription which gives the date A.H. 886 (1481 A.D.) and announces that this is the burial place of a certain Bayindar Bey, son of Rustem Bey. Unknown otherwise to history, he is described as a great king and propagator of the Moslem faith, a ransomed emperor and a master of the sword and the pen.[2] From this tomb the great graveyard stretches southwards. There are acres and acres of lovely tall rectangular tombstones, some of them nearly two metres high and not all of them upright. They are all carved in relief with intricate designs, usually around a pointed panel in the lower part of the stone face. The reverse side of the stones often has a curious and unusual arrangement of symbols. The extent of the burial ground and the number and the beauty of the stones effectively record the prosperity, good taste and fine craftsmanship of medieval Ahlat. This long-abandoned graveyard is one of the strangest sights in Turkey and should not be missed. The forest of tall scrolled and lichened stones seen against the background of the lake and the far mountains seems no longer to have any reference to life or death but a strange and absolute beauty.

South of Ahlat the mountains recede and a road leads inland to Lake Nazik and the Kurdish village of the same name. Lynch found it the haunt of all kinds of water-birds and the presence of pelicans indicated fish. I have not been able to visit it but the map gives a motorable dirt road, only possible in summer, which goes through to Bulanık, on the road from Muş to Patnos.

The road from Ahlat to Tatvan[3] now crosses a considerable stream, which comes down from the direction of Nazik, and is here so low-lying that a flood or one of the unexplained rises in level of Lake Van covers it with water to a disconcerting depth. Before reaching Tatvan the road skirts the railway terminal and the jetty where the train for Van is put on the ferry-boat.

[1] Such a tomb or *türbe* is often known as a *kümbet*, the word for vault or dome or projection. This is also a slang word for the human backside.

[2] Lynch, op. cit., vol. II, p. 293.

[3] The v is locally pronounced as w, so don't be surprised at the pronunciations Wan and Tatwan.

TATVAN

Tatvan is a straggling, characterless town which alternately suffers from mud, slush or dust according to the season. An asphalting of the roads in the little town would make it more attractive to visitors and tolerable to its inhabitants. If you are planning to stay there, make for, having phoned in advance, the Denizcilik Bankası Hotel, which is pleasantly situated in a garden away from the town centre and near the lake shore and the old jetties from which the passenger ferries run. This is comfortable and cheap but if you fail to get in there are other possible hotels in the centre of the town. The restaurants of Tatvan are good but they must be the noisiest in the world. Young waiters dash about between the tables shouting orders to the kitchen at the back and uttering cries which can only be an encouragement to order or an attempt to create an atmosphere of furious and efficient service. The result is an endless cacophony in sharp Kurdish and rather worse service than one gets elsewhere.

With its abundant rain and its sun-trap situation, Tatvan is surrounded, except for the lake side, by green hills. Red-legged partridge (*keklik* in Turkish) abound and breed here and are trapped by townsmen and villagers. One method is to set out a hen with a covey of chicks, trapped for this purpose. Its alarm cries attract scores of gallant cock birds, which are then easily netted. A shopkeeper from whom I bought hand-knitted socks was about to go out netting into the hills and he showed me his equipment. These handsome birds will live quite long as pets and I have seen them uncaged in grocers' shops in Istanbul. Tatvan Fair is held annually from June 30 to July 14 and this is a good time to buy country-made things, weaving and knitting. Otherwise, the odd countryman who brings in a *kilim* or a saddle-bag is apt to have an exaggerated notion of its worth to the visitor and I have found such things cheaper in the market quarter of Gaziantep.

Tatvan is the base for the ascent of Nimrut Dağ, over which you may have flown on your way to Van. This ascent can only be done in the midsummer months since up to the beginning of July snow remaining inside the crater blocks the road. But until the new snow comes in the autumn a jeep, which can be hired in Tatvan, will take you through a gap in the crater rim and down to the lake shore. No one lives inside the crater but Yuruks camp and graze their cattle there in the summer months. Steam still issues from fissures near the summit and one of the three lakes is hot, whilst in a cave on the far side things freeze quickly. There's a rocky island in the main lake that's easy to swim to but tricky currents are apt to make the return difficult.

There's a local belief that the main crater lake is connected by an underground link with a little lake some distance to the west which is the source of the Kara Su, a headwater of the Murat branch of the Euphrates. The usual story is told of a shepherd who threw his staff into the crater lake, walked to the Kara Su spring, sat there a few days and then saw the stick come up. Another story is told of the origin of this spring. In Christian times there was a little monastery at Kara Su in charge of a monk who had a pretty daughter. One day she was washing clothes at a little spring near the monastery wall. Her father happened to look down from the wall and was scandalised to see his daughter being kissed on the mouth by a shepherd. The girl then pushed the young man away, gathered up the clothes and came back into the monastery. That night the father said nothing. The next day the girl was outside the wall once more, this time baking bread in a *tandır*.[1] The monk was watching and he saw the young man approach again and, after exchanging a few words, kiss her on the breasts. The father could stand it no longer and stormed out through the gate to see the young man disappear over the hill. He turned on his shamefaced daughter.

—Shame on you for allowing such a thing. Who was he?

—I don't know. He came yesterday and asked to kiss me. I said certainly not. Then he said, for God's sake let me kiss you.
    So what could I do?

—And today?

—The same thing happened. He wanted to kiss my breasts. Of course I refused. Then he said, for God's sake let me kiss your breasts . . .

Hopping mad by this time the monk shouted, For God's sake jump into that *tandır*. This the girl did and it immediately became a pool into which she disappeared. The pool is still believed to be in the form of a funnel. Stories of a volcanic region, of sudden lakes, fires and

---

[1] The *tandır* is a big earthenware cylinder set upright on the ground, with a draught hole at the bottom. A wood fire is lit inside it and when that subsides flat pieces of dough are stuck on to the inside of the pot with a cushion called a *mazraka*. Lake Van fish and gobbets of lamb are cooked in the same way, as well as the little flat loaves of the region. Delicious *tandır*-cooked meat is served in some restaurants in Istanbul and Ankara.

underground water and where one religion has replaced another, leaving elements of an earlier faith submerged in folklore.

Not far from here, at Sason or Sasun, a little town difficult of access in the mountains south of Muş, Lynch reports the presence at the end of the nineteenth century of a tribe called the Baliki or Beleke, speaking a language which is a mixture of Arabic, Kurdish and Armenian. They made oaths by the name of a church or monastery but they had neither churches nor mosques and could not be classed as either Christian or Moslem. They had no institution of marriage, women went free and unveiled but could be bought and sold. Lynch took them to be a pocket of original Anatolians not greatly affected by Armenian and Seljuk domination.[1] I cannot say whether they still pursue this way of life.

[1] op. cit., vol. II, p. 430.

Hakkari

Van is the obvious base for a visit to the Hakkari (pronounced Hakkyari) in the extreme south-eastern corner of Turkey, unless you are with an organised alpinist party, in which case you will probably make Yuksekova your base. You can also stay in Hakkari town but if you do so observe whether a balcony rail protects the balcony outside your bedroom window. When I was there the balcony was a flat slab of concrete with a straight drop to the street.

From Van a good hard road goes southwards away from the lake, over the hills and down to Gürpinar in the fertile valley of the Engel Çayi which runs into Lake Van. Soon after leaving Van a road goes off to the east a few kilometres to Yedi Kilise (the Seven Churches) and to the abandoned church of the old Armenian monastery of Varag. The mountain behind is Mount Varag, which faces you as you look southwards from Toprak Kale. Here are buried King Senekerim and his wife, daughter of King Gagik who built the church on Aghtamar Island.[1] The church looks westwards to Lake Van from its three-arched narthex and still has traces of fresco painting inside its walls and its central cone-topped dome. It was here that Archbishop Khrimean established a printing press in an attempt to raise the standard of education of the Armenians and from here he encouraged them to take a greater pride in themselves and their traditions.

Back on the Hakkari road, instead of going on to the little settle-ment of Gürpinar and a very rough road through the mountains to Hakkari, we turn eastwards up the Engel valley. Soon after this, south

[1] Lynch says, op. cit., vol. I, p. 237, that Senekerim in 1021, distressed by his son's defeat by the Seljuks, abdicated in favour of the Byzantine Emperor Basil II and retired to Sivas, which he was given in exchange. He is much reviled for this cowardly act, comparable to that of the King of Ani in 1022.

of the road and immediately east of the well-watered village of Atbaşı, a conspicuous spur running parallel with the road is the Urartian site known today as Cavuştepe, possibly the ancient Sardurihurda. A track runs up to the eastern end of the citadel, motorable except after rain, which is apt to swamp the lower part, but the citadel's not a long walk from the road. This typically long and narrow Urartian fortress is completely surrounded with fine masonry which excavation conducted by Professor Afif Erzen of Istanbul University is now revealing. First one comes to the eastern wall across the ridge, then to a temple with beautiful black basalt frontage and cuneiform inscriptions which are perfect because they have been until recently protected from the elements by tumbled mud-brick from buildings, perhaps the upper walls of the temple itself.[1] From here dressed blocks of stone have been tumbled down to the field below by foraging builders, a form of quarrying which is still going on here, facilitated as it is by the nearness of the road. From the temple, streets of mud-brick houses run lengthwise along the ridge to the royal palace which, as at Toprak Kale and Van Kalesi, is mostly underground. These underground rooms have not yet been cleared and are uninviting. Urartian seals have been found here and recently bull's head rhytons and a boot-shaped drinking vessel.[2] Professor Erzen has found signs of destruction and fire at the base of the north wall and indications of possible Phrygian occupation of the site.

Here again the fortress dominated a fertile valley. The air is wonderful and in summer there are birds which I have never seen before. One, about the size of a pippit, seemed to be all blue and gold and red as it made short swoops between the dried thistles and herbs.

From Cavuştepe the road follows the Engel Çayı upstream to the village of Güzelsu (Sweet Water), formerly called Hoşap, an obviously Indo-European name of either Kurdish or Persian origin. The bridge we cross to reach the village was built in the year 1500 by a Kurdish ruler, Zeynel Bey, and the castle which towers over the village and valley in 1643 by another Kurd, Sari Suleyman. The castle, which is approached by walking down on the left, after crossing the bridge, as far as the police station and then by a path up to the right, is the main stronghold of a completely walled town of considerable area, the extent of which can be realised as we walk uphill to the main gate on the north side. This is a rosette-decorated door in a great round tower.

[1] See Plate 5.   [2] *A.J.A.*, vol. 74, no. 2. Mellink's digest.

19. Seljuk cemetery: Gevaş

0. Seljuk tomb: Gevaş

21. *Seljuk cemetery: Ahlat*

22. *Mardin*

Don't be deterred by the gloom of this entrance. A careful picking of one's way over tumbled stones (a torch is useful here) for a few yards brings one out to daylight and the interior of the citadel. From the far side you get a vertiginous view on to the village roofs and the road. The castle has hundreds of rooms, two mosques, baths, wells, store-rooms and dungeons.

The village below has a few mud-brick and mud-roofed shops and a teahouse with a few chairs and tables outside. It's obviously an important shopping and staging centre for the Kurds of this part. Women move freely amongst the men to do their shopping (and window-shopping even here) but do not sit on the teahouse terrace.

From Hoşap the road swings south from the Engel valley along a wide plain and then climbs to a pass before dropping down to the creamy turbulent greater Zab river which cuts its way southwards through the mountains to join the Tigris in Irak. The road leaves the valley to rise to Başkale, the highest town in Turkey. It is purely Kurdish today, though Lynch reports the presence of twenty-five Jewish families here late in the nineteenth century. Kurdish music blares öpenly from radios around the square, though whether broadcast from Russia or from Irak, both of which have programmes for Kurds, I wasn't able to discover. A very able and pleasant Kurdish lawyer whom I met in Van and who lives and practises in Başkale, invited me to stay and shoot there on some future occasions. He could promise me shots at wild goats and wild sheep, and of course partridges. Başkale, very much a man's town, with hardly a woman venturing into the streets, is a very busy market town and has a modern-looking hotel in the wide main street. The Dörtyol Oteli on the corner of the square is very prettily painted and old-fashioned. The ruins of a castle overlook the town. Near Başkale I saw six and eight cattle yoked together to ploughs.

The Zab now becomes wilder and more dangerous looking and the road which clings precariously to the scree of the valley side is much at the mercy of floods and landslides. At times it passes very close to the narrow old road and the polished rock side shows how animals rubbed against it to keep away from the precipitous drop. There are traces of abandoned terrace cultivation on the eastern bank of the river and some rice was being grown on a flat patch in a bend of the river, near a ruined Nestorian house. Then an abandoned Nestorian village and, about ten kilometres from Hakkari and just past a little castle, an old Nestorian church almost opposite a police post. Its very dark, vaulted interior is now used for the occasional housing of cattle and I could see no trace of decoration or of ritual arrangements.

The huge bulk of Sümbül Dağ now looms over the east bank of the river as we approached Hakkari. *Sümbül* means hyacinth and the adjective *sümbüli* cloudy or overcast. There was still a lot of snow on it in mid June and our Haci and driver swore there were lions on it. Perhaps he meant mountain leopards.

Hakkari town, capital of the *vilayet* of that name, is perched above the Zab River in the middle of fresh green pasture, when it isn't deep in snow, and ringed with tremendous mountains. The eternal snow of Cilo Dağ is visible to the east and the peak, rising to more than 4,000 metres, is in fact only about 30 kilometres as the crow flies from the town. But this is not the direction from which the Cilo-Sat Mountains are usually approached by climbers.[1] Hakkari used to be known as Çölemerik, presumably a Kurdish name, and the region was known to the Arabs as Hakkariye. In spite of the wildness of the region it has long been inhabited and there are primitive drawings of uncertain date and in a stick technique on a rock face near Gevaruk Lake, at a height of 2,920 metres. For the sportsman, or nature observer, there are red-legged partridges, hares, foxes, jackals, wolves in plenty and especially visible in hard winters, bears, wild goats and wild sheep. Robin Fedden reports seeing snowfinches and a wealth of flowers, a bright yellow umbelliferous flower, tall purple vetch, white hollyhocks, mammoth poppies, tulips, primulas, gentians and buttercups.[2]

The town, which has little of interest to offer except its situation[3] and its people, has increased its population from one to seven thousand since 1927. It now has a resident governor and the improved road has brought more traffic and business. Hakkari has a very good and cheap restaurant known as the Kent, which means Town, and a dusty, angled street of small shops selling the usual haberdashery, domestic utensils and horse trappings. I failed to find any local craft products and the excellent local weaving seems to be unpurchasable here. The men wear suits called *şal çepik*, which means jacket and trouser in Kurdish, in an attractive, striped angora wool material said to be of Nestorian origin, the jacket tight fitting, the trousers short and wide, but the material is not for sale here. I was greatly disappointed, for it would

---

[1] See Appendix on climbing, pp. 240–43.   [2] *The Times*, 19 November, 1965.
[3] Lord Warkworth has some lovely photographs of the country near the town, which he knows as Julamerk, in his *Notes from a Diary in Asiatic Turkey*.

make wonderful trousering. The only local thing I managed to buy was a pair of woollen socks, white with a little cruciform device in colour on the toes, a design which is surely another Nestorian relic. Men galloped along the main street on horseback but I only saw two women, both heavily covered in black and not Kurdish. There were a few lorries but I saw no sign of the bus which is said to run between here and Van. It must be a slow service, stopping for lone travellers and tribal movements, and I was glad to have acquired the knowledge-able and experienced Haci Muhittin as driver and guide.

On the way back from Hakkari to Van, Haci stopped at a trickle of water by the roadside above the Engel Çayi, saying that it was the best water he knew and that he planned to build a proper wayside fountain here, with his name on it. Turks love spring water and a Turk who has driven to Mecca values it the more. This was certainly lovely water and we scooped it up in our cupped hands. The usual summer thunder-storm in the mountains had suddenly filled the rivers, the road below the bridge at Hoşap was a foot deep with flood water and further down the valley we had some difficulty with a torrent which was cutting the road. Nature is apt to spring at you in the Hakkari and is tough for the inhabitants too. There are not many bridges over the turbulent rivers and on the greater Zab countrymen going to market, women too for that matter, suspend themselves by a pulley to a rope fixed across the torrent and work their way across the valley and back.

A few kilometres north of Hakkari a bridge over the river leads to a road which takes you down the Zab valley 78 kilometres, except when it's cut by floods or landslides or blocked by snow, through very wild country, to the little town of Çukurca, remote in the mountains near the Irak frontier. But this is not a frontier post and there is no motorable road through to Irak this way.

Alpinists who plan to attempt the great Cilo and Sat peaks will turn eastwards over another bridge about half way between Başkale and Hakkari and make for Yuksekova as the base, where they will hire guides and pack animals. This little town in a great high plain has little else to offer the traveller but will probably benefit from the com-pletion of the Cento road to Iran. Though built for a strategic purpose this road will open up the marvellous country, with its always snow-covered mountain ranges, its high lakes and glaciers, its nomads and wild animals and the lovely flowers which grow up to the snow line.[1]

[1] See Appendix on climbing, pp. 241–2.

Westwards from Tatvan through Bitlis

I went by bus from Tatvan to Siirt. I had booked a seat on a bus due to leave at one o'clock, so there was time for a good lunch of grilled *köfte* and rice, *otlupeynir* and yoğurt, after a last swim off the wooden jetty into deep silk-soft Lake Van water. The bus had come from Van and the through passengers had scattered all over the little town. An amplifier called them from the bus company office, runners were sent out to the market and the teahouses, the bus-driver yelled and hooted. Unhurried and calm, the passengers appeared from all directions. The driver threatend to start, half an hour late already, and two Arabic-speaking women covered in black clothes let out squawks. Their man, husband and son-in-law probably, got on with two children. A Kurdish woman swung past my window to the rear door in her gaily coloured exhibition of clothes, followed by a bedraggled little future beauty, and got in. The company was complete and we were off.

The road rises from Tatvan to the skirts of the not quite extinct Nimrut Dağ and the pass is quickly reached with its sixteenth-century Ottoman holding fort and its ruined *han*. We drop quickly into the Bitlis valley which will shuttle us fifteen hundred metres down into the foothills of upper Mesopotamia. Bitlis is one of the great towns. It lies in a well-treed gorge, the sides of which admirably display the stepped houses in their green surrounds. There is cultivation on ancient Armenian terraces and arched bows of stone take you to the other half of the town, high over the tumbling Bitlis River, now in a great and surely rather foolish hurry to join the Tigris. But the houses are the wonder of Bitlis, tall, rectangular, with flat undecorated façades of exact and solid masonry. The stone is the local chocolate-coloured rock of which the island church of Aghtamar and the tall Selj uk tombstones of Ahlat are made. It is said to be easy to work when quarried and then to become as hard as iron.[1] Each house is separate, each in its own green setting of garden: no Welsh industrial valley rows here. The skyline of the northern side of the town is formed by the high, grim ramparts of the incredibly long castle, a palimpsest of fortification on a Byzantine foundation. At the foot of the hill, the town's centre and end, squats the early twelfth-century Ulu Cami, the great Mosque, with intricately carved doorway and blunt square drum where one expects a dome.

Bitlis was Armenian until the Seljuk conquest and the Ulu Cami was built by an Artuk emir in 1126. The Gökmeydani Cami is Seljuk of 1216 but the beautiful Şerefiye Cami belies its late date of 1528, during the reign of Emir Şeref IV, one of a long line of Şerefian rulers who lasted from the early thirteenth century to 1670. Other notable late Seljuk buildings are the two sixteenth-century *medreses*, the Hatibiye and the Şeref Han. There is a sixteenth-century bath, the Paşa Hamam, and an Ottoman mosque, the Alemdar Cami.

Bitlis is famous today for its Virginia-type tobacco and for a light-coloured honey of exquisite flavour. The whorls occurring in the local walnut trees were profitably exported to France in the nineteenth century for use as veneer in furniture. There used to be a very important trade route up from Mesopotamia through Siirt and the Bitlis valley to Van, and at the end of the nineteenth century there was a British consulate here. But the valley, though possible for pack animals in summer, was too wild and steep for rail and road, so that Bitlis sees little through traffic today. But when the present widening and surfacing of the road from Diyarbakır is completed Bitlis may return to something like its old commercial importance. The road will certainly offer a spectacular drive and is already motorable.

Up to the time of the troubles, the Armenians formed rather less than half of the population of Bitlis, the majority being Kurds. During the second half of the nineteenth century schools were established here by the flourishing Protestant American missionary colony, whose proselytising purpose aroused opposition from the Armenian church, until the missionaries concentrated on education only.[2] William Saroyan's family came from Bitlis and he was well received by the

[1] In the older buildings one or two layers of wooden beams between courses of masonry reduce the danger from earthquake. This is an ancient Anatolian practice.
[2] Lynch, op. cit., vol. II, pp. 153-4.

now almost entirely Moslem population when he visited the district a few years ago. People joked with him about his coming back to look for the treasure his family must have buried when they left in the desperate hurry of Armenian flight. Buried gold is an obsession in eastern Anatolia and the illicitly excavated Urartu bronzes and Byzantine coins, as well as the more recent Armenian trinkets which one is offered, have always been filed to make sure they are not gold.

The origins of the name and the town of Bitlis are unknown, though it seems once to have been called Bagesh or Pagesh. Local legend ascribes the foundation of the castle to a certain Budles, a general of Alexander the Great, and Greek coins have been found here to testify to hellenistic penetration. The town is 1,600 metres above sea level but in spite of its cold winter the plentiful rain, melting snow and summer heat encourage a vegetation which, as Lynch remarks out of his knowledge of the behaviour of sheep and goats, 'even the Kurdish shepherds have failed to destroy.'[1]

After a stop at Bitlis we hurtle on. The mountains seem to get higher as the valley increases in fertility but not in width. There's an ominous moment. The driver slows down for a word with an approaching Highways Department lorry. 'Is the road open?' The answer is a blunt and unsympathetic no. A few kilometres further and we come to the barrier, with one bus already pulled up against it. A hundred yards short of it, at a bend, there's another bus, empty, surrounded by the lumps of rock which in Turkey signify a breakdown or an accident. Our driver pulls cautiously past it and we stop under what appears to be a small café. Either two hours or four hours to wait until the road is opened, no one is quite sure. We climb up rough stone steps on to a flat earth platform under huge cherry trees. A stream of clear cold water runs from a yard-high waterfall at the back across the terrace to disappear into a culvert under the road. To the left is a flat-roofed building with living-room and kitchen. It's a mountain inn, run by as villainous looking a set as I have ever seen. Not a woman to be seen among them. The few women from the bus go higher behind trees to a place reserved for their sex. I order tea at one of the rough wooden tables. It's a staggering place. From the curve of the road below, the hillside dives precipitously hundreds of metres to the valley floor. Facing us is an unbroken mountain slope rising thousands of feet sharply to a snow-covered peak, past steep pastures, green and smooth

[1] ibid., p. 145.

from this distance, scattered trees and a long scree crossed by a hazardous track. Higher up I pick out possible cultivation terraces but not a single house or village. Then more pastures, rocks and finally snow. We are already in the shadow of the mountain behind us but this mountain which faces us is in full cloudless afternoon sunshine. There is no animal and only one human being to be seen in this vast sweep of landscape. He is scything some grain crop on one of a series of stepped terraces near the river immediately below us, stopping occasionally to bind what he has cut. All round his two or three fields there are tall trees, some of them poplars, useful for building. His house must be concealed by trees in full leaf. He works steadily on.

The inn is now doing good business at its dozen or so little tables and the rough wooden chairs are all taken. I drink another glass of tea. It's served in the eastern Anatolian fashion, the little glass upside down on the saucer, to be righted with a flourish and set in front of you in the normal arrangement. Some people are eating, little dishes of stew or rice with small chunks of meat on top, probably goat. A man brings a large earthenware jar of yoğurt and settles it in the stream near the waterfall to keep cool. A nightingale is singing in the tree above me. There is no mechanical noise but there are raucous cries from the unsavoury, unprofessional waiters, put on their mettle now by this sudden clientele. They shout orders to the Stygian kitchen. Lorries and petrol tankers have piled up to beyond the bend.

I go for a walk along the road in the sweet mountain air. A little vineyard on a terrace above the road is in full leaf. The shadow of the mountain has reached the little fields below but the lonely man is still cutting and binding. Our driver is now arguing with the Highways foreman at the wooden barrier across the road whilst two soldiers look on with deadpan lack of interest. Two vehicles have come through from the other direction but one is said to have carried a doctor and the other a sick woman. Our driver thinks we should invent something of that kind. A woman passenger is about to have a baby (this is not infrequent in buses and taxis in Turkey) or the foreigner (that's me) has to catch a plane at Diyarbakır. Nothing serves. It's now five o'clock and we've been here for two hours. The foreman stubbornly insists that the road is closed till seven, when the men go off work.

I turn back. Something is happening at the bend of the road under the inn. A policeman has come from Bitlis on a petrol tanker and is now taking measurements of the position of the abandoned bus. It seems that a man was knocked down before we arrived but his head has been bandaged and he is said to be all right. He had crossed the road in front of the bus but had turned back when the driver thought he had reached the other side. The nightmare of drivers in Turkey. There is no excitement, but for the locals who have now gathered from somewhere this is drama and they have a front-row seat in the balcony of the inn terrace. I look up. The rim of the terrace is now thick with tables and seated men, none of them travellers. One of them, I can't see which, is singing a Kurdish song. The rather high, almost monotonous wavering line of the melody, the long-held notes, this is unmistakable. I go back on to the terrace and drink more tea at a table near the back. I can see the singer now, a bare-headed man in his twenties sitting at the middle table near the edge. He has a strong sensitive voice. I feel that his singing there above the policeman, who is still making notes, is a defiance of authority.

Here, at this mountain inn, I sensed this Kurdish singing as the only audience participation in the happening below. The whole thing was theatrical, the audience, men only, on the natural balcony, the curved segment of road with the policeman moving about amongst the little groups of standing men, the superb backdrop of mountain side and peak. The singer ended a series of songs with a long-held quavering note like that of a shepherd's pipe. When I looked again he had gone.

Still an hour to wait. I went back to my seat in the bus and read until seven o'clock. There was a minibus as well as the original bus in front of us now and our driver was eager to be off as soon as the barrier was opened. He was called Hajji something, since like so many bus and taxi drivers in this part of Anatolia he had driven parties to Mecca. He outmanoeuvred the minibus at the start and tried to get past the bus but failed at his first attempt. The road was narrow and winding. Oncoming traffic was meeting us now and the bus driver in front was punctilious in pulling in at a wide enough place to give climbing lorries an unbroken run. This infuriated our Hajji and he swung his bus past the other on a corner where it would hardly have been safe for a motor bike to overtake. Then away he hared down the precipitous road, hardly slowing up for oncoming traffic but judging to a hair's breadth the position of his wheels. I found it better not to look down from my window. There were encouraging cries of 'Hajji, Hajji' from the back of the bus. Most of the passengers were Arabic-speaking and rather more demonstrative than Turks usually are. The fact that their driver had been to Mecca must give them confidence, I thought, and they were doing their bit by displaying this confidence. When the oncoming traffic had dwindled to almost nothing and we had passed the stretch of road that had been closed for excavation,[1] the Hajji slowed down to a more normal speed. I think he must have been as anxious as I was to get out of this lovely but dangerous Bitlis valley while there was still some daylight left. He was ruthless in getting his passengers away from Baykan, the only small town between Bitlis and Siirt, and he suddenly became talkative as he swung us through the darkened foothills to Siirt. This is still bandit country. To our left, over the Hakkari mountains, there was almost continuous lightning but above us the sky was cloudless and we kept returning to the direction of the Scorpion, with its great yellow star. Siirt at last. A cool wind was whipping up the dust, there was room at the hotel that had been recommended to me (the Özgen Palas, quite comfortable) and a restaurant was still open. Only reheated *lahmacun*, the Syrian *pizza*, was still on and I felt that I had dropped halfway to Arabia.

[1] I don't remember going through a road tunnel, so the famous Tunnel of Semiramis, said to have been commanded by the Assyrian queen, may have been destroyed to widen the road here, about 7 kilometres west of Bitlis.

Siirt and Tillo

Siirt is an ancient and unexplained name, perhaps of Syrian origin. The region has been occupied by all the invaders of this part of Turkey, and had a period of Arab occupation which was successfully challenged by Byzantium in the tenth and eleventh centuries. But the only buildings of interest in Siirt today date from the Seljuk occupation and the subsequent Moslem lordships up to the time when the town was added to the Ottoman Empire early in the sixteenth century.

The Ulu Cami, dating from 1126, now being repaired and restored, has a beautifully tiled minaret, the blue Seljuk tiles patterned against the red brickwork into chevrons, spirals and diamond panels. Because until recently the mosque was disused and because of its beauty, the *mimber* was taken to the Ethnographical Museum in Ankara, but it will presumably be restored to its original place now the courtyard has been cleared, the minaret repaired and the prayer room cleaned up. In the work of restoration the floor of the interior has recently been cleared of rubble to a depth of two metres, and two old Seljuk *mihrabs* with lovely tiles of simple geometric shape which catch the light like jewels have been revealed.

Other old buildings are the thirteenth-century Asaker Çarsı Cami, the Cumhuriyet Cami, a recent name for a mosque said to have been founded by the Arabs in the eighth century, and a very early Seljuk bath, the Kavvam Hamam, of the late eleventh century. There are some beautiful old houses in Siirt, tall, with receding plastered walls, in a style one associates with Arabia and North African oases.

The new town is developing at the foot of the hillside on which Siirt is built but the old buildings are to be sought through arches and along narrow streets with tall windowless houses and intriguing domes. The new streets are wide and are said to be used sometimes by rival Kurdish bands to shoot out their differences. I saw nothing of this but there were several hold-ups on the roads east of Siirt soon after I left the district. This is where life in Turkey comes nearest to a film western.

The land around Siirt is mostly pasture and there are the usual sheep and goats, with smaller numbers of cattle. East of Siirt, tributaries of the Tigris cut back up to Çatak and past the 2,945 metre Herakol Dağ to the almost impassable Hakkari uplands. Siirt is a good place to buy locally made Kurdish things of mohair, rugs, handbags and saddlebags, much more cheaply and with a much wider choice than in the covered bazaar at Istanbul.

But for me the main reason for revisiting Siirt would be to go once more up to Tillo, eight kilometres uphill and north-eastwards from the town. I was taken up there by a friendly journalist who is devoted to the cult of Ibrahim Hakki, the eighteenth-century sage of Tillo. Tillo was recently renamed Aydınlar, which means the educated or enlightened ones. The name is justified, for all the boys here go to school, not to a state school but to an old established religious school where Arabic grammar is taught as well as other subjects. Students still come here from Iran and Irak to study. But the inhabitants of the little town are enlightened enough to insist on the retention of the old name, whatever may be its meaning and origin. They are people of independent mind and when I was there they were preparing to boycott a general election, having no interest in a government which refuses to give them a proper water supply. I found it hard to understand how such a considerable settlement should have grown up in a place so desperately short of water but I suppose that when the population was smaller the local springs must have been adequate.

We went up to Tillo in a lorry which sometimes plies in this way in between transporting stone. It leaves from a café at the eastern end of Siirt and is a great help along a dusty road steep enough to be wearying even in this clear sharp air. It runs infrequently on Sundays, a quiet day in these parts, very like Wales, and, since there was some uncertainty whether it would make another journey up in the afternoon, I walked most of the way back with a soldier going on leave, until the lorry passed us on its way up and picked us up on its return journey. On the way up, in an oasis on the hillside, is the fine village of Bağtepe. This too is a new name and it means Vineyard Hill. The old name is Halenzie. Bağtepe looks like a fortified township with

high flat walls and a few arched entrances. There are lovely houses in
Tillo too, where all the buildings, old and new, are plastered inside and
out with a material called *jast*, which sets very hard and imposes an
effective unity on the architecture. It is a limestone cement which is
quarried locally at places easily visible from the road near Tillo. It is
burnt and then mixed with water for application. But here as everywhere today concrete blocks are beginning to replace this pleasing
method of surfacing stone or mud-brick walls. The doors of the houses
are sometimes arched in a Seljuk manner, with lovely decoration in
stucco and wood. Young Turkish architects might well study Tillo.

Once off the lorry, the journalist led the way straight to the contemplation room of Fakir Ullah, Ibrahim Hakki's master, past a two
hundred year old pomegranate tree in a little courtyard near an old
mosque in the centre of the township. Then in through beautifully
carved walnut wood doors into the dark little domed prayer and
contemplation room, with its simple *mihrab* niche. Ibrahim Hakki was
born at Hasankale, east of Erzurum, and when he was nine his father
took him southwards in search of a good teacher for him. When they
got to Siirt, on the old route to Mesopotamia and Mecca, they heard
of Fakir Ullah and they went up to Tillo in search of him. The young
Ibrahim Hakki went and stood at the door of the prayer room, where
the philosopher was at his devotions before his *mihrab*. Without
turning round Fakir Ullah said, 'Come in, Ibrahim Hakki.' There
Ibrahim Hakki spent the rest of his life, learning at first and then going
on further than his master had ever dreamt, into the worlds of philosophy, mathematics, science and sociology. From this simple but
impressive and well-kept shrine we were taken to the house of two
descendants of Ibrahim Hakki and first of all the young student,
Feyzullah Toprak, and then his elder brother showed us the relics of
the great thinker. They entertained us charmingly too with coffee in a
spotless room on lovely rugs. They brought us the sage's manuscript
books and his astronomical and mathematical instruments. We turned
over the pages of Ibrahim Hakki's book on the universe, *Marifet
Name*, full of detailed and complicated charts and diagrams. This was
another world from Adilcevaz and its Caucasus-dominated world-
view, this world of Islamic continuity from Aristotle. We handled
beautifully worked walnut wood quadrants and astrolabes and then
Feyzullah read us passages from Ibrahim Hakki's classification of human
types, physical characteristics and their psychological counterparts, the

physical qualities of a beautiful woman, four things curved and four straight, four black, four red, four white and so on in a balanced and eventually convincing statement of perfection. Then the relationship between hair colour and other physical characteristics and character in men. A monastic atmosphere but a humane and by no means ascetic interest in mankind alongside a probing of the stars and the surface of the earth. A most agreeable polymath.

Fakir Ullah, his sons and Ibrahim Hakki were all buried in a tomb which has recently been restored, uphill and to the west of the school, mosque and contemplation room. A wall on the ridge to the east of the village has a hole in it through which the sun used to shine on the morning of March 21 directly into a hole in the dome of the tomb, on to a mirror and then in a beam on to the coffins. All this, designed by Ibrahim Hakki, worked until the recent restoration by German architects, since when the trick has failed and nothing so far has got it to work again. In the cemetery below the tomb there are huge trees called *butum* in Turkish. This is the turpentine nut tree (*pistacia terebinthas*), which has all kinds of useful medical properties and a very pleasant smell when the leaf is broken in the fingers. It makes excellent soap, which you can buy, and it is said to purify the air so that there is no tuberculosis in Tillo. People suffering from sunburn or fevers used to be wrapped naked in its leaves for immediate relief. Pistachios grow in the gardens of Tillo and they are claimed to be bigger than those of Antep.

The men of Tillo are famed circumcisers and still go far into Irak and Iran in the practice of their craft. In these parts of Turkey there is much fellow feeling with the Arab world and I have seen pictures of King Hussein of Jordan where one would expect photographs of Ataturk.

Siirt to Diyarbakır

Siirt to Diyarbakır looks easy on the map but is a rough journey by car and a difficult one by any other means of transport. A three-hour journey by bus took us across rolling uplands, past new oil rigs to Batman, the great oil centre, with a stop at Kurtalan, the railway terminus in this part. This station is the end of the western world. When I said at Siirt that I was in a hurry to get to Diyarbakır people assured me that there would be a train at Kurtalan. There was one in a day and a half. Trains leave here three times a week and eventually get to Istanbul. The departure must be a moment of great excitement but otherwise the station looks like an abandoned siding. The bus, however, made a ritual pause here. But Beşiri was lively enough: a village street pullulating with people, fragmented sunlight through vine-covered trellises and children erratic in the raised dust like tadpoles in a pond. A spindle-legged boy catherine-wheeled across in front of us and the bus-driver stopped as though he'd hit a wall. But he hadn't hit the boy, no one showed much concern and we weren't delayed. Approaching Batman in the dusk we just missed an erratic homing tractor. Look out for tractors which turn across the road without giving a sign in eastern Anatolia. These new monsters are not yet under control there.

Batman looked and smelt as one expected it to and has become very important to the Turkish economy. The Turks hope soon to produce all the petrol and oil they require. Here we bargained for a landrover to take us to Diyarbakır since there was no bus or *dolmuş* so late in the evening. The young driver complained bitterly of the state of the pot-holed road, saying that all the asphalt by-produced at Batman was used for roads in Istanbul and Ankara, a typical neglect of places far from administrative centres. Soon after reaching the Bitlis–Diyarbakır road we passed the lovely Artuk Seljuk bridge with its great central arch over a tributary of the Tigris near Malabadi. The driver suggested a stop at Silvan for an excellent meal in a spotless restaurant with a little fountain inside, on the north side of the road through the town. Silvan was called Miyafarikin in earlier Moslem times and was once a capital city of the Eyyubi Kurds, but little of its grandeur remains save some traces of defensive wall, an old mosque and a minaret. It may or may not have been Tigranocerta, the Armenian capital city of this region, but it became Martyropolis at the end of the fourth century when the church secession from Byzantium took place under Persian domination. It was retaken by the Byzantines at the end of the sixth century and lost in the seventh century to the Arabs, who held it until the coming of the Turks in the eleventh century. The Artuk Turkomans governed it for most of the twelfth century and it was duly sacked by the Mongols in 1260. Once more the Persians returned, but Miyafarikin was taken by the Ottomans in 1515. The Ulu Cami, in the centre of the town, dates from 1227 and is an interesting building with a dome supported by four stalactite pendentives.

The road from Silvan to Diyarbakır is due for re-surfacing and you may be lucky enough to find it has been done.

Muş and Bingöl

Muş and Bingöl are on the motorable, though patchy, road from Tatvan to Elazığ. From the pass above Tatvan and the plateau beyond, with its fine view of Süphan Dağ to the north-east, the road drops down to the fertile plain of Muş and to the upper waters of the Murat branch of the Euphrates. The town of Muş, capital of its *vilayet* and a mile south of the main road, so that you can by-pass it if you like, looks northwards to the plain from the mouth of a gorge at the foot of great mountains. The plain was until the end of the nineteenth century populated mostly by poor, ill-housed Armenians, with Kurds in the mountains and the hill villages skirting the plain. According to Lynch the women of some of these Kurdish villages were noted prostitutes.[1]

The town of Muş has little to offer the tourist. Hardly anything is left of the Armenian castle above the town. The minarets of the Seljuk Alaeddin Cami and Haci Şeref Cami are decorated in coloured stone, the chocolate-coloured and hard white sandstone of this region, done into spirals, chevrons and diamond shapes. There are interesting Armenian stone carvings in high relief in the ruined monastery of Surb Karapet, known locally as the Çanli or Çengelli Kilise, the Church of the Bell or of the Hook. The Seljuk Arslanlı Han is the most interesting of the old caravanserais.

Armenian tradition states that Muş was founded in the sixth century A.D. by Mushel Mamikonian (hence the name, they say), a member of an important Armenian family. It was invested by the Arabs in the seventh century, at the same time as Ahlat on Lake Van, and called Tarun by them. Different Armenian families, some in league with the Arabs, and then the Byzantines held it until the Seljuk victory of Malazgirt, which is in the north-east of Muş province. Like everywhere

[1] op. cit., vol. II, pp. 163–4.

144

3. Mardin: Şehidiye Cami

24. *Tombs near Eski Van*

25. *Siirt: repairs to Ulu Cami minaret*

else in these parts it was sacked by the Mongols in 1260 and by Tamburlaine at the end of the fourteenth century. Sultan Selim took it for the Ottomans in 1515. It suffered during the First World War and was occupied by the Russians for some time.

The Muş province produces excellent grain crops, maize, chickpeas and potatoes as well as meat and butter from its flocks and herds. Tobacco is also grown. At Varto, some seventy kilometres to the north of Muş, occurred the fearful earthquake which drew the greatest response ever to a radio appeal in Britain. Some at least of the food contributed by some western countries was unsuitable and is said never to have found its way to the earthquake victims. Varto is on an earthquake belt which runs across Anatolia. Gediz and Burdur, further west, have suffered recently and the town of Bingöl has been destroyed since I began to type this page. Money, to be put to use by responsible people who understand local requirements, is the best one can offer to alleviate such disasters.

A difficult road runs northwards from Muş through Varto to the Erzurum road. Short of Varto a feasible road turns east, up the main Murat valley, past Bulanık and Malazgirt to Patnos. This must be a very ancient route for a little way along it, just before the Murat river is joined by a big tributary and turns south, is the Urartian citadel of Kayalıdere.[1] Bulanık is again in a fertile area which was peopled mostly by Armenians until seventy years ago. It was then called Gop.

Fifty kilometres west of Muş the road, having climbed out of the Murat valley, crosses the 1,640 metre pass of Buğlan and then reaches Bingöl. This old town used to be known by the Kurdish name of Çapakçur but the new town alongside it—a town which will now have to be rebuilt—has been given the name of the mountains to its northeast, the Bingöl or Thousand Lake massif. The streams and lakes of this region abound in trout and the mountains are not entirely lacking in bandits. The road through these mountains northwards to Erzurum is said to be spectacular, of frightening difficulty but motorable with care. Lynch speaks poetically of the solitude and fertilising streams of these mountains, finding in the region one of the homes of the human imagination.[2] He found blue gentians and delicate yellow mullein growing in profusion here, and sweet-scented violets at the edge of the snow. And his keen eye was more than usually caught by evidence

[1] See C. A. Barney, *Anatolian Studies*, vol. XVI, p. 55.
[2] op. cit., vol. II, pp. 361–2.

of volcanic and glacial action on this great mountain which rises to 3,250 metres. The western peak of the main mountain is known as Bingöl Kale or Castle and is not a difficult walk from the south in summer, when the snow has melted. A base for this could be the appropriately named Karliova, snow-covered meadow, on the road to Erzurum, or, further east and nearer to the summit, Çaylar, on a motorable dead-end from Varto. Bingöl town is in the middle of mountains and only three per cent of its province is cultivated. It's a pastoral region of sheep, goats and cows and the swing from extreme heat to cold results in widespread transhumance and a semi-nomadic way of life. Neither the old nor the newer town of Bingöl offered much to delay the traveller. The town now to be rebuilt will speak for itself.

Elazığ and Harput

❧❦❧

Elazığ is easily reached by air and rail from Istanbul and Ankara or by a good road which continues eastwards to Muş and Van.

It was founded in 1862 by the Sultan Abdel Aziz and was named Elaziz after him, later to become Elazığ under Ataturk, to dissipate the Ottoman association. *Azığ* means food or fodder. Most of the population of the ancient city of Harput, three miles to the north, then moved into the new and more easily approachable town. Elazığ still has a pioneer air, with its main east–west boulevard only recently acquiring big modern buildings, and with streets running off north and south. An important street runs from the centre down to the railway station. The road westwards has administrative and educational buildings along it, including a big new engineering college and the prison. The children's prison looks damp and dreary. The town has a number of possible hotels and restaurants (I stayed at the Turistik, quite adequate) but has little of interest to offer except for a minute museum up some dangerous concrete stairs in a building behind the central Post Office. This has a few specimens of local crafts and some Bronze Age and other prehistoric finds, of little appeal except to the expert, from the Altınova district about to be drowned by the Keban Dam. What makes this museum well worth a visit is the group of grain storage jars of recent making from Fatmalı, up the Murat River from Keban. The value of these is enhanced by the fact that they won't be made there much longer for the potteries will soon be deep down under the waters of the projected reservoir. These jars are beaker shaped, open at the top, tapering slightly towards the bottom and of unglazed pottery. They have a hole about six inches wide near the bottom for the extraction of grain. They vary in height from about a metre to one metre twenty centimetres. The main decoration is a

147

sun symbol about twenty centimetres across and made of two concentric raised bands with spikes sticking out all round. All the raised parts have little circles stuck in at intervals. Two of the five jars have stylised human figures which give the impression of being male, one of them simplified to the degree of resembling an Egyptian *ankh* standing on a spiked sun disk.

At certain times of the day the town seems to be milling with students, school boys and girls and country people, mostly men, in for the market. But Elazığ has its industrial workers too. It has an important sugar factory to cope with the beet production of the vicinity, a cotton thread-making factory and other enterprises. It is famous for its grapes, which are wonderful to eat in late summer and autumn, the long white *keçikmemesi* (goat's teat) and the *okuzgözü* (ox-eye), a full midnight blue grape from which the excellent red Buzbağ wine is made at the Government Monopoly factory here. (*Buzbağ* means ice vineyard, not bagpipe.)

Daylight comes early in eastern Turkey and even in November the boys are out at 5.30 in the morning crying the buses. Elazığ is a great bus centre, a modern caravanserai, and one is well advised to shop around before deciding to which company to trust oneself. I always like to book a seat on a bus that starts from the place, not a through one from somewhere else to Ankara, to be sure of my seat. I've found the buses to be comfortable and mostly well driven. But we have come to Elazığ in order to visit the ancient city of Harput. To do this, unless you have your own car or have time to walk and savour this marvellous view, you should take a taxi (25–30 liras to the top of the rock and back including time for you to see all the monuments). If you're driving you'll find that a fine new road has been constructed to the village centre of the old site.

Harput is an ancient Anatolian name, possibly of Armenian origin. The Arabs first knew it as Khartabirt. The oldest remaining buildings are the Castle and the little Meryem Ana Church near its north wall, both of early Byzantine construction.[1] The city was taken by the Arabs in the tenth century and by the Seljuks after the Battle of Malazgirt (1071). For some years towards the end of the eleventh century it formed part of an Armenian kingdom and then was occupied by a succession of Turkoman conquerors, Artuk and Ak Koyun, by

---

[1] See Plate 13.

Tamburlaine and by a Persian shah. In 1515 it was taken by Selim I's army and became part of Ottoman Turkey.

Harput was built on a great ledge of rock, less accessible than the new road makes it appear today, looking southwards over a fertile valley to the Karaoğlan and Maden Mountains. Behind it, to the north, is rough, high, deforested country within a curve of the Murat reach of the Euphrates, a one hundred and thirty kilometre stretch which will be flooded by the Keban Dam to add a sheet of water to the already spectacular view to the south-east. The best way to see Harput is to leave your car in the square outside the Sara Hatun Mosque and walk from there. The air is good and the distances short. The mosque you are near, a simple square shape with a central dome and a plain tiled *mihrab*, was built in 1463 by the Lady Sara, mother of an Ak Koyun chieftain. From here follow signs eastwards and downhill to the Ulu Cami, the Great Mosque, a long rectangular domeless building put up in the twelfth century by the Artuk leader Melik Kara Arslan. It was closed for restoration while I was there but I imagine it must follow the pattern of its kind, with rows of columns or sturdy piers of masonry to support a flat ceiling. It has been given a slightly pitched corrugated roof and its stubby minaret, also twelfth century, has a new muezzin's balustrade and a conical top.

Continue downhill from here to the Castle, a Byzantine[1] fortification, impregnable, one would have thought, on its great rock, towering over the valley below with immensely high flat walls and projecting, semicircular bastions. Had it a weak point, some treacherous postern, or was it reduced by starvation and thirst? It looks impossible to take by force. Across the road from its north-west corner, a chapel without the walls, is what remains of the Meryem Ana Kilesi, the Church of Mother Mary, uncared for now, its door open to the winds and to stray animals, its decoration gone.

Walk back directly uphill to the square and, west of Sara Hatun Camii, visit the thirteenth-century Seljuk Tomb of Arap Baba. The interior is plain except for a lovely blue-tiled *mihrab*. Outside, at the back and overlooking a fearful drop into the valley, there is not much more than a cupboard door which the gentle old *imam* opened and encouraged me to enter after him. This involves crawling through after removing your shoes. Inside the dark room, and underneath the

---

[1] The Castle was restored by the Artuk rulers of the thirteenth century and the architect Nizamettin Ibrahim.

mihrab which we had looked at in the prayer room, is a long plain wooden coffin. The *imam* raised the lid and began to lift and pull aside beautifully clean grave clothes. Reluctantly I looked down on an embalmed, naked, hairless body, brown as leather, with the back of its head bashed in. There was nothing to suggest rest in the attitude of the body but rather a striving to rise, to escape from this long imprisonment. Arap Baba, Father Arab, is much revered locally and is thought to do great good to those who seek his help, but the unhappy body seemed to me to beg for the release of disintegration. It gave me a new view of death, of the death of the body.

Still further west, on a spur of rock, is the fifteenth-century Kursunlu Mosque with its handsome black and white banded minaret. Near it and overlooking the plain and the town of Elazığ. is a modern equestrian statue in white stone of Battal Gazi, a legendary hero and defender of this region of Turkey. I met his name again at Eski Malatya, where he is said to have been born.

There is also an old Turkish bath to be seen, if you have time for it, and a simple but friendly café for a glass of tea before leaving Harput. It is hard today to believe that when it was abandoned a hundred years or so ago this seeming village had eight hundred shops, ten mosques, ten religious schools, eight churches, eight libraries, twelve caravanserais and ninety baths.

The Keban Dam

The Keban Dam is the greatest project in hand in Turkey at the moment of writing. Keban is a little town fifty kilometres west of Elazığ, perched above the confluence of the Firat River (Euphrates) and a tributary that runs into it from the south-east and whose channelled water makes possible the luxuriant green of this suddenly well-known little place. If you have no car an Elazığ taxi will do the round trip, including an hour or so for the visit to the dam and the construction headquarters, for ninety liras. The dam is being built at a point above this confluence and where the valley narrows to a cut through the rugged mountains. It's a pleasant ride from Elazığ on a good asphalt road through gaunt treeless hills. Until the project is completed and a circuit of the dam arranged one is expected, and indeed well advised, to go straight to the Administration Offices on the far side of the valley, beyond the more temporary construction camp of the French engineers. I was met by a pleasant and helpful man called Atil Bey who explained the project, taking me round the explanatory charts and graphs, and gave me the explanatory brochure published in several languages by Devlet Su Isleri Matbaası of the Turkish Government, an interesting and beautifully produced booklet. Unforeseen geological difficulties have caused the work so far to be running about eighteen months late. The top of the barrage will measure 1,155 metres across. The southern section, based on a spur of rock and containing supply chutes and the permanently open tunnels, is being made of concrete, whilst the northern part, which will block the original water-course, will be rock-filled, with a core of clay on a concrete foundation. But the French contractors have run into troubles not predicted by the original surveyors of the scheme. (American accents were common in the admin offices, so this part of the work may have been done by

Americans working with Turks.) For a foundation to the rock-filled section the builders have had to go down through more alluvium than they expected to find the schist foundation and then to pour in concrete. The rock above the schist is all limestone in this region and of the karst type, honeycombed with holes, tunnels, pits and cracks that all have to be washed out before being filled or grouted with concrete. One hopes that all the cracks have been found.

Another problem was presented by the alarm occasioned in Syria and Irak at a possible hold-up in their normal irrigation water during the six to twelve months it will take to fill the reservoir. This has been met by the construction of two immense tunnels at the original river level. These will remain permanently open and the water running through them will satisfy the minimum normal requirements of these countries. The plan now is to fill the hundred and thirty kilometre-long reservoir during the flood season from about February 1972. Since the purpose of the dam is purely hydroelectric no attempt is being made to use the accumulated water for irrigation within Turkey, though it must be remembered that the water has a good three hundred kilometres to flow before it reaches the frontier. No concern is felt over the agricultural land to be drowned by the dam, since the people to be dispossessed only feed themselves, sending nothing to the big cities, and their economy is therefore unimportant. The dam will double Turkey's present electrical capacity and will chiefly serve the growing needs of Istanbul and its new factories. Yet another sacrifice of small communities to the megamachine. Coming from a country, Wales, which has suffered terribly from English demands for water, I am conscious of the destruction of these simple communities. They are, of course, being compensated by the Government, payment being related to the production value of the land. Some families have already left and have acquired smallholdings elsewhere. Others will move to the big cities and merge into their cultural anonymity and emptiness. The human sacrifice, to my mind, is considerable.

A curious side effect of the dam is on the fish of the river. Carp have been accustomed to go up in their season to breed in the upper reaches and tributaries of the Euphrates. They are now unable to enter the tunnels and the huge fish mill around in stunned confusion, the easiest fish in the world to catch.

More fuss than that over fish and men has been made of the archaeo-logical possibilities of the area to be drowned, particularly of the prehistoric sites which proliferate here, a region which may have important information to offer on the early development of man, particularly before and during the Neolithic Revolution. Teams from many countries are using the summer digging seasons left before the waters rise to investigate the more promising sites, but, although every excavation contributes something to our knowledge of a region which is one of man's earliest homes, there seem so far to have been no spectacular discoveries, certainly little of aesthetic appeal and nothing yet like Çatalhüyük. The Chicago University excavations at Korucutepe under Professor M. Van Loon have revealed evidence of a great conflagration about 3000 B.C., the end of the Chalcolithic period. Then came Hittite occupation levels, late Hittite, and others on to Seljuk.[1] During the early Hittite period (1750–1570 B.C.) Korucutepe was fortified with a wall-and-tower system. A good deal of pottery of the middle Hittite period has been found and there are signs that the site was abandoned by the Hittites without destruction of the town.[2] The Bronze Age finds by Dr. Hamit Koşay at Pulur have already been referred to.[3] The moving to higher ground of the mosques at Eski Pertek, organised by the Middle East Technical University, Ankara, would appear to be more a sop to Moslem sentiment than an essential safeguarding of architectural treasures, since they are of no particular interest. What I most regret is the passing of the potteries of Fatmalı and the simple and courteous decencies of life in Altınova and the eighty-nine villages to be drowned.

[1] *A.J.A.*, vol. 72, no. 2, p. 211. [2] ibid., vol. 74, no. 2. [3] See p. 37.

Elazığ to Diyarbakır

Diyarbakır is easily reached by road, air or railway. (The railway goes on through the new oil centre of Batman to die quietly at a sleepy little station called Kurtalan.) From Elazığ to Diyarbakır by bus costs ten liras and takes four hours if you're lucky. The road is good except for corrugation and construction work between the eastern end of Lake Hazar and Ergani but it will soon be easy motoring. It runs for about twenty-five kilometres along the north shore of Hazar Gölü, a lovely stretch of water twelve hundred metres above sea level and a changing blue against the bare mountains. You can swim almost anywhere in the saline water and the restaurant at the eastern tip of the lake serves lake fish and eels. From here the road rises to Maden, accompanied by the railway. Maden means mine, mineral or metal and this is a great centre of copper and chromium mining. Maden rises in stepped streets of old-fashioned houses from its confluence of gorges and the town can be avoided if you don't want to go over the bridge and sharply up to its little market square. The great copper works above the town puff steam and exude hot water and running green copper oxide. The road south rises to a pass and drops to Ergani. We are now among the headwaters of the Dicle or Tigris River. Ergani is an undistinguished town with a big *lycée*, across whose football field my bus for some reason drove, perhaps a short cut to pick up an old man who had gone off to say his prayers and who did soon turn up at the point where we regained the main road. Not far from the town the Hila Caves have prehistoric rock drawings, which I had no time to look for, and there are other evidences in the district of prehistoric and Assyrian occupation. The plain of Diyarbakır is from here on dotted with obvious *hüyüks*, habitation mounds which pinpoint early villages and townships. This is the region where copper was first used by man, some thousands of years before the so-called Bronze Age of the third millennium B.C. which until recently was thought to be the earliest time when copper was used. About twenty-two kilometres from Diyarbakır and on the west side of the road we pass near a lovely early Ottoman bridge called Devegeçidi, the Camel's Passage.

We reach Diyarbakır by the long straight road leading to the northernmost gate of the walled city, the Dağ Kapısı, or Mountain Gate. This is also known as the Harput Gate and was once called Bab el Armen, since in Arab days it led to Armenia. At this point the effect of coming to a walled city has almost been lost and a much more spectacular approach is by air, particularly the view from the plane if you fly from here to Van. You then see the old town on its rock in a bend of the Tigris, the black walls untrammelled and grim.

The name you might well take to mean Copper Land, since *bakır* is copper, but it seems to be a recent version of an earlier Diyar Bekr, the country or province of the Bekr, a famous Arab tribe. The ancient name was Amida.

The mound on which the Citadel or inner castle is built in the old city is evidence of very ancient habitation on this well-placed rock. It has been occupied by Hurrians, Mitanni, Assyrians, Medes, Persians, Seleucid Macedonians, Parthians, Romans, Byzantines, Arabs, Kurds,[1] Seljuks, the Artuks, the tribes of the Kara Koyun and Ak Koyun (Black and White Sheep Turkomans) and finally the Ottomans under Sultan Selim early in the sixteenth century. Relics of these different occupations are to be seen at the Museum in the Zinciriye Medrese.

The most notable feature of Diyarbakır is its great enclosing wall, over five kilometres in circumference, grim, dark and strongly bastioned. A circuit of at least the western half of these fortifications should begin your visit to Diyarbakır, for which at least two days should be allowed. (I stayed at the very comfortable Demir Oteli, just inside the main entrance to the old city. It has an excellent roof restaurant with a wonderful view of domes and minarets you might easily miss whilst wandering through the streets.) Unless you have your own car the visit to the walls is best done by horse-carriage or *fayton* (phaeton). I paid twenty liras an hour, without much argument

---

[1] The Marwan dynasty which ruled here from 990 to 1096 was Kurdish, though it is often referred to as Arab because these Kurds had adopted Arabic as their language for official purposes. The Eyyubi kings of Miyafarikin, present-day Silvan, were likewise Kurds who used Arabic officially.

over extra time, and the driver knew all the good places to stop. The walls are Roman in origin, repaired and fortified by the Byzantine Justinian in his great rebuilding sweep of his empire in the sixth century. Further repairs and rebuilding on the old foundations were carried out in the twelfth and thirteenth centuries by the Seljuks and Artuks, when most of the present decoration, inscriptions and reliefs, as well as the castellations, was added. Walls and bastions have clearly suffered from recent pilfering from ground level for building material. The rock on which the walls are built is itself black but could hardly have provided enough stone for this immense construction. The plain west of Diyarbakır is covered with such stone. Two kinds of black stone have been used, a porous-looking rock and a basalt capable of a fine polish. The walls are most conveniently followed from within, starting at the north gate and taking the new boulevard past the Urfa Gate in the west and round to the Mardin Gate in the south, with at least three stops in between, at the Urfa Gate and at the bastions of Ulu Beden (the Great Wall) and Yedi Kardeş (the Seven Brothers). The Ulu Beden is also known as the Evli Beden or wall with houses.

The Harput or Northern Gate is between two well-preserved bastions. Reliefs and inscriptions in Greek and Arabic have been incorporated at different times into the building and rebuilding. The two pilasters and the arch of the doorway are Byzantine. From here we go westwards towards the gardens within the wall and swing south to the Urfa Gate. Two of the three entrances of the immense portal are thought to have been closed in the twelfth century by an Artuk chieftain and the two iron folding doors are also of that period. The tremendous Ulu Beden bastion, at a point of the wall projecting westwards and measuring twenty-five metres in diameter, has reliefs of a double-headed eagle and human-headed lions. A Kufic inscription indicates an Artuk king of the early thirteenth century as the restorer and decorator of this great tower. It is possible to climb to the top of the wall here. The southernmost tower is the Yeni Kardeş, the interior of which can be visited. Inscriptions on the Mardin Gate announce its restoration in the year 909, under the Abbassid Caliph Muktadir. Here, as at the Harput Gate, a breach in the wall has recently been made to facilitate traffic.

From the Mardin Gate some pleasant excursions can be made, one to gardens of Ataturk's kiosk or summer house, out along the Mardin road and then a few hundred yards to the right. About two kilometres from the Mardin Gate a turning left takes you to the old bridge over the Tigris. This splendid ten-arched bridge in black basalt is probably of Roman origin, and improved early in the sixth century during the reign of the Byzantine emperor Anastasius. On the near southern side an Arabic inscription of 1065, during the Kurdish Marwan occupation, also records a restoration.

Just inside the Mardin Gate is the Deliler Han, a fine late sixteenth-century building in basalt, with two lovely square panels of almost abstract Arabic script high on the far inside wall, facing the entrance. The *han* is now an open market for metal junk and for the local carpets, which are spread out for your inspection. All round are tin-smiths and blacksmiths.

You should now visit as many as possible of the buildings within the walls. The Tourist Bureau brochure, which you can usually get at your hotel, will help you locate them, or anyone will direct you to them. A *fayton* driver will know them all.

The Ulu Cami or Great Mosque is said to have been founded by the Arabs in the seventh century on the site of the Christian Church of St. Thomas. The form of the mosque, however, is purely Moslem and is important in the development of the Anatolian mosque since it carried into Turkey the plan of early Syrian mosques. An inscription on the outside of the main building says that it was restored by the Seljuk Sultan Melik Shah in 1091. The mosque suffered from earth-quake and fire in 1115. Over the main entrance to the courtyard are a long inscription in Kufic and two relief plaques of lions attacking bulls, probably Seljuk of the late eleventh century. The courtyard has two ablution places with pointed roofs raised on stone pillars. Beyond these and facing the main entrance is the most extraordinary double-tiered façade, Seljuk arches separated by tall Corinthian columns, above which rise shorter carved Seljuk columns. The blend of classical column and capital, Kufic lettering and Seljuk arch and stone carving gives a staggering anachronism of baroque effect. The main body of the mosque is a three-aisled interior running across the face of the *mihrab* or prayer direction. The ceiling is flat and timbered and the central cube of masonry is topped with a flat square decorated ceiling. The minaret, outside the mosque, is in the tall square form typical of Diyarbakır, with a thin pepperpot top.

Adjoining the Great Mosque is the Zinciriye Medrese, a Seljuk building dating from 1190, in use as a theological school until this present century and now the town museum. It is closed on Mondays but even on this day the courtyard, with stone sculpture, the black and white sheep of the Kara Koyun and Ak Koyun graveyards, Byzantine sarcophagi and the more ancient cuneiform and hieroglyphic inscriptions, can be visited. The rooms contain costumes, coins and arms, Hittite, Urartu and Roman remains and one of the quadrants of Ibrahim Hakki, the sage of Tillo.

The Behram Paşa Camii, the biggest mosque in Diyarbakır, is an Ottoman building erected in 1572. In the middle of its courtyard is a roofed ablution fountain with an interesting knot design in the supporting columns. The mosque entrance has a fine double row of columns, a beautiful stalactite doorway and a *mihrab* inside which repeats the stalactite design. There is lovely stained glass in its windows. This mosque is reached by a narrow street off the Melik Ahmet Caddesi which leads from the centre of the town to the Urfa Gate. Behram Paşa was a governor of Diyarbakır. The Mosque of Fatih Paşa, the first Ottoman governor of the city after the Ottoman occupation, is in the eastern part of the town and has very beautiful tiles.

The Peygamber or Nabi Cami, the Mosque of the Prophet, was built in 1524. This pretty little mosque is at the much used crossroads near the Harput Gate and the prayer room and minaret are in the Diyarbakır style of alternate black and white bands. (Symbolising the black and white totem sheep of the Turkoman tribes?) It has a row of Iznik tiles along the left-hand wall of the interior. It has been much restored and looks incredibly neat and new.

The Kale Cami, or Mosque of the Citadel, was built in 1160 but the original Seljuk building has been much restored and altered. The minaret must once have been square. The Citadel enclosure, entered through its own gateway, down the road past the Demir Hotel and the T.H.Y. office, is a pleasant place to walk in, silent and peaceful after the hurly-burly of the busy streets. The mound indicates the antiquity of this site as a place of human habitation. The Citadel is of early Byzantine foundation, strengthened by the Artuks of the twelfth century and again by Soliman the Magnificent in the sixteenth. There are ruins of a Church of St. George and its guesthouse within the Citadel. There is a Syrian Christian church in the south-western part of the old town, not far in from the walls and between Lale Bey and Şaytanpazari. Its altar is said to be Byzantine.

One of the most famous and photographed structures in Diyarbakır is the Dört Ayaklı[1] or Four-legged Minaret. This is square, with broad bands of white stone in its black basalt, has the usual pepperpot top, and stands rather oddly on four stubby columns. It's the sort of thing that gave me faith when the thought of earthquakes occurred to me in Turkey.

There are any number of old *hans* and caravanserais in the old town and it is only from a height like that of the Demir Restaurant that one realises from the little domes how many Turkish baths there are. Some of them are still in use and may be visited with confidence. Diyarbakır today is almost equally ancient and modern. In the northern part of the town, within and outside the walls, one meets the sophisticated Turk and a variety of foreigners connected with education and petroleum. In the centre of the old town one meets the rural shoppers for whom Diyarbakır is a great, time-honoured and satisfying market centre. The narrow streets are great fun to explore since there are not many streets in the old town where motorised traffic can go. My *fayton* driver one day took me down a street that got too narrow even for him and we only managed to reverse into a high-walled lane with grilled house-windows by lifting the carriage wheels.

The food is good in Diyarbakır, excellent lamb, good cheese and butter, the best *ayran* (whipped yoğurt) I have ever drunk and good fruit from its orchards and vineyards. Its melons and watermelons, grown along the Tigris, are famous throughout Turkey and the Diyarbakır Basin to the north-east produces wheat and other cereals.

Diyarbakır has recently become the base from which all those connected with the expanding oil industry visit the Batman refineries and carry on the continuous search for more oil. These days the town is enjoying the best of both worlds, industrial and agricultural, and the people, whom I've found very friendly, look happy about it. There are other flourishing industries, woollen carpet making, silk and serge weaving, a *raki* factory, an ice factory and one for processing rice. The wonder of Diyarbakır, the walls, are likely to preserve old architecture and commercial ways in the old city whilst encouraging new developments to take place outside, an admirable arrangement which will make of Diyarbakır a place of perennial interest.

[1] The popular name. Officially it is the Şeyh Matar Minaret.

Mardin

✦✦✦

Mardin, ancient Marida, is a beautiful stone-built town strategically placed under a great and fortifiable rock on a hillside that dominates the heart of northern Mesopotamia. It is about one hundred kilometres from Diyarbakır on the road to the Syrian frontier and is only about thirty kilometres from Syria. It has much that is Syrian in its architecture and it has been an important Syrian Christian centre. It enjoyed or suffered similar conquests and occupations to those of Diyarbakır and up to the twelfth century A.D. was always dwarfed by Diyarbakır's greater strength and importance.

The hilltop Citadel was a Roman and Byzantine fortress but it failed to withstand the Arab attack of 640. After two and a half centuries of Arab rule it was taken by the Kurdish Marwans, at the same time as Diyarbakır. Captured by the Seljuks in the late eleventh century, it was held by the Artuk Turks during the twelfth, thirteenth and fourteenth centuries. Under this regime it resisted attack by Saladin and by the Mongols, but fell to Tamburlaine in 1395. During the fifteenth century it was held by the Ak Koyun and Kara Koyun, and it was briefly occupied by the Persians in 1508 and was taken by Selim I, the Grim, who added it to the Ottoman domains in 1517, after a year's siege of the Citadel. The glorious days of Mardin were those of Artuk rule, when it became a capital city.

The Citadel crowns the hill on the left as we enter the town from the west and up on the left too is the ruin of a great bastion, once a part of the lower city wall which linked up with the Citadel at either end. A road to the right leads to the Kasim Paşa Medrese, a fine fifteenth-century Ak Koyun building with a high, stepped doorway, fluted domes in the front corners of the courtyard and a slightly pointed dome over the prayer room, to which a passage leads from the entrance. Stairways

26. Tillo: Ibrahim Hakki's house

27. Tillo: pistachios growing

28. Urfa: Halil ur Rahman Mosque

29. Urfa: sacred carp

allow one to go up to the gallery of the courtyard and the students' bedrooms.

The Citadel in its present form is of fifteenth-century Ak Koyun construction, the arched entrance, the walls, the vast ruined palace and the mosque all belonging to that period. In some places the sheer rock was sufficient fortification and houses were built on its edge, their walls in turn providing a further deterrent to attack. From the walls there is a fine view southwards to the Syrian plain.

Not far from the central square of the lower town, down a narrow street, is the Ulu Cami, the Great Mosque. Founded by the Seljuks in the eleventh century and much added to later, it has a roof supported by two rows of columns. The central section, facing the *mihrab*, is surmounted by a stone dome and is out of line with the rest of the mosque. Much damage was done by an explosion during a Kurdish revolt of 1832 and the cylindrical minaret, with its interesting raised decoration, was rebuilt in the nineteenth century. An inscription on the square base of the minaret gives the date equivalent to 1176, during the Artuk period. North-east of the town and backed by the Citadel is the Sultan Isa Medrese, a balanced masterpiece of Artuk construction dating from 1385. To the east of the town too is the thirteenth-century Şehidiye Cami, much restored but with beautiful stone carving in its doorways and windows. It has a fluted minaret with two balconies. The houses of Mardin, facing southwards and stepped against the Citadel hill, are well built and show a great variety of arched window and doorway. Dr. Arnold Toynbee, no mean traveller, has called Mardin the most beautiful town in the world.

Still further east and about ten kilometres outside the town the imposing mass of the Syrian Christian monastery of Der Zafaran rises above terraced fields and a conspicuous fortress. This is a fifth-century foundation and it indicates the importance to early Christianity of this part of Mesopotamia. The great plateau to the north and north-east of Mardin is known as Tur Abdin, a region which seems to have been to the Monophysite Christians of Syria what Mount Athos was to the Greek Orthodox Church: there are any number of churches and monasteries scattered about this area. There were still monks in residence in some of these at the beginning of the twentieth century, as there were in the cells of Göreme further west. The involvement of the Syrian, Nestorian and Armenian churches in international politics during the past hundred years or so has led to a sad break with history.

Midyat, in the centre of this region, can be reached by a slow road through Savur and has the ruins of an ancient church, Mar Philoxenos. Between Midyat and Kerburan many of the villages have remains of churches and monasteries but the most interesting is the monastery of Mar Gabriel at Kartmen, or Kartamin, south of Kerburan on a poor road to Idil. This fifth-century foundation once housed four hundred monks, some of whom came from as far off as Egypt.

A difficult road northwards from Midyat leads to Hasankayf, which may also be reached by a shorter but much more difficult road from Batman in the north. A Roman foundation, known to the Byzantines, who made it a bishopric, as Kiphas and to the Arabs as Hisn Kayfa or Kayfa (Kiphas) Tower, it became an Artuk capital from the end of the eleventh century to 1231 and from 1232 to 1524 the home and capital of a long succession of Kurdish Eyyubi kings. This city too was an important Syrian Christian centre but declined steadily after the destructive Mongol invasion of 1260. The Citadel has a staggering situation on a cliff top overlooking the southern bank of the Tigris and encloses the ruins of a twelfth-century Artuk palace. In the lower town there are a number of ruined mosques and a very beautiful tomb of the Eyyubi Zeyn el Abdin, Persian in style with a pattern of blue tiles on red brick giving a cross-stitch effect.

Urfa

From Diyarbakır to Urfa a well-metalled road runs over an undulating plain strangely strewn with roundish lumps of stone which vary in size from a Rugby football to a sack of potatoes. These lie almost everywhere on the surface and where they have been cleared there is good cultivable soil. When trimmed the stone is almost black and this is the stone with which the great walls of Diyarbakır were built. When used for the construction of houses the stone looks dull and dingy if not colour washed, and the little groups of huts one passes give a depressing effect. Roughly half way between the two cities we pass through the undistinguished town of Siverek in its setting of vineyards and with the ruins of a little castle of Byzantine origin. The road we are following drives straight into the modern end of Urfa and offers little promise of the delights in store.

Urfa is a point at which the Anatolian foothills meet and are able to dominate a large area of Mesopotamian pasture land, and its situation has therefore made it important since very early times in human history. Early forms of its name are Hurri and Orhai, the latter Aramaic. The ancient Greeks knew it as Orrhoë or Osrhoë. The Seleucid followers of Alexander the Great named it Edessa after a city in their native Macedonia,[1] keeping the original name for the surrounding kingdom of Orsoene, and this name, Edessa, was taken up again by the Crusaders who settled here. The Arabs called it Ruha, another version of the ancient name, and from this, by a kind of metathesis, came the Turkish form Urfa.

In the second millennium B.C., the town became one of the centres of the Hurrians, the people of Hurri, Indo-European warrior aristocrats who formed part of the southward and westward drive from the

[1] One reason is said to be that the new Edessa, like the old, was liable to flooding.

Caucasus and the mountains of western Persia of which the Hittites were another notable element. They were associated with the Mitanni, who had established themselves here in northern Assyria. Urfa's coveted grazing grounds have been and are still today famous for horse-breeding and for the flocks of sheep which give the excellent Urfa butter. In a sense a bastion of the western world against the eastern plains, it has also been occupied by Babylonians, Persians, Seleucids,[1] Parthians, Sassanians, Romans, Byzantines, Arabs and Crusaders. It was an important crossroad between trade routes from the Mediterranean to Persia and north–south from Anatolia to lower Mesopotamia and Egypt. The Crusader Counts of Edessa occupied and fortified it from 1098 to 1146 and it was successively ruled by Baudoin (Baldwin) I and II and Jocelin I and II. Then came the Turks. The town was taken by Nurretin Zengi in 1144 (to be briefly restored to Jocelin II) and it was then occupied by Artuks and Eyyubis. In the thirteenth century it came under the domination of the Mameluks but as a result of their defeat by Sultan Selim I in 1516 Urfa became a part of the Ottoman state. It has remained Turkish since that time, though briefly occupied by Mohamed Ali's army in 1837 and by the French, after the British entry into the town in March 1919. After two months of bitter fighting early in 1920 the occupation forces abandoned Urfa to the Turks. Apart from the official Turkish, the languages one hears most commonly spoken in the street today are Arabic and Kurdish.

Urfa is a friendly, gay and bustling town, a market and shopping centre for a considerable area, from the Syrian frontier thirty miles to the south to a similar distance in each other direction. Boys run wildly across the road, women wear marvellous costumes and the men too, proudly upright in richly embroidered jackets and baggy trousers. Early one morning whilst waiting for a bus in the main square of the modern town I saw a taxi approach with horn blowing and the other waiting men crowd towards it. It slowed down as though to invite inspection. It was a wedding party with the bride seated between two other girls in the back. They were dressed beyond the invention of a film producer doing a harem scene, the bride covered in shimmering

[1] There is evidence that Edessa had native rulers from 132 B.C. and that many of the settled Greeks married women with Aramaic or Persian names. A. H. M. Jones, *Cities of the Eastern Roman Provinces*, p. 221 and p. 224. The settlement brought other Macedonian place-names to this region, e.g. Amphipolis, Anthemus, Ichnae, etc.

gold, whether real or fake I couldn't tell, the other two girls in white. All three were bare-faced, beautiful and smiling. It was a sight to cheer one's heart at seven o'clock in the morning.

I don't think the official Turkish hotel list gives one for Urfa but there are several possible ones. I stayed at the Doğu Oteli which I found clean and cheap. The best approach to the exploration of Urfa is to take a buggy from your hotel to the foot of the Citadel, along Urfa's main thoroughfare. The horse-carriage fare from the main square to the sacred fish pools is three liras and it's enough to ask for the fish, *balıklar*. Everyone will know where you want to go. You should walk back afterwards to look at the shops and the many interesting buildings. The frequent minibus dolmuş is much cheaper but is apt to be crowded so that you don't see much. You go west-wards towards the old town along an undistinguished street except for glimpses of lovely carving in stone on the southern side, where demolition for new building has broken into and revealed the court-yards of noble houses. One wonders whether anything is being done to preserve some of these beautiful buildings. I thought of what Gayer Anderson did with the Beit el Kretleya in Cairo. There are mosques with interesting minarets, very different from either the Seljuk or Ottoman minarets of Turkey, often not one pure conception like those of Sinan or the anonymous Seljuk architects but some of them giving the impression of having been built in parts, in sections of diminishing width, with sometimes a layer of blind arches. This is not true of all of them, however. There is the fine campanile (one can call it nothing else) of the Halil ur Rahman Cami, built in 1211, square and well proportioned with its eight tall open arcades in the top section. There are other exceptions too. In fact one could make quite a collection of minaret styles in Urfa.

A turning right takes us into the shine and clatter of the tin bazaar, with a great rectangular many-chimneyed *han* on our left. More turns and soon we reach an open area which seems to be all gardens and mosques. The great rock of the Citadel, with its two tall Corinthian columns, towers above. To our right is a fine rectangular stone-enclosed pool with an elegant seventeenth-century Ottoman mosque on the far side and an equally elegant kiosk at the end. This pool and the other lesser pools and channels that lead from it are full of carp that no one is allowed to catch and eat. There is a story of a Laz who came to Urfa from the Black Sea coast, was unable to resist the temptation and caught one of the carp. The townspeople were angry but the Laz unashamedly cooked and ate the fish, remarking that he would eat anything that came out of water, even his father. It is better not to angle for these sluggish fish, up to a kilo in weight, which become a swirling, fighting mass in response to a handful of chickpeas. There is always a boy to sell you these. It is correct to feed and photograph the fish.

A spring of sweet water emerging from the foot of the rock and known to the ancient Greeks as Callirhoë has made this spot sacred to any number of gods, but the people of Moslem Urfa have another explanation of the holiness of the fish. They say that Abraham, an important figure in Islam, fell here when he was catapulted from the rocks above by Nimrod. God opened a spring to break the prophet's fall and when cinders from the fire in which Nimrod had failed to burn Abraham fell after him they turned into fish. Urfa has a traditional story of the life of Abraham which doesn't agree with that given in the Bible. The Babylonian king then in occupation of Urfa dreamt of a rising star and the interpretation was that a child would soon be born there who would be greater than he. Nimrod went further than Herod in a similar situation for not only did he order the destruction of all male infants but the absolute segregation of the sexes so that there should be no further conceptions and births. Abraham's mother hid in a cave under the great rock to give birth to him. You can visit this cave if you go a couple of hundred metres southwards along the foot of the Citadel rock, past woodyards to the Dergah Mosque or Mevlidid Halil Camii Şerifi. Go through to the far right-hand corner of the courtyard and you will be allowed to enter this obviously very holy and much revered shrine. Be careful to remove your shoes. When you come out, look up at the rock from the middle of the courtyard and you will see another cave outside the back wall of the mosque enclosure. From here a deer is said to have come and suckled Abraham when his mother was forced to leave him in the cave. So Abraham grew up to disapprove of the polytheism of Nimrod and the people of ancient Hurri. He had a divine visitation but refused to accept it as a vision of the true god until a miracle had been performed. He was told to take four different kinds of bird, kill them, clean them, cook them and pound them into paste. Then he should bake them in a pasty, take the pasty out into the open and throw it up in the air. This he did, the four birds flew away and Abraham believed. His father was an idol maker but the young man decided to smash the idols in the temple. (Think what Freud would have said.) He spared the biggest of them and hung his axe about the god's neck, a symbolical assertion of monotheism. Nimrod was furious, Abraham was caught and condemned to death. A great fire was lit between the tall columns on the cliff top, a spot traditionally known as Nimrod's Throne, but the fire was too hot for the executioners to approach with their victim. Nimrod caused an engine to be brought and Abraham was projected to his intended death, only to fall into the miraculous spring. The place where he fell is a very holy Moslem shrine, protected today by an iron grille inside the Halil ur Rahman Mosque at the far left-hand corner of the big pool, conspicuous for its elegant square minaret. The jumble of religions incorporated into that tradition (and typical of the creeds that have sprung up in the Near East) is symbolised in the decoration of the *mimber* arch in the central room of the little mosque itself. This has sun and moon symbols almost identical with those found at Sultantepe and Sumatar. We remember, however, that Sabian moon and planet worship continued in the Urfa region up to the eleventh century A.D. In yet another cave near here J. B. Segal in 1952 discovered an interesting Sabian mosaic of the third century A.D.[1]

There are two good restaurants back in the main square of Urfa and a decent little shop across the road that specialises in the eastern Anatolian breakfast of boiled milk, flat crisp bread, excellent butter and honey. The restaurant I went to for dinner one night turned out rather different from what I'd expected. It was curtained from the street, suggesting some kind of entertainment rather than the unlikely concept of privacy, and it was so full of men when I peeped inside that I thought it must be good. And it was. But as I went in I noticed that most of the men at the little tables were facing me. Their interest was not in me but in six young women who were sitting on settees on either side of the door, facing the tables. They were pleasant-looking girls, rather dolled up except for one dressed in severe grey, and they looked cheerful and well fed. Plump enough for an Arab's dream. Occasionally one of them would get up and walk down the room to the toilets at the far end, I thought a parade of charms. They were clearly well known to some of the men. At about 9.30 I looked up from my excellent grilled kebab and raki to find that all six had left,

[1] J. B. Segal, 'Pagan Syriac Monuments in the Vilayet of Urfa', *Anatolian Studies*, vol. III, p. 117. The mosaic is now in the Urfa Museum.

and most of the men too. Arrangements for the night had been dis-
creetly made and the restaurant had lost its cachet.

From Urfa some places of great importance and interest can be
visited, notably Sultantepe, Sumatar and Harran. For these you start
out along the highway leading to the Syrian frontier at Akçakale,
passing, as you leave Urfa, some remnants of the Crusader city wall.
The roads to these places are usually motorable, except after heavy
rain, but it may be safer to hire a jeep in Urfa for the journey. Prices
should be compared. I paid sixty liras for the trip to Harran and back
by jeep, with time to go over and round the whole site, two and half
hours in all.

SULTANTEPE

Some sixteen kilometres south of Urfa a turning left signposted
Yardımcı takes one past the great mound of Sultantepe, the most
conspicuous object in this vast plain. It is said to be called the Sultan's
Hill by the Turks because Murat IV camped here on his return from
the sack of Baghdad in 1638. This mound, like others of its kind,
incorporates a number of cultural levels from prehistory to Hellenistic
and Roman times and as a result rises about fifty metres above the
plain, but the most important discovery made here so far has been that
of the hoard of unbaked clay tablets which carry, in cuneiform
Assyrian and Sumerian, versions of some of the greatest poems of
antiquity.[1] One tablet fills a gap in the epic of *Gilgamesh*, almost
certainly, says Seton Lloyd, the oldest poem in the world,[2] and is therefore a major literary find. *Gilgamesh* takes us back to the mysterious
beginnings of civilisation in Mesopotamia and to man's first articulate
facing of problems posed by the elements, by love and friendship,
by the practice of living in towns. The story of how Enkidu was
trapped into abandoning the wilds for an urban existence is an alle-
gory of the taming power of woman over man. The adventures of
Gilgamesh link the lower culture centres of Mesopotamia with the
Anatolian highlands from which their water and possibly their first
impulses towards civilisation came and the poem has a description of

[1] See 'The Sin-Temples of Harran' by Seton Lloyd, *The Listener*, 24 April 1952,
for the excitement of his discovery of the unbaked tablets stacked near empty wine
jars in an outbuilding of the great Assyrian palace.
[2] ibid., p. 670.

the eruption of one of the eastern Anatolian volcanoes active at that time. Here too, at Sultantepe, were found copies of the great *Creation Poem*, prayers, ritual, medical, astrological and historical texts. There is a terrific poem of the sufferings of a hero which reminds me not so much of the Book of Job as of the old Welsh saga of Llywarch Hen. It is in Akkadian and is known as 'The Poem of the Righteous Sufferer'.[1] The depth of this man's despair can be gauged from the lines:

> *A halter is laid on my mouth*
> *And a gag on the utterance of my lips.*
> *My 'gate' is barred, my drinking place blocked,*
> *My hunger is prolonged, my throat stopped up.*
> *When grain is served, I eat it as filth;*
> *Beer, the life of mankind, is distasteful to me.*[2]

When a man no longer enjoys his beer he is clearly in a bad way. There is also a fragment of the Assyrian *Descent of Ishtar to the Nether World* and a fascinating late Assyrian version of the *Nergal and Ereshkigal* story.[3] This poem tells of a strange love affair between the god Nergal and the goddess of the Underworld. There are memorable lines in Dr. Gurney's translation, for example the description of a shock suffered by Namtar, Ereshkigal's messenger.

> *Namtar's face turned pale like a cut-down tamarisk.*

There are unfortunate lacunae in this version and one misses the details of the goddess's preparations in the bathroom for the reception of the god Nergal.

These poems are thought to have been set down in the seventh century B.C. shortly before the collapse of the Assyrian Empire. Sultantepe (we do not yet know what the Assyrians called it) was probably destroyed by the Scythians in 610 B.C. at the same time as Harran. Scythian burials have been found on the mound and these Assyrian tablets in their fragile unbaked form are lucky to have escaped the accidents of later burials and the digging of grain pits.

[1] W. G. Lambert and O. R. Gurney, 'The Sultantepe' Tablets, *Anatolian Studies*, vol. IV, 1954.
[2] ibid., p. 87.   [3] O. R. Gurney, *Anatolian Studies*, vol. X, pp. 105–131.

SUMATAR

A few kilometres beyond Sultantepe and near Yardımcı is Sumatar, an ancient watering place for nomads on their annual transhumance to the winter grazing grounds of the Tektek Mountains which rise to the north-east, a practice still followed. Sumatar has enough wells of sweet water to make it of perennial importance, for there are few ancient sites unconnected with springs of good water. On a hill here J. B. Segal noted and identified, with the help of Syriac inscriptions on niches and rock faces, a semicircle of buildings of different shapes dedicated to the Moon and the planets, a worship carried on here, as at Harran, well on into Christian times. On a hill a few hundred yards to the west Segal identified a temple of the Sun and, some distance to the north-west, the remains of other temples sacred to planets. Not far from here there are caves with relief sculptures and Syriac inscriptions of the second and third centuries A.D.[1]

HARRAN

Back on the main road to the Syrian frontier take the next turning left, signposted Altınbaşak. Harran is a conspicuous long mound with a minaret which can be seen for miles before we even leave the main road.[2]

Harran is the Haran or Charan of the Bible, where Abraham is said to have gone with his family from Ur of the Chaldees and where he remained until he was inspired to take over the land of Canaan. Abraham had ranged freely as a rich nomadic chieftain between Asia Minor, Egypt and Babylon and he must have had a shrewd idea where he could settle with least resistance from the natives. This probably happened about the beginning of the second millennium B.C., before the Hittite invasion of Mesopotamia and Babylon. Abraham's father, Terah, died and was buried at Haran and his youngest brother was named Haran, according to the Bible.

[1] J. B. Segal, op. cit., pp. 97 ff.
[2] T. E. Lawrence mistook the minaret for a campanile. 'The tower of Harran cathedral was in sight for four hours.' *Oriental Assembly*, p. 12. Lawrence was doing this trip from Aleppo on foot and this records his first impression in his diary of the walk. He talked about the mosque and its minaret later in the diary but didn't bother to correct the earlier impression. The diary was edited for publication by his brother.

After the destruction of Nineveh by the Medes in 612 B.C. the Assyrian court fled to Harran which briefly became, in Seton Lloyd's apt words, 'the posthumous capital of Assyria',[1] before it was destroyed by the Scythians. The growth of Urfa, which became the great city of Edessa under the Seleucids in 304 B.C., slowly killed Harran by taking away its water for its own requirements. Harran lies between the two streams known today as the Jullab and the Balıkh which converge and now dry up completely to the south of the site. These streams once supplied water to the city and irrigated the fertile soil of the surrounding plain. Today there is only one good well in the vicinity, that known as Bir Yacub, Jacob's Well, about a kilometre north-west of the site. All the others are brackish. At this well occurred the fateful meeting of Jacob and Rachel[2] and here Rebecca drew water for Abraham's servant.[3] So even four thousand years ago this must have been the best well in the district. The water is still approached by an inclined shaft and stone steps. Lawrence was offered water by women here and found it cool and clear and good to drink.[4] I haven't drunk from it myself and can't add it to my personal list of famous and unknown springs.

A tablet of about 2000 B.C. found at Mari, a very ancient city south-east of here in Mesopotamia, mentions the Temple of Sin, the Moon Goddess, at Harran and the signing of a treaty there. In the fourteenth century B.C. a Hittite king signed a treaty with the Mitanni at this temple. The gods of Harran, Moon, Sun and planets, must therefore have been widely revered and their authority powerful in peace-making. This temple was many times destroyed and rebuilt and is now thought to have stood on the site of the Castle, Citadel or Qalat, on the city wall to the south-east of the site. The castle is thought to have Hittite foundations and has been added to by Romans, Arabs, Kurds and Crusaders, but no pre-Islamic building is visible today. Its south-eastern gate, and you should go outside to try to puzzle out this hotch-potch of defensive architecture, has an arch with a Kufic inscription of A.D. 1049 and a relief of hunting-dogs on either side.[5] The present arch is rough and later than the original, higher, horse-shoe arch of

---

[1] *The Listener*, 24 April 1952, p. 670.
[2] Genesis, 29:10.
[3] Genesis, 24:45.
[4] Op. cit., p. 17.
[5] Finds which have been removed from Harran are now at the Hittite Museum, Ankara.

Islamic construction. There is some twelfth-century Crusader decoration in the stonework of Room 45 on the south corner.[1]

Harran has therefore been an international religious and diplomatic centre, a trading post and a fortress at the junction of important routes from east to west and from north to south-east and south. The Castle is the biggest remaining building but a good deal of defensive wall is left and many of the ancient gates are recognisable. You will probably enter as I did by the Aleppo Gate on the west side. This still has its arch and an inscription on it, Year of Hegira 588, A.D. 1192, the year before the death of Saladin. The Romans knew Harran as Carrhae and from it was made the most disastrous sortie in their history. Marcus Licinius Crassus regarded his governorship of the province of Syria more as a means of adding to his wealth than as a duty to Rome, but he also felt that he needed a military success to balance those of his fellow triumvirs Caesar and Pompey, so in 53 B.C. he marched out from Harran to meet a Parthian army under Surenas. Crassus was defeated, thousands of his men captured or slain and he himself was killed and decapitated during an interview with the Parthian general.[2] Orodes, the Parthian king, had liquid gold poured into the mouth of the dead Roman's head as a comment on his passion for that metal. The Battle of Carrhae was a black day for Rome.

At Harran too the Emperor Caracalla was murdered, after a life of slaughter and plunder, by the prefect Macrinus, as he returned from a temple of the Moon thought to have been outside the city. Caracalla was killed on April 6, the day on which the Sabians were wont to sacrifice a bullock to the Moon. What a capital calf he made! Harran seems to have been an unlucky place for the ruthless and acquisitive to visit, with its memories of ancient peace-making and civilised living. The Emperor Julian, glad to see paganism flourish, worshipped the Moon here in A.D. 363 but the Christian Theodosius destroyed the Harran temple in 382. In spite of this, Sabian worship of the Moon, Sun and Planets continued here alongside Christianity until the eleventh century, the Christians, to judge from the church remains, living in the north and east, the Sabians in the south of the city. There are church ruins near the Mosul Gate in the east and not far from the north wall.

[1] See Seton Lloyd and William Brice: *Anatolian Studies*, vol I, pp. 77 ff., and D. S. Rice: *Anatolian Studies*, vol. II, pp. 36 ff. T. E. Lawrence considered the walls to be indefensible and all post-Saladin, 'possibly post-Crusade', op. cit.

[2] Freya Stark gives a colourful account of this sad sequence of events in her *Rome Beyond the Euphrates*.

Justinian, in his remarkable building sweep of the Byzantine Empire, repaired the walls in the sixth century.

The next conquerors, the Arabs, tolerated the Sabians until in revulsion against their strange practices they forced upon them the choice of adopting either Islam or Christianity. Arab writers report animal sacrifices to the goddess Sin and the sacrifice of a pregnant woman to the goddess Balthi and her male attendant. There was also a water-god at Harran.[1] Harran was occupied by the Arabs in 639, early in their outsurge of conquest, and the Ulu Cami or Great Mosque, also known as Cami el Firdaus, the Mosque of Paradise, whose great square minaret we saw from a distance, was founded by the Khalif Marwan II in the middle of the eighth century. Saladin may well have embellished it during the last quarter of the twelfth century. Only part of the wall, one fine doorway and the great free-standing, now truncated minaret remain of what must once have been a noble edifice. As usual, earlier stonework was used in its construction and in 1956 Dr. D. S. Rice lifted the steps of the doorway and some paving slabs to discover stelae of the sixth century B.C. with inscriptions in Babylonian cuneiform. These stelae belong to the restoration of the Moon Temple by the Babylonian King Nabonidus. They help to explain his mysterious ten-year retreat from his kingdom and people and in one of them he justifies his seizure of power in Babylon. Another, erected by his mother, records how Nabonidus was told in a vision to rebuild the Temple of the Moon at Harran and how he did this. Nabonidus, whom Seton Lloyd in the *Listener* article already noted calls 'this eccentric antiquarian', clearly brought new life to Harran at this time. Each stela is surmounted by a half circle of sculpture in low relief of quite extraordinary interest. Right of centre the king stands in profile. He holds a rough staff taller than himself in his left hand and raises his right hand in a gesture of adoration towards three symbols in the top left half of the tympanum. In order away from him these represent the Moon, the Sun and either a planet or the goddess Ishtar, equivalent of Aphrodite. Otherwise the space is empty and one gets the impression of infinite space, an empty sky, a universe dominated by the three principles these symbols represent and worshipped by the Divine King.[2]

[1] Seton Lloyd and William Brice: op. cit., p. 91.

[2] C. J. Gadd, 'The Harran Inscriptions of Nabonidus', *Anatolian Studies*, vol. VIII, 1958, pp. 35–92. There are similar stelae, some of unknown origin, in the British Museum (No. 90837) and the Louvre (No. AO 1505), the latter from Taima in north-west Arabia.

These things at least have been preserved by Moslem re-use up to the thirteenth century.

Harran was destroyed by the Mongols in 1260 and never recovered as a city. Today it is a village, or rather a scattered group of hamlets, all built in the north Syrian style of conical beehive-shaped mud-plastered domes and unbroken, inward-facing stone walls, like compact termite colonies. My driver was disinclined to approach these curious windowless houses, perhaps out of contempt rather than fear, and I am sorry now that I neglected an opportunity of discovering whether the women are still as friendly and informal as T. E. Lawrence found them half a century ago. He was well received by the Sheikh of Harran 'who has offered me two first-class wives in his gift. The women here are extremely free, handling one's clothes, and putting their hands into one's pockets quite cheerfully.'[1] The houses huddle against and even over the Castle and spread out north-east of it. There is another huddle outside the walls at the north-west corner, near the little mosque and tomb of Sheikh Hayat el Harrani. This tomb has also been said to be that of Aran, eponymous founder of the city. The house of Aran, where Abraham took Sarah to stay, is said to be on the hill as you go up from the Aleppo Gate to the top of the mound. The villagers of Harran today are semi-settled Arabs, with other nomads pitching their tents and tending to settle on the outskirts. The shepherds take the flocks to graze on Tektek Dağ, sixteen kilometres to the east, in December and they return in the spring to help sow beans, sesame and millet and to harvest the summer crops, the barley and wheat which are sown in the autumn and the cucumbers which are gathered in July. Horses are still bred and graze freely outside the walls. You may think Harran hardly worth the visit, as some people think of Troy, unless you allow yourself time to ponder over the antiquity and strangeness of its history and to photograph its termite houses.

Harran is an evocative place. The rim of hills to the north and the flat horizon to the south have made it a point of hesitation and decision from the earliest times of human movement. So much that is strange and significant happened there, the peace conferences of the dawn of history, the heroic, romantic and sometimes squalid adventures of Abraham, the visits of such egregious persons as Nabonidus, Julian and Saladin and the sticky ends of Crassus and Caracalla. The cedar-

[1] op. cit., p. 19.

built Temple of Sin must have been the centre of a kind of Assyrian blend of Sybaris and Geneva. But the city the Mongols finally wiped out was an important Moslem centre of learning and had its architectural and sculptural glories too. It is no longer very impressive. Seton Lloyd finds that the fortifications now form 'a sort of retaining wall to this vast platform of accumulated human debris. . . . The Assyrian city, we reckoned, must in places be buried as deep as thirty feet beneath the present surface.'[1] There must be a great deal more history awaiting discovery at Harran, as at Sultantepe and scores of other such mounds in this culturally important part of the world.

[1] *The Listener*, 24 April 1952, p. 670.

Urfa to Gaziantep

A very well surfaced road runs from Urfa to Gaziantep. It climbs quickly to the limestone plateau, affording a splendid view of Urfa and its citadel and revealing the citadel as the key to the fertile plain to the south. Here at the top of the hill, on the edge of the plateau and north of the citadel, signs of the ancient importance of this place are everywhere, quarries, rock sanctuaries, tombs, roads. From here to Birecik men are thin on the ground but when they appear they are tall and swarthy and wear black and white Arab headdress. We drop down suddenly into Birecik,[1] a neat town which slopes down to the Euphrates and a fine new bridge. The remains of the little castle can be seen on the rock overlooking the Euphrates to the north of the bridge and the town. At the western end of the bridge there are petrol stations, a restaurant and a motel. In Hellenistic times a Seleucid bridge spanned the river here on pontoons and it is from here down that the Euphrates is navigable. This crossing was held by the Crusader settlers to protect the road from Edessa (Urfa) to Antioch, and the castle belongs originally to that period. An important ancient road ran from here down through Karkemiş to Aleppo.

We go on through Nizip, a straggling untidy town on a tributary of the Euphrates, the site of ancient Belkis, some remains of which are curious rock reliefs on cave walls. Nizip is an important market centre. We have now reached olive-growing country and Nizip has olive-oil and soap factories.

From here a road and railway run down to Karkemiş, thirty-odd kilometres away on the Syrian frontier, near the Turkish village of Barak. The discovery, identification and excavation of this ancient

[1] The Aramaic *birsa* became Arabic *bira* meaning fort or castle. The Turks added their diminutive *-cik* to make it Birecik, Little Castle.

30. *Houses at Harran*

31. *Tobacco drying at Eski Malatya*

32. Diyarbakır: the walls

33. Diyarbakır: Deliler Hau

city on the Euphrates, the capital of a late Hittite kingdom, has been the work of British explorers and archaeologists. The railway crosses the Euphrates here on the Turkish side of the frontier but the road bridge is on the Syrian side. Karkemiş, being a frontier site in a region much given to smuggling, is not easy to visit unless you go to some trouble in recruiting official help. Cattle are smuggled from Turkey into Syria, where they fetch good prices, in spite of extensive mine-fields on the Turkish side. An old donkey is usually sent first. If that gets through all is well, if it's blown up it has made a gap in the mine-field and the others pour through.

Karkemiş became important after the fall of Hattusas (Boğazköy) and the considerable archaeological remains reflect the blend of northern and southern elements, Hittite, Aramaean and Assyrian, in this neo-Hittite culture on the north-western edge of Mesopotamia. The plan of much of the city has been revealed and a great deal of sculpture in relief recovered. This is mostly on flat slabs of stone placed against the side walls of ceremonial ways and it shows a decline from the formal excellence of the work at Boğazköy and a curious mixture of styles. The goddess Kubaba (Cybele), a nun-like figure seated in a simple chair poised on a lion's back and holding her symbol, the pomegranate, is dignified enough, but not so an unnamed and naked Syrian goddess, a comic figure wearing a very twentieth-century man's felt hat, a pair of Egyptian vulture wings and a very formal suggestion of a garment falling either side of her to her outward-pointed feet. She holds her ridiculously small breasts. She looks an arrant fake and it's difficult to imagine how she could have been worshipped, since she so obviously represents a breakdown in faith and a grotesque attempt to bring together two religions, a thing done much better in Ptolemaic Alex-andria. There was also a monstrously ugly god in the round that was destroyed during the fighting of World War I. Part of the base is in the Hittite Museum at Ankara and one of the rather nice lion's heads is in the British Museum. Some of the Karkemiş reliefs have Hittite hieroglyphic writing and these have been deciphered following the discovery at Karatepe of such an inscription in this hieroglyphic form and in Phoenician. The hybrid neo-Hittite culture exemplified by Karkemiş, Karatepe and Arslantepe was roughly contemporary with that of the Phrygians in western Anatolia and the strong Assyrian power in the south, that is the first four centuries of the first millennium B.C.

After Nizip there are vast stretches of olive cultivation, more and more interspersed with thick dark-green-leaved pistachio trees as we approach Gaziantep. Obviously a fertile region with a considerable variety of trees. There are more vineyards too.

Gaziantep is a fine new town with a prosperous bustling air and good air to breathe. The appellation Gazi, meaning conqueror or hero of the faith, was granted to the town by Ataturk in recognition of the struggle of its people against the French occupation after World War I. Antep is from the Arabic Ain Tab. *Ain* means spring or source and Tab is presumably a personal name. Today it's the in thing to refer to it informally as Antep, rather as one says Leamington, not Royal Leamington Spa. Antep, let us therefore say, has splendid new streets and buildings whilst contriving to preserve its old market quarter with its lovely houses and streets of craftsmen's shops.

Antep, in its fruitful plain and with its defensible hills, has been an important centre since the fourth millennium B.C. The hill on which the castle stands is a habitation mound which has given pottery fragments of Tel Halaf type. The castle is of Byzantine origin, much rebuilt by Seljuks and Ottomans. Antep has suffered and benefited from the usual invaders of this part of the Near East and relics of the different cultures are displayed in the town museum, together with sculpture from the neo-Hittite sites of the region and specimens of local crafts. Antep is a great commercial centre and a shopping centre for old and new things. It is here in the market quarter that I have found the widest and most reasonably priced selection of woven articles, particularly of Kurdish *kilims*, saddlebags and socks. Its nearness to Syria makes it an attractive shopping place for car owners in Aleppo and even for people there who find it pays them to hire a taxi to Antep for the consumer goods which are scarce and expensive in Syria. It is probably best known to the Turks as the centre of pistachio-nut production, the greatest in the world, but it also has almonds, walnuts and very good fruit, notably figs, apples and apricots. It has carpet factories and the Antep *kilim* is famous all over Turkey. Wine is made here and *raki* distilled and its *baklava* and other sweets are of the finest quality. The plentiful olive groves enable the province to produce good soap, chiefly at the lesser towns of Kilis and Nizip. Antep today is a lively town, very much on its commercial toes, and an important centre of bus communication.

Gaziantep to Malatya

From Antep road and railway run northwards to Malatya. At Narlı (Pomegranate) a road goes off to Maraş, capital of the province of that name, a town with a history which goes back to the neo-Hittites but which has little of interest to offer the traveller today. Backed by a range that rises to nearly 2,500 metres it looks southwards to the fertile valley of the Aksu, tributary of the Ceyhan River, a district important for its production of rice and red pepper. The famous arms industry of Maraş, which once turned out very fine guns, pistols, swords and daggers, has now declined but embroidery in silk and silver wire is still made to decorate garments and headdresses for countrywomen happily reluctant to give up the old ways of dress. It is the centre of spirited folk dancing and one looks forward to the Maraş group at any folk festival.

Making once more for Malatya, the road from Narlı winds through the quiet foothills of the Anti-Taurus past Pazarcık to Gölbaşi with its long Lake Gölçuk running parallel to the road and at the foot of the mountains. Perch grow to a great size here and are good to eat.

From here a difficult road goes off to Adıyaman (check its condition on the latest Highways Department map) and eventually Kahta, the base for Nimrut Dağ.[1] There is a great deal to see here, if you have time for it, and that means at least two days, but the mountain and the strangeness and beauty of the monuments erected by Antiochos I of Commagene in the first century B.C. more than justify the time and effort. Jeeps may be hired at Kahta to take you to Eski Kahta and the sanctuary on Nimrut Dağ, and for the mountain itself horses or mules may be used if you prefer them. There are some fine bridges near here, a Roman bridge, with standing columns, over the Çendere Su, about

[1] Not to be confused with the mountain of the same name near Tatvan.

eight kilometres from Eski Kahta and beyond the village, on a road which goes northwards to Alut, a beautiful Seljuk bridge over the Kahta Çayı. The Kahta Çayı is the ancient Nymphaios River and is a tributary of the Euphrates. Here, to the south-east of the village, is the site of the Commagene Hellenistic city of Arsameia ad Nymphaios, known today as Eski Kale. It can be reached on foot by crossing the Seljuk bridge over the river and following a path, uphill on the left, to what remains of the ancient city on its successive terraces. A good deal of excavation has been done here and at the mountain sanctuary during recent years by German and American scholars and the advice and help of the archaeologists should be sought if the digging season is on. At any other season you will find it difficult to get to these places. The sanctuary itself was constructed by Antiochos I, in honour of his ancestors and of his own hybrid faith, on the 2,000 metre mountain top, with a great artificial mound behind it and on terraces facing north, east and west. Antiochos himself is probably buried under the mound. The blend here is an impressive and successful one of Hittite, Greek and Egyptian styles, reflecting the corresponding blend in the integration of faiths which Antiochos adopted in the broad-minded manner of hellenisation. The gods and kings sit square and solid on their thrones, rustic versions of the colossal Pharaohs of Upper Egypt. The heads have tumbled off but they have been righted and they stare confidently, with unperturbed, bland curiosity, upon the lower world. The humans have become gods in this shared elysium of summer sun and winter snow. Zeus and Herakles are moustached and bearded and have a distinctly Celtic look. Apollo and Antiochos are clean-shaven and only Antiochos himself looks at all Levantine. A goddess of fertility, wearing grapes and other fruits on a crown of plaited barley, has a straight Greek nose but otherwise a Phoenician opulence of feature. A tumbled lion's head guards them. The most impressive thing about them is the equal degree of humanisation of the gods and deification of a human—in its way a great statement on life and death. It makes one wonder what modern civilisation has lost with the passing of decent polytheism and how many neuroses spring from the divine father image of most monotheisms. Disturbing thoughts in clear Anatolian air.

From Gölbaşı, back once more on the highway, the road rises alongside a river that looks good for trout to me and then climbs into wild mountain country with torrents and some natural pine forests, before dropping from the Reşadiye Pass down to the plain of Malatya and the Euphrates once more, a good enough road all the way.

Malatya is a big new town with nothing older than some good nineteenth-century houses. It dates from 1838 when the old town, Eski Malatya, was fortified to resist Mohamed Ali's advance and the population was moved out to a camp where the modern town now stands. It has grown considerably since the construction of the railway from Ankara through Sivas and Malatya to Diyarbakır. I found the Keban Hotel comfortable and very good cooking at the Kantar Restaurant nearby. The people of Malatya are lively and friendly and very proud of their clean and well-treed town. It has an important cotton textile factory and a big government tobacco factory. There are good schools but a shortage of teachers, since well-qualified young teachers are not paid enough by the Government to isolate themselves from the attractions of Istanbul and Ankara. The little market quarter, behind the Keban Hotel, is interesting, as such places always are, even in new towns, with local craft products, ironwork, leatherwork, *kilims* and saddlebags and the work of goldsmiths and silversmiths. I bought two old brass shoehorns, which I always do when I can get them for a reasonable price—five to ten liras according to the casting— and a cartridge belt for Gwydion. The antique man gave me a glass of tea in his tiny shop and the gunshop owner spoke with enthusiasm of the Welsh soccer team when I told him where I came from. I tried to explain in what way Rugby was a superior game and though a soccer fan he took this well and we parted firm friends. The apricots of Malatya are claimed to be the best in the world and its apples have been famous for many centuries. No wonder the fertility goddess on Nimrut Dağ a little to the south fills her skin so sleekly and is crowned with such plump fruit. The seventeenth-century Evliya Çelebi in his Travels[1] has a good deal to say about these apples. He says there are seven kinds of them, all more delicious and clear-coloured than the famous apples of Izmit though smaller than those of Kefe in the Crimea. A few of them will perfume a whole house and even a person's mind. The nobles of Old Malatya and their ladies had the habit of cutting couplets of verse on the peel of the apples or sticking on cut-outs which when removed from the skin of the apple, after it had ripened, would leave a pale thought in Arabic script against the fresh colour of the fruit. The apples were then sent as greetings and gifts, even sometimes

[1] *Seyahat Name*, vol. IV, p. 16.

to the Sultan. I was told that it is impossible today to buy a true
Malatya apple since a family which has trees in its garden keeps all the
fruit for private consumption. But the local apples I bought had a high
red colour that polished beautifully and were crisp, sweet-scented and
tender. They are thought in Malatya to get their lustre from moon-
light and their freshness and tenderness from the summer air.

Malatya has very good tap water too, pure and unchlorinated,
coming directly, without any exposure to pollution, from springs in
the mountains to the north. The people are justly proud of it, but
they're worried too. So far the springs have given a sufficient supply,
but any increase in demand, especially by industry, could require other
methods of supplying the town, with inevitable chlorination and the
loss of this lovely water, now on tap in every house and every hotel
bedroom and bathroom.

There are two places near Malatya which will take you back into
the early history of the district, Arslantepe and Eski Malatya. Arslantepe,
Lion Hill, so called in Turkish because of the stone lions found there, is
about seven kilometres from Malatya and is reached by turning right,
into a good earth road from the Eski Malatya road. This turning is
unsigned at the moment of writing, so you should ask for the way to
the village of Ordu Su. Arslantepe—we must call it by its Turkish
name since the Hittite name has not yet been discovered—was the
capital of a new Hittite kingdom after the fall of Hattusas (Boğazköy).
Of all the new Kingdoms it preserved most purely the older Hittite
art of sculpture and the lions which gave the site its modern name are
thought to be of the eleventh century. These solid, bland creatures,
with beautifully stylised manes, were the guardians of the north gate,
which has now been reconstructed, with the lions, in the Ankara
Museum. The figure of a king, cut from a block of limestone over three
metres high, was found tumbled and roughly buried near the gate and
has now been restored to its original form in the Museum, a fine-
looking man in the prime of life, with a curly beard, a beautifully
draped and stitched garment and sandals. Set well above ground level
in the wall of the gate were little panels of scenes in relief from Hittite
life and religion, a king pouring a libation to the Weather God, but
carefully into a jar since it is probably wine, the same god attacking the
flaming Dragon,[1] and scenes from lion and stag hunting.[2] The hunting

[1] See O. R. Gurney, *The Hittites*, pp. 180–183, for the myth represented here.
[2] See Seton Lloyd, *Early Highlands Peoples of Anatolia*, Plates 102–6.

is being done from chariots and this is thought to be an Assyrian influence, an influence to be detected also in the colossal figure of the king, probably eighth century B.C.

Italian archaeologists are now working at Arslantepe every summer and for the moment what is visible is for the uninitiated confusing and of no great interest except for some puzzling stone foundations at ground level, but there is still a great deal of detritus hill to be dug away and there must be things of beauty and significance yet to be revealed. Storage jars are still embedded in the ground at a high level on the site and these must be much later than Hittite, one imagines. The situation is lovely, overlooking a green valley, soon to join that of the Euphrates, and facing quite high mountains to the south, the direction of Commagene Nimrut Dağ. Arslantepe was never a natural fortress, not the sort of place the Urartians would have chosen, but the Hittites were master wall builders, the first great military engineers, and in their day Arslantepe was strong enough for a regional capital, in years when these new Hittite Kingdoms of the south-east were alternately under the domination of Urartu and Assyria before disappearing completely from history.

Eski Malatya, about twenty kilometres from Malatya and to the north of Arslantepe, is mostly Roman and later and most of the ruins are lost in the luxuriant greenness and cultivation of the scattered present-day village. Much of the rectangular protective wall remains but within living memory it was much higher. It has suffered from ruthless re-use of its masonry in buildings. Since the place has been Moslem most of the time since the seventh century A.D., in between sacking by Byzantine emperors and by the ubiquitous destroyer, Tamburlaine, not much is left above ground of Roman and early Byzantine Milidia. This name comes from the Hittite Milid, the ancient name of the region of which the city at Arslantepe was probably the capital. The most imposing ruin is that of the Ulu Cami, a thirteenth-century Seljuk mosque built on a seventh-century foundation and with fourteenth- and fifteenth-century modifications. This very impressive building is behind the present village school and is made conspicuous by its fine though truncated brick minaret. There is another similar minaret not far to the south and, apart from the detailed brickwork, they look rather like factory chimneys. Of course factory chimneys can be fine too and sometimes have detailed brickwork. The entrance to the mosque at the south-east corner is of the simple stalactite design and has been partly restored. This leads to a high vaulted interior covered by a great central dome on an eight-sided brick drum. An archway leads northwards out of the prayer room to an open courtyard with abstract blue tile decoration and lovely lettering on tiles. This must have been extremely beautiful in its heyday and is still of the greatest interest to the student of architecture and interior decoration. All round the arched courtyard too there are remains, high up on the walls, of similar decoration. Built during the Danishmend occupation, suffering from the descent of Tamburlaine in 1395, then restored and added to, this mosque requires a detailed study to reveal its importance in the development of the *ulu cami* or great mosque in Anatolia.

From the school a road runs northwards along a narrow street to the present village square. A hundred yards to the west of the square and at a lower level is a fine seventeenth-century Ottoman caravanserai which is now being cleaned up and restored. Along the outside wall and facing the village is a line of little shops which supplied the needs of travellers. The interior is gloomy when one enters from daylight, perhaps to soothe the eyes after a long day's journeying, and is lit by an octagonal opening in the shallow central dome. There are other smaller lights along the two sides. The roof is supported by two lines of masonry pillars, making three long aisles. There are fireplaces all along the four sides of the interior, one for each party staying the night, and each surmounted by a tapering, scalloped, stone canopy, in the strangely Gothic style that delights us in the Topkapı Saray at Istanbul. This *han* is by no means as beautiful as the earlier Seljuk ones of central Anatolia but its size and good state of preservation make it interesting and impressive. With great fires burning it could have been quite snug in the travelling season and even in winter, grim though it may seem as a night's resting-place to a traveller today. At least one could sleep with one's feet towards glowing embers, and an Anatolian hotel in autumn can be pretty chilly today.

A lesser road goes off along the well-defined south wall of the old city past two Seljuk tombs of no especial interest and an old ruined minaret. On a fine big house here tobacco leaves were strung across the end wall.[1] Battal Gazi, whose statue rears its charger at Harput, was an Eski Malatya man and a legendary hero in its defence, though against what enemy I am unable to say.

[1] See Plate 31.

Gaziantep to Malatya

Both roads from Malatya to Ankara through Sivas are very rough at the moment of writing and buses and *dolmuşes* are infrequent on them. You can of course make this journey by a daily train service. The road to Kayseri is better but not good right the way through. It takes you through wild country and over several passes through the Tahtali Mountains, an offshoot of the Taurus range. A turning to the south-west, about seventy kilometres along the Malatya–Kayersi road, will take you to the beautifully situated little town of Elbistan, fifty-four kilometres from this turning along a motorable road, and on the upper Ceyhan river, that reaches the sea near Adana. The valley here produces good crops of rice and sugar-beet. Elbistan has been a very important centre of Turkish trade and culture and was the capital city of the Dulkader Turks in the fourteenth and fifteenth centuries. It has a number of interesting ruined mosques and *hans*, the most important buildings being the Ulu Cami and the Himmet Baba Cami. It is immediately backed by the Şehir Dağ, the City Mountain, on the western spur of which stands the fine castle known to the Turks as Kız Kalesi, Girl Castle. At Karahüyük in the Elbistan plain, not to be confused with Karahüyük near Konya, also a Hittite site, Hittite hieroglyphics and cuneiform writing have been found in excavated mounds.

Erzincan and Altıntepe

Erzincan can be reached by road, rail or air direct from Istanbul and Ankara. It can also be reached by road from the south. There are not many ways of driving from the southern half of eastern Anatolia to the northern. One, which has already been traced, is through Van, Patnos and Eleşkirt to Erzurum. Another, the E99, from Elazığ to Erzincan, goes through some of the most beautiful mountain scenery in Turkey and is regularly done by cars and buses, except when blocked by snow. I am not sure what will happen to this road and its bridge over the Murat River at Pertek once the Keban Dam is completed and the waters rise here. Slightly off this road and about half way across to the Erzurum road is the town of Tunceli, which used to be called Dersim, then Kalan, and has now been given the name of the province of which it is the capital. There is little to detain the traveller in this town today but it has a couple of possible hotels which could make it the base for a short fishing holiday. I haven't fished here myself but the streams of this province, particularly the Munzur Suyu and the Pulumur Suyu, are said to swarm with trout. And though this is a very mountainous region, there are some very fertile valleys where volcanic soil produces good grain, vegetables, cotton and sugar-beet. Ovacık, the Little Meadow, over to the west from our road and walled with wild mountains, is such a place. Immediately north of Ovacık there are natural pine forests and springs of very good fizzy water in the Munzur Mountains. And at Pulumur, on our road northwards, there are hot springs (Kaplıca-lar). Before reaching Pulumur the many-tunnelled road follows the gorge of the Pulumur River for many miles. Altogether this could be marvellous country for an unspoilt rambling, fishing, camping holiday. Climbing too, for the Munzur Mountains offer little-known and, for the experienced climber, not difficult peaks up to 3,300 metres.[1] From Pulumur the road drops down to the road and railway at Tanyeri, where one turns west for Erzincan, east for Erzurum.

Erzincan is today a new town rebuilt after the fearful earthquake which destroyed it in 1939. But it is a very old site, the centre of a fertile plain in its circle of mountains, with the upper Euphrates flowing through it. In ancient times it was called Aziris and then corrupted to Erzingan by the Turkoman invaders of the eleventh century before it became the modern Erzincan (pronounced Erzinjan). It is on one of the great trade routes between East and West. Marco Polo went this way and praised the wool, the weaving and the copper craftsmanship of the region. Erzincan still has excellent workers in copper as well as industries, including a great sugar refinery for the recently extended cultivation of sugar-beet. Evliya Çelebi said that in the seventeenth century Erzincan had seventy mosques and in the nineteenth century it was thought to be one of the most beautiful cities of Asia.

At the end of the third century A.D. King Tiridates of Armenia was converted to Christianity and made this the official religion of Armenia. He and St. Gregory toured the country destroying the shrines of Mithras and endowing the new church with the wealth of the pagan temples. This campaign culminated in St. Gregory's destruction of the golden statue of the goddess Anahid at Erzincan and of the Mithraic temples there. St. Gregory, known as the Illuminator, spent his last years as an anchorite near Erzincan and was buried near the village of Tortan. At the end of the nineteenth century Armenians still numbered about one-sixth of the population of Erzincan.

The town has had a not entirely fortunate history for the Turks, for the Seljuks were defeated here by the Mongols in 1243 and as a result became dependants of the Ilhan rulers of Persia. During the First World War Erzincan was occupied by the Russians for eighteen months in 1916–18 and then in 1939 came the obliterating earthquake.

ALTINTEPE

The important Urartian site of Altıntepe (Gold Hill) is near the road and railway about half way between Erzincan and the junction with the road from Tunceli at Tanyeri. The discovery came when a tomb

[1] See Appendix on climbing, pp. 237–8.

was found in a cutting made for the railway in 1938; and since 1959 Turkish archaeologists have recovered a wealth of objects and of knowledge about Urartian life and architecture. These less disturbed and fuller finds at Altıntepe have helped to explain the significance of remains at the other Urartian sites of eastern Anatolia and are an alarming indication of what may have been smuggled abroad as a result of permitted excavation, quite apart from peasant pot-hunting. As elsewhere, the masonry here is exact and well trimmed. The tombs built into the side of the hill are vaulted in stone and have several little rooms. In one completely undisturbed tomb a man and a woman were found in stone sarcophagi. The woman had been buried in all her finery of clothes and jewellery and with her favourite household things in gold, bronze, pottery and wood. Weapons were found too, mostly of iron, and equipment for horses and chariots. The Urartians loved horses and a winged horse engraved on a bronze belt found here is a prototype of Pegasus. Another prototype, and the ultimate source of a household or ritual object, which the hellenised Aegean coast later popularised and the Romans vulgarised at Pompeii, is a splendid bronze cauldron standing on a three-legged iron stand. The cauldron has four bull's head handles and the stand has the cloven-hoof feet regularly associated with this piece of furniture in classical times.[1] (The Altıntepe cauldron is now in the Ankara Hittite Museum.) The popularity of this originally beautiful conception shows a curious progression, or to my mind recession, in the history of taste and a monograph on it could throw light on other sources and lines of development in art and architecture, apart from the evolution of domestic monstrosities. Similar Urartian cauldrons found at Gordion are evidence of trade with the Phrygians.

Bronze belts engraved with horses, human beings and gods, similar to those found at other Urartian sites, were found at Altıntepe, as well as lovely gold filigree and pottery which seems to imitate things originally made of bronze.[2] The tombs are dated about 700 B.C. and all these interesting objects are presumably of about that date too.

The discovery of the tombs led to the investigation of the hilltop fortress above and here again important finds have been made. A temple, a palace and a great hall are more complete here than at less fortunate

[1] See J. M. Cook, *The Greeks in Ionia and the East*, for later forms of this object.
[2] See Piotrovskii, op. cit., for these and similar objects found at Karmir Blur and other sites.

sites. The temple is small, built of mud-brick on a foundation of very well cut masonry, like that of Cavuş Tepe, with a courtyard that might have been roofed and with traces of mural painting within. More complete and once brightly coloured murals were found in another building. The immense assembly hall had a roof supported by three rows of wooden columns and probably had a pediment-shaped gable end or frontage.[1] Professor Tahsin Özgüç has revealed spacious houses with three to six rooms on terraces below the hilltop temple site. The tombs are on a terrace to the south-east.[2] The citadel at Altıntepe, whatever it was called in its great days, must have been the administrative centre of the north-western region of the Urartian empire. Was it from here that the cultural leap to Europe was made, the trek to the coast and the sea journey to Etruria and the Etruscan foundation to much that was good in Rome? The path from Altıntepe to Rome and Florence has seen more than the passage of a three-legged cauldron.

[1] See Seton Lloyd, op. cit., Fig. 130.   [2] *A.J.A.*, vol. 72, no. 2, p. 212.

Divriği

Divriği, in the wild upper reaches of a western branch of the Euphrates, is best reached by train and no one travelling in eastern Anatolia is likely to attempt it in an ordinary car unless in the meantime the rough mountain road from Sivas to Elazığ has been re-made. You could, of course, buy a seat in a minibus or jeep *dolmuş* from Sivas.

Originally Tephrike, of which Divriği is a Turkish corruption, and a Byzantine stronghold, it became the centre of the Paulician heresy which was persecuted by Byzantium but encouraged by the Arabs as a rift in the Christian front. It was taken by the Byzantines in 872 and an end was put to the Paulicians, who were thought to have Manichean tendencies. Divriği was occupied by the Seljuks after Maznikert and ruled by the Menguçoğullar dynasty and beautified with some of the most lovely and unusual of Seljuk buildings. The Mongols spared the mosques and *medreses* when they took the town in the thirteenth century but they dismantled the citadel which towers above the town. It then came under the emirs of Sivas and was taken for the Ottomans by Selim I in 1516.

For the seventeenth-century traveller Evliya Çelebi, Divriği was chiefly remarkable for its cats. He writes, 'In the lands of the Rum (i.e. the Byzantines), the Arabs and the Persians there are no cats like those of Divriği, which are beautiful, playful and lovable. They hunt and they are generally well behaved. The cats of Egypt, Trabzon and Sinop are also famous but these cats of Divriği are fat and big and their fur is as good as that of the otter and very colourful. They take these cats as gifts to the *vilayet* of Erdebil in the land of Persia, where market criers carry them on their heads in cages and sell them to the highest bidders. Some of the bankrupt *kadis* (judges) of Divriği are great misers and they have fifty to sixty of these cats killed every year to provide them with fur. The fur has a reddish shade and cannot be distinguished from the famous squirrel fur of the land of Moscow.'[1]

Even if you don't spot a Divriği cat of the right colour there's a good deal to see so long as architecture interests you. Within the ruined citadel there is a mosque built in a fine reddish stone about the year 1180 by the Menguç ruler Seif et Tin. In the town the two most important buildings are the Ulu Cami and the adjoining Hospital, both of the early thirteenth century, the latter at the command and expense of Turan Malik, daughter of the Emir Behram Şah. The main entrance to the mosque is by the north door, which is surrounded by a rich decoration of plant forms and abstract shapes in high relief, closer to Armenian and even Far Eastern stone carving than Seljuk work usually is. The interior has a roof supported by four rows of columns, the basic *ulu cami* form. The *mihrab* is also extraordinarily opulent in its stone carving. The decoration of the Hospital is equally rich and its complex plan of great interest.

I have said that Divriği is best reached by train and anyone fond of wild country should once do the train journey from Sivas to Erzurum. From Sivas the line runs up the Tecer valley, tributary of the Kizilirmak, then climbs through the mountains before dropping down into the valley of the Çaltı Su, tributary of the Euphrates. At the top of the pass, near a little station called Kara Göl, Black Lake, there is a little circular lake obviously full of trout. I have never seen so many rings made by rising fish early in the morning of an autumn day. The train hurtles by groups of neat, mud-plastered houses with domes of hay and cow-dung fuel cakes perched on the corners of the roofs. At Çetinkaya there are great mounds of iron ore ready for transport to the new steelworks at Karabük, a long way to the west. Down past Divriği to the junction with the Euphrates the country is savagely wild, treeless and almost uninhabited. So also up the Euphrates to Kemah no road to speak of accompanies the railway until we join a reasonably good road from Kemah to Erzincan and Erzurum. A deep wild gorge hardly encourages human passage or habitation but did provide a way through the mountains and up to the Erzurum plain for the railway engineers. Kemah is built against a cliff, with the remains of an ancient castle around the flat-topped towering hill. There are a few trees near the river but the colour here comes from rock and earth, ash-grey, ochre and green. To the south one gets exciting glimpses of the snow-topped peaks of

[1] *Seyahat Name*, vol. III, p. 213.

Munzur Dağ. Road and rail level out to the great high plain of Erzincan in its ring of mountains and then together wind up the upper Euphrates valley, here known as the Kaṛa Su, Black Water, for a hundred kilometres before separating to cross the Dumanlı Mountains and reach the even higher plain of Erzurum at Aşkale.

34. *Diyarbakır: the Tigris from the walls*

5. *Minaret at Diyarbakır*

36. *Erzurum: interior of Ç*
    Minare Medrese

37. *Doğubeyazit: Ishak P*
    Saray and old village

Erzurum

From Altıntepe road and railway follow the narrowing Euphrates eastwards, against its flow of course, separate to find their several ways through the Dumanlı mountains, then rejoin each other at the high plateau level of Askale, where there is a ruined castle and a fine Seljuk *han*. At Ilica, seven kilometres from Erzurum, there are hot springs and a huge new sugar factory. The airport is over to the left as we approach the town across the plain.

Erzurum has a situation which has made it important in war and trade, since it can control one of the great routes between the West and Asia. It is for this reason probably that it has been occupied by the Russians on two occasions during the past hundred years. It is a natural stage in the land route between Trabzon (Trebizond) and Persia and as early as 1690 there was a British commercial agent stationed here. At the end of the nineteenth century Lynch reported that between thirty and forty thousand head of camels annually passed through the city, bearing goods loaded and to be unloaded at Trabzon for the sea journey to Istanbul and Europe. Now a railway line and an air service link Erzurum with the rest of Turkey but the road to Trabzon is still an important connection with the ships of the Turkish Denizyollari which call regularly there. Buses leave Erzurum daily for Tabriz in Iran.

The first known name of the city is Theodosiopolis, after the Byzantine Emperor Theodosius II who fortified it as an outer bastion of his empire at the beginning of the fifth century A.D. The Armenians knew it as Karin. It may also have been the Arzen which existed in this part and which was known as Arzen Rum (Roman, meaning Greek) by the Arabs to distinguish it from other towns known as Erzen or Arzen.[1] Or it may have been called Arzer Rum, the Land of

[1] See Lynch, op. cit., II, p. 223.

the Greeks (Romans),[1] by the first Turkoman invaders and this credibly gives us Erzurum.

Apart from the walls of the citadel there is nothing in Erzurum which predates the Seljuk conquest of the eleventh century. The Armenians have since that time been in the minority in the town and have never erected any notable buildings there. A number of severe earthquakes have damaged or destroyed buildings over the centuries. But in spite of earthquakes and Russian bombardment there is still architecture of great beauty left in Erzurum.

The Armenians are said to have considered Erzurum a second Garden of Eden and a visit in early summer might do something to justify that view, but to anyone coming from a kindlier, less violent climate it seems to be a city which never quite recovers from winter. The first snow comes in October and for five or six months from mid or late November the ground is snow covered. Even in early November water from the washing of cars and horse carriages freezes into glaciers which make it hazardous to cross streets. Spice is added to university life by the wolves which range the campus in the winter months. Yet there's plenty of water and great heat during the short summer and gardens could flourish here almost as well as at Van but for this apparent abandonment of the population to the depression of winter. Evliya Çelebi's famous story of the cat which was frozen on its way home over the rooftops in November and came to a brief life again in April typifies this attitude. Trees have recently been planted along the new boulevard as a gesture of faith in the possiblity of greenness and summer shade, but the drabness of the town is being accentuated by the new tendency to roof new buildings with corrugated sheets painted black. Erzurum would be the better for the red tiles which have such a pleasant and unifying effect on the domestic architecture of western Turkish towns. But the flat mud roofs of the old houses make for an interesting vista of steppe terraces from which minarets and domes rise uncluttered. Each earth roof has its roller of marble or sandstone for use after rain and with this care the roofs provide good insulation against heat and cold. In summer grass grows on them and they are used for fattening sheep and keeping poultry. A good view of these roofs is from the wall of the citadel.

Erzurum has always been famous for its craftsmen and you can still

[1] A confusion which arose from the fact that Byzantion, the Eastern Roman Empire, was in fact Greek.

buy things handmade in leather, iron, copper, brass, silver and gold. The market quarter is to the south of the citadel and downhill from the Çifte Minare. The carriage lamps and samovars are good and a speciality of Erzurum jewellers is the setting of jet, known here as *Oltu taş*, in gold. The jet is obtained from Oltu, in the mountains to the north-east, and this handmade jewellery is incredibly cheap.

The citadel, now released from military occupation, is perhaps the best point from which to begin a tour of the important buildings, since you see them from above and get a sense of the arrangement of the city and of its position in relation to the plain and the mountains. The citadel walls were originally erected by Theodosius II and there was also an outer wall which enclosed all the main parts of the town but which has now almost completely disappeared. The open court-yard of this commanding building has been cleared and the storerooms along the western wall are being restored. I cannot report whether the threatened municipal café has been installed here but if it has I hope that the prevailing odour of spices hasn't entirely succumbed to redecoration and that the carved wooden pillars that supported the roof haven't been replaced by ugly modern structures. This citadel was for long years the stronghold in eastern Turkey of the dreaded Janis-saries, the instruments of Ottoman power, and Lynch says that the only time a pasha of Erzurum ever entered it was to have his head cut off.[1]

The thirteenth-century Seljuk tower in the north-eastern corner was given a wooden belfry and clockhouse early in the nineteenth century. The bell, cast at Croydon, is still there but the clock, of which the inhabitants were once inordinately proud, though it never went well,[2] is said to have been taken away by the Russians in 1830. Removal by the Russians is a handy explanation in Erzurum for any-thing that has gone. Near the tower, steps lead up to the roof of the storerooms and to the top of the wall with its view of the town. Here too is a fine cone-shaped Seljuk tomb and one can look through the little windows down into the mosque below.

Downhill from the citadel are the conspicuous Çifte Minare Medrese, the theological school of the Twin Minarets, and the less visible Ulu Cami. The Ulu Cami was built in 1179 for the Saltıkoğlu Turkoman

---

[1] op. cit., II, p. 210.

[2] James Morier reports that the clock was striking 'with sufficient regularity in 1809'. *A Journey through Persia, Armenia and Asia Minor to Constantinople*, London, 1812, p. 322.

Chieftain Melik Mehmet. It is a severe, squat building covering a great area of ground, for it measures fifty-four by forty-one metres, with a flat roof upheld, until it fell in, by columns forming seven long naves. It is in a dangerous state of repair and was not open to the public whilst I was at Erzurum. Its walls are plain and undecorated, except for an unusual architectural feature, a huge round column built into the back left-hand corner of the exterior.

In great contrast to this primitive solidity is the splendid frontage of the nearby Çifte Minare Medrese built for the Seljuk Alaettin Keykubad in 1253, one of the masterpieces of Seljuk art. Set off by the flat masonry of the walls is a high stalactite doorway surrounded by a rectangular sequence of scroll work in stone, the top part of which has recently been restored. The sides of the doorway are flanked by great bastions of masonry which support the twin minarets, with panels at the foot of each bastion carrying a stylised branch in high relief. The minarets are of fluted brickwork, with eighteen narrow pilasters rising to the cap and with typical turquoise-blue Seljuk tiles worked into them. Lynch found this use of brick with stone 'an architectural solecism' but for me it is an Urartian device raised to a very high point of balance and beauty. So true is the balance achieved that I find it hard to believe the story one is told in Erzurum that the minarets are unfinished, and the reason why. According to this one minaret was being built by the master architect and the other by his apprentice. One day the master saw that his pupil had outdone him and he threw himself from the point his minaret had reached down on to the flagstones below. When he learnt the reason for his master's suicide the apprentice threw himself from his minaret. At that stage the minarets were given their conical caps and left without a muezzin's balcony.

At the far end of this building is a huge tomb, the Hatuniye Türbe, built for herself in 1255 by a daughter of Alaettin Keykubad. The main building, the theological school, was for years a military store but it has now been released and cleared and the beauty and balance of the interior can be appreciated, a courtyard with a covered walk along its sides with pointed arches opening out and a corresponding gallery above.[1] The central part of the courtyard was open to the sky and all round it are the rooms where the students lived. Chillier even in winter than the two quads I had to walk through at Oxford to get a bath. Some of the little rooms, on the right-hand side as you enter, now

[1] See Plate 36.

house a fascinating little museum, with interesting and sometimes puzzling local finds of all periods. I was shown a lovely alabaster model used by masons when they cut cornices and the inside of arched door-ways. The curator said there used to be more of these but the Russians took them. There are curious sculptures and a terracotta sarcophagus which seems in its decoration to imitate a cremation coffin of woven reeds. This too has signs of fire around one of the holes in the lid and may itself have been used for cremation.

Behind the Hatuniye Türbe, in an open space where children play, there are three restored and rather highly coloured Seljuk tombs which are to me slightly comic. I expect them to begin to move about, like something in a cartoon film, rather pretty Daleks.

Slightly downhill from a garden near the middle of the new boule-vard is the very remarkable Yakutiye Medrese and minaret built in 1308 during the occupation of Erzurum by the Ilhan Mongol rulers of Persia. The now topless minaret is on a circular stone base and has a boldly interlaced pattern of brickwork and blue tiles. The entrance is a low arched doorway in a stalactite recess within a tall rectangular frontage lined with scrolled stonework. The ground level has risen outside it and now gives it an unnecessarily subterranean look. The interior is more unusual and amounts to a rare architectural experience. The central area is covered by a square dome raised on pillars of masonry and capped with a square cage to let in light. The light is beautifully caught by high-relief stone carving of stalactite type but giving a rich floral effect inside the dome. To look up to this sudden beauty takes one's breath away. Until recently and since it was abandoned by teachers of religion and their students, this building too was an army storehouse, but it has now been happily released from this unworthy use.

Downhill again from here, on the winding street that takes you down to the hotels, restaurants and vegetable market, a very impressive *han* with severe walls and conical corner turrets was being restored but I have not been able to discover its date of construction.

Off the main boulevard, not far from the point where we started downhill for the Yakutiye Medrese, is the Ottoman mosque of Lala Mustafa Paşa, built in 1563 by a governor of that name to plans by the great Sinan. A public garden in front of it sets off its well-proportioned arcaded frontage, cupolas and central dome. The minaret is modestly stubby and I should be surprised to hear that it is the work of Sinan, whose minarets are usually of an unrivalled elegance.

Erzurum

The University of Erzurum, a state institution founded in 1958 and growing steadily, is a partial fulfilment of Ataturk's dream of a university for eastern Anatolia. He himself wished this to be at Van and many people today think that Van would have been a happier site for it. It has been difficult to staff the new university. The winter is so severe and entertainment so limited in Erzurum that university teachers trained at Ankara and Istanbul are reluctant to go there, unless they are dedicated to archaeology, agricultural experiment or the medical problems of such a region. The result is that outside these three fields the level of teaching and achievement is apt to be a good deal lower than at the older universities. The Faculty of Agriculture has 10,000 acres (about 4,000 hectares) for research and is linked to the University of Nebraska in the U.S.A., an arrangement which has brought enthusiastic scholars and teachers to this remote centre. It has sought to improve stock, by breeding in new strains of cattle, sheep and poultry, and crops by the introduction and development of new types of wheat and potato suited to the altitude and short summer. Sugar-beet growing and beekeeping have been encouraged. The main difficulty has been to persuade the inhabitants of the region, mostly Kurds today, to depend less on their old pastoral ways and to do some farming, to become food suppliers for the big cities rather than just follow their age-old practice of only growing what they needed to eat and depending on the sale of horses or cattle for the purchase of their other requirements. Open days are arranged on the university farms and local people are encouraged to visit them to see what can be done with their land. A recent rector of this university was ideally suited to the job, since he bred horses and lived on his own farm outside Erzurum, while keeping in touch with the cultural life of western Turkey.

I imagine I must be the only person ever to have given a public lecture on Shakespeare in English at Erzurum. I went expecting a small audience of people who understood English and were interested in drama, an atmosphere in which I could cosily air my rather unconventional view of the Bard. Nothing of the kind, for this was a showing of the flag of culture rather than a moment for the communication of knowledge or ideas. It didn't really matter what I said since a large part of the considerable audience in the great university hall didn't understand a word of English. I had hardly begun to speak when a murmur in the back rows, high above my eye level, grew into quite a hubbub and the makings, I thought, of a riot. The front rows of important people seemed prepared to ignore this commotion but a member of the English Department came forward to tell me that the protest was because the microphone wasn't working and they couldn't hear me at the back. I said I didn't need the microphone and that if they kept quiet they would hear me perfectly well. An electrician, or at least someone prepared to fiddle with the wires, now climbed on to the dais and began to work at my feet, out of sight of the audience but making it very difficult for me. I now re-started, raising my voice a little to reach the highest level of the theatre. At this the students in the back rows got up, marched noisily down the hall towards me and left, uttering remarks which I didn't understand, by the big doors on either side of me. I learnt later that the reason for their protest was that the lecture was in English and that it was the afternoon of November 10th, the anniversary of Ataturk's death. An insult therefore to the memory of the great man and something I should have wished to avoid, for I had not suggested the date. I ruthlessly cut short my talk, a brief translation of its main points was read and the occasion was considered a success by all except a Dutch journalist I had met on the train a few days earlier and who was horrified at the whole of the proceedings. After experiences in Egypt I hadn't found it especially disturbing.

Erzurum has a pioneering air today and seems to be not quite certain of itself. Its people are famous for their taciturnity but their commercial prosperity must be assured by the growing importance of the town as the centre of a region which is certain to develop agriculturally and touristically. You will eat well in this capital of a pastoral area. Meat, butter and cheese are very good, as are the potatoes, cabbages and turnips, but you will miss the variety of fruit, vegetables and salads common in western Turkey. The local *bastırma*, meat sun-dried in a paste of spices, is famous. The tanneries of Erzurum provide leather for saddles and boots that are highly valued all over Turkey. It is a town which is very close to the earth it lives on. Horse-drawn vehicles are more frequent than motors in its streets and the smell of horse dung is more powerful than petrol fumes. The ox-drawn cart unashamedly takes its time up the middle of the street to the market. With its excellent air and these country odours, Erzurum smells a good deal better than it looks. Erzurum always seems to have enjoyed a rustic air. James Morier, after his visit in 1809, wrote, 'The streets are mostly paved; but, as in Turkey, in that manner which is more calculated to break the passenger's neck than to ease his feet.'[1] It had then only three churches, two Armenian and one Greek, and very many mosques. It was, however, capable of some sophisticated elegance. He enjoyed, 'a dinner under tents at the Büyükdere meadow, and a ball and supper at night, in a house borrowed for the purpose.'[2] On his second visit, a few years later, he writes of the Governor of that day, a former prize-fighter and wrestler who has risen as a soldier, and comments, 'We never find the Turks ashamed of their origin, however great may be the rank to which they may afterwards attain.'[3]

[1] ibid., p. 321.   [2] ibid., p. 365.
[3] *A Second Journey through Persia, Armenia and Asia Minor*, London, 1818, p. 400.

Eastwards from Erzurum

A fine new road rises eastwards from the Erzurum plain over a low pass known as the Camel's Back and descends into a tributary valley of the Aras (ancient Araxes) River and the fertile plain of Pasinler. Pasinler is well treed and green and is known for its curative water and hot springs. A new hotel has been built there at the springs and the domes of its Turkish baths are visible from the road. But it seems to me an unlikely place for a Turk or a tourist to go for a cure, though it might prove rewarding in its very remoteness, calm and simplicity. And for anyone travelling by road to or from Iran it might be a very pleasant place to clean up and rest in. The domestic architecture of the town is primitive and rural, the flat roofs and mud-plastered chimneys sometimes level with the road, like the semi-troglodyte dwellings in which the country people here live out the winter snugly enough. Living underground is an old practice in these parts and Xenophon, having travelled through this country in the snow, described how animals and poultry were kept there too and fed over the winter with hay and grain kept indoors.[1] It was in one of these houses that Xenophon first drank beer, which he called barley wine, sucked up from great bowls with straws or reeds, yet another ancient custom of Anatolian origin.

Near the town and overlooking the road is the fine castle of Hasan Kale, an Armenian fortress restored by a certain Uzun Hasan after the Turkoman conquest of the eleventh century but now in a ruined condition and offering little of interest to the traveller apart from its domination of the highway. A road from Pasinler goes southwards to join the rather better road which runs from Çobandede Bridge down to Varto and Muş. Köprüköy, near Çobandede, has a pool of curative

[1] op. cit., IV, 5.24.

water where people go to bathe and then dry off in the sun, a double therapy which is good for rheumatism. A village in the hills near here has a noted thief-catcher who sniffs the ground and follows tracks, pretends to have second sight and puts two and two together in successful detection of criminals. The advantage he offers over the police and the law is that he actually recovers and restores the stolen goods—much more important surely to the one who is robbed than the punishment of the thief, often without the recovery of the property. You should pause at Çobandede (shepherd grandfather) Bridge to admire the fine Seljuk stonework and to wonder whether you will ever take the winding road through the wild bandit country of the Bingöl Mountains down to Muş through earthquake-shattered Varto.

You must make another choice at Horasan, for one road and the railway turn left towards Kars whilst the main road to Iran climbs the 2,475 metre Tahir Pass. It is worth pausing before you reach the top of this pass for the splendid view of mountains to the south and west.[1] The road drops to the village of Tahir and soon to Eleşkirt (once Armenian Alashkert). Once from this road near Tahir I saw a party of bride-seekers on their way to the village, a spirited Kurdish cavalcade led by two mounted women with four men behind. They would enquire into the character and family background of a young girl sought as wife for a young man of their family. The young man might have seen the girl at a market or a well and the terms of the marriage would now be arranged if all proved suitable.

Eleşkirt is an important shopping centre for the mountain Kurds. Groups of taciturn men in patched suits and caps stand about while their women busy themselves with huge bundles wrapped in cloth and with what window-shopping this miserable place offers. Oxen which draw the wooden disk-wheeled carts are resting before the laborious return home.[2] There are trees and some gardens and to the north towers the tremendous hump of Köse Dağ, the bald or bare mountain.

I found the next town, Karaköse, a good stopping point and the Acar Oteli there clean and cheap. (Acar, pronounced Ajar with stress on the first a, means brave, self-reliant.) The name of the town has recently been changed to Ağrı, in line with the unfortunate practice of giving up an old name and knowing the chief town of a *vilayet* by the name of the district. Ağrı is the Turkish form of the ancient name Ararat

---

[1] Plate 10. [2] Plate 8.

and means pain or ache, and the Turks have no love for Ağrı Dağ, Mount Ararat. Karaköse or Ağrı is a convenient base if you are planning to spend some time in the Ararat area. The grilled meat in the restaurants is excellent and the butter served with your simple breakfast at the pastrycook's across the road from the Acar Hotel is as good as any in the world, fresh creamy stuff. Three kilometres out of the town is the village of Küpkıran, which is said to offer excellent skiing; but I am unable to recommend any dwelling where you could keep warm at night, unless there are chalets at Küpkıran or you are invited into some snug semi-underground dwelling. This is a very cold part and a temperature of minus 43 Centigrade was recorded here in October 1940. In contrast, July 1957 gave a reading of 37 plus. A good place to do your Xmas shopping, however. On the street there I was offered a fine live white goose for ten liras. Even if you don't stay there you should certainly stop for a meal in one of the restaurants in the street which runs north from the main crossroads of the town.

ARARAT

After Karaköse one just looks out for the first glimpse of Mount Ararat and there's little to distract one from this interest. If you are lucky enough to get a first sight on a cloudless day of this permanently snow-covered volcanic cone, which increasingly dominates the land-scape as you approach Doğubeyazit, it is something you will not forget. In summer the snow line retreats up the mountain but after the autumn snowfalls the mountain is white down to the fearful band of broken lava that rings its lower flanks. The volcano has long been dormant, for two thousand years or more, and it appears deceptively easy to climb. But remember that when you look at it from the roadside you are probably at least twenty-five kilometres away from it. Its flanks are not as smooth as they look and the lower zone of broken lava is frightfully difficult to negotiate. The Turks believe that it cannot be climbed and my friends at Erzurum University begged me not to attempt it. I had no intention of doing so, but a young Oxford man who set out to climb it alone a few years ago disappeared without trace. When James Morier saw it on his travels early in the nineteenth century it had not been climbed. He writes, 'Nothing can be more beautiful than its shape, more awful than its height. All the surrounding moun-tains sink into insignificance when compared to it. It is perfect in all its parts, no hard rugged feature, no unnatural prominences, everything is in harmony, all combines to render it one of the sublimest objects in nature. . . . No one since the flood seems to have been on its summit, for the rapid ascent of its snowy top would appear to render such an attempt impossible. . . . We were informed that people have reached the top of the small Ararat (or, as it is called here, *Chuchuk Agri dagh*); but as all the account which they brought back was a tale (like that told of Savalan) about a frozen man and a cold fountain, we must be permitted to disbelieve every report on the subject which we have hitherto heard from the natives.'[1] But of course it has been climbed, first of all from the north-west by a Professor F. Parrot and his companions in October 1829, then by a number of German, Russian and British mountaineers and recently by Turks as well.[2] But it is a dangerous mountain, not to be attempted alone and without advice and preparation. Falls of rock, sudden changes of weather bringing fierce winds and mist, the hazards of snow, ice and the tremendous boulders of volcanic rock, all these call for care, circumspection and physical toughness. Neither Lynch nor Warkworth has anything to say about the wild beasts which are said to inhabit the mountain but the leopards and great snakes are unlikely to be entirely mythical. Lynch has an account of a fearful earthquake which occurred on the mountain in 1840. There hasn't been a bad one since but a smell of sulphur still hangs about the mountain and it may still have a surprise in store.

Armenian tradition dating back to the third century A.D. gives Ararat as the landing place of the Ark, at a point between Ararat and Little Ararat. But when we are reminded that the kingdom of Urartu, or Ararat as the Prophet Jeremiah calls it (Jer. 51:4), extended southwards to the upper limits of Mesopotamia, we realise that a far-sighted character like Noah might well have escaped by boat from the Flood, which Sir Leonard Woolley has found evidence of, and come to shore on the foot-hills to the north of wherever Noah lived.[3] In spite of this, there are people who search for and claim to find and even photograph traces of the Ark at this most unlikely height. The summit of Ararat is 5,165 metres above sea level, nearly 17,000 feet; Little Ararat, a more perfect volcanic cone on the flank of the great mountain and to the east

[1] *A Second Journey through Persia, Armenia and Asia Minor*, London, 1818, pp. 312–13.

[2] See Lynch, op. cit., I, p. 199; D. C. Hills, *My Travels in Turkey*, Chap. 7; and Appendix on climbing, pp. 238–40.

[3] See Lynch, op. cit., I, p. 197.

of the summit, is 3,925 metres high. The Armenians know the mountain as Masis.

The main road comes nearest to Ararat at Doğubeyazit and about a kilometre south of the present village is the old village and the fortress-palace of Ishak Paşa, the Ishak Paşa Saray. The old village is scattered over the slope rising up to the palace and looks like an ancient ruin today, chiefly because the roof timbers and all the woodwork have been removed.[1] The village was destroyed and its population dispersed by the Turkish Government because of its involvement in a Kurdish revolt against the Ataturk régime, in 1930. A photograph taken by Lord Warkworth in 1897 shows it as quite a little township built around the road that winds up to the palace, flat-roofed houses, built of stone and mud-plastered, with the usual huge stacks of cow-dung cakes on the roofs for winter fuel. There were many Armenians living here at that time but by 1930 it was entirely Kurdish. The new roadside hovel township of Doğubeyazit has replaced it and is still Kurdish in character. It's a very ancient site, due no doubt to its commanding position on the road from Anatolia to Iran and the East. The ridge above it has an Urartian fortress and there are relief carvings and cuneiform inscriptions on the rock face. But the present fantastic fortress dates from the late seventeenth and early eighteenth century and thus predates other bold and fanciful attempts to recapture and combine older architectural styles, such as Horace Walpole's Strawberry Hill and Thomas Johnes's Hafod. The whole structure has an exotic air, a Xanadu of the Ararat region. Here the architect brought together Ottoman, Seljuk, Armenian, Georgian and Persian elements, making it fun to spot the sources and wonder at the juxtapositions. But there's nothing shocking or really offensive to taste in all this and one forms the strong impression that it must have been a pleasant and interesting place to live in. It has been a Turkish army barracks and the Russians have occupied it at different times and are said locally to have been responsible for the signs of cooking left in rooms designed for more elegant and serious purposes. Restoration carried out in 1956 has ensured the preservation of this happy anachronism in its present state at least for the immediate future. It has all the features of a Turkish *saray*, inner and outer courtyards, guardrooms and servants' quarters, mosque, kitchens, Turkish bath, harem, court-room and reception room. The last must have been a fine though perhaps draughty salon

---

[1] Plate 37.

for it once had mirrors all along its walls to catch and re-convey sunlight from a hole in its ceiling. Of course this hole might have been glazed. The mosque still has much of its original decoration in the stone carving of ceiling and columns, some paintwork and the original lamp chains. The acoustics are marvellous, strengthening and deepening the voice, and it's worth getting someone to go up the stone steps to the *mimber* to demonstrate this. No offence will be given as the mosque is no longer in use for worship and is hardened to much more desecration than this. You can also go up the steps to the balcony of the minaret for a view of the layout of the palace. Otherwise the view is little different from what you get from the fortress walls. Living at such a height in relation to the village and travellers along the road must have generated a kind of megalomania in the Kurdish bey who built the palace, and this is best demonstrated by the position of the master's water-closet. This has an open window, high up in the sheer wall which overlooks village and road. Squatting there, face towards the window and the western spur of Ararat, Ishak Pasha must have felt that he was doing it on the world. A cleverly devised water system flushed the conventional oriental marble slab down the outside wall. Hygienic and contemptuous.

Across the little ravine to the east of the palace more fortifications and a little mosque can be made out with some difficulty because of the identical colour of rock and buildings. An ancient fortress was rebuilt here by the Genoese to protect their trade route from Trebizond to Persia and the Far East in the thirteenth and fourteenth centuries and this was used for the same purpose by the Turks, who changed the little Genoese church to a mosque and added the minaret.

DOĞUBEYAZIT

Unless something new has been built in Doğubeyazit or its frontier post with Iran since I was there, the flat-roofed, drab little town has nothing else to delay or delight the traveller, unless he wants to hear Kurdish spoken and drink a glass of tea. The tea at the teahouse (men only but they would probably not object to an accompanied foreign woman decently dressed to their eyes) is excellent and they told me that it is smuggled from Iran and blended with tea from the Black Sea coast of Turkey. After some whispering and comings and goings to the hole in the wall through which the glasses of tea were served I was able to buy a tin of this smuggled Persian tea. We still use the tin as a tea caddy, liking the gaiety of its pictures, a man working in the fields on the lid and a luscious girl with a basket on one side, but the tea turned out to be poor, dusty stuff. My Iranian doctorate student completed my disillusionment back in Istanbul by telling me that in Iran they always drank Indian tea and by bringing me a packet which made excellent brews.

Kars

After Horasan both road and railway from Erzurum veer north-eastwards to follow the Aras River for a few kilometres before swinging northwards to Kara-urgan. They then negotiate the skirts of the 2,800 metre Çamdar Dağ, and pass pine-forested Sarıkamiş, 2,100 metres above sea level, once a resort of the Tsar of Russia and today a winter sports centre, to come down to the upland plain of Kars. This plain is drained by many tributaries of the Arpa Çayi, the Barley River, itself a tributary of the Aras (Araxes) which curves round southwards to form the boundary here between Turkey and Soviet Russia. Kars itself is 1,750 metres above sea level. The name is probably from the Georgian *kari*, meaning gate, and the valley of the Kars River is one of the ways through the mountains of north-eastern Anatolia. The railway line goes on to make the link with the Russian system.

The strategic importance of Kars has led to its changing hands often in the course of history. It has seen most of the invaders of Anatolia and it was for many centuries an important Armenian centre. Alp Arslan took it for the Seljuks in 1064 as a prelude to the conquest of central Anatolia, and early in the thirteenth century it became part of the kingdom of Georgia. During the past hundred and fifty years it has several times been occupied by the Russians and Kars's moment of glory came in 1855, during the Crimean War, when a Turkish force of 15,000, with a British general called Williams and British officers and a doctor, withstood starvation and a large Russian force for five months.[1] The town was restored to Turkey at the end of the war but was taken again by the Russians in 1878 and held by them until 1920, when they were driven out by the Turks. Lynch visited Kars while it was in Russian hands and he gives an amusing account of

[1] Lynch, op. cit., I, p. 393.

38. Ararat from Doğubeyazit

39. Gümüşhane

40. Trabzon: Aya Sofya

41. Trabzon: Gülbahar Hatun Mosque

riding a tall horse at the head of a Cossack regiment and of winning a race on it. When he was there most of the population was Armenian and unhappy, the place being a city of refuge for Armenians in flight from the Kurds,[1] who had about this time been allowed licence by the Turkish Government to attack the Christians in return for Kurdish acceptance of the central Ottoman authority.[2] Lynch and Warkworth were not allowed by the Russians to take photographs and even today, though there are officially no restricted areas, the Citadel hill is not easy to visit and should not be approached without permission.

One old Armenian church is now a cinema and the beautiful tenth-century cathedral at the foot of the Citadel hill was until lately abandoned to weeds, filth and decay. This Church of the Holy Apostles, built by a Bagratid king in 930, has an unusual plan. The main structure is square, with five-sided projections, semicircular inside, on each side of the building, the entrance being through one of these. A ribbed, tiled conical roof is supported by a circular masonry drum with twelve well-proportioned blind arches. There are figures of the twelve Apostles in high relief between the tops of the arches. This drum, with its blind arcades and conical top, surely represents the origin of the typical Seljuk tomb. As well as being an Armenian cathedral, the church has served as a mosque, a Russian Orthodox church with some modification and redecoration, and a storehouse, and has recently been put to good use as a museum.

The citadel is squat and ugly on its tremendous rock but it has obviously been a fortress of great strength. An Armenian foundation, it has been modified by Seljuks, Ottomans, British and Russians. James Morier, who visited Kars during the years 1808–1816, found the citadel in a ruinous state and the town not a happy place for strangers. 'It is built upon a rocky bank, exposed to the south-east. A castle upon a steep rock, in a picturesque and commanding position, overlooks it; and its dark towers, which are now ruinous and running into decay, give it an appearance at a distance of more strength than it really possesses.' He has little to say about the town. 'A stone wall, with square turrets at stated intervals, encompasses it on every side, and it is furnished with gates, which according to Asiatic custom, are closed at sun-set and opened at sunrise. Its inhabitants are a race of bigoted Mussulmans, intermixed with Armenians, and it enjoys the reputation

[1] ibid., I, p. 405.
[2] Warkworth, op. cit., p. 133. For Kurdish pillaging, ibid., pp. 115 ff.

of being a place of call for the many thieves and marauders, Kurds, Yezidies, and others who at various times and seasons infest the highways, and who are and have been from time immemorial the dread of caravans and travellers. The exactions made upon passengers, and the petty despotism to which they are exposed from the authorities, render a visit to Kars disagreeable and even dangerous. . . .'[1] Morier set his novel *Ayesha*, published in 1837, in this town and the romantic tale is still readable, partly because of the authenticity of the background material.

Kars and its citadel are at a point where the Kars Çayı, on its way to join the Arpa Çayi, enters a narrow gorge. Near the entrance to the gorge there are a seventeenth-century bridge and an old Turkish bath and there are trees and gardens, rare things in this region and highly thought of by the people of Kars when summer permits excursions on Sundays and holidays. For half the year Kars is under snow and horse-drawn sledges ply for hire in the winter-gripped town, giving it for us a distinctly Russian air. During their occupation the Russians laid out the wide boulevard of the town but neglected to line it with suitable buildings. The ugly Russian Cathedral, built during the last quarter of the nineteenth century in the centre of the modern town, has been put to several uses by the Turks since 1920.

The long winter makes the harvesting of grain and other crops difficult and they are liable to be caught by early October snow and frost. Fruit-growing is almost impossible. Wheat is grown and Kars has a flour mill as well as a factory for powdered milk. The butter and cheese are famous all over Turkey and the meat from the plentiful flocks and herds is excellent. There are few goats, perhaps because they don't take kindly to the indoor, semi-subterranean life of winter or to indoor feeding. When one has seen kids capering in winter sunshine on outcrops of rock on the Aegean coast of Anatolia it is hard to think of them accepting this indoor life with the docility of sheep, cows and horses. Hay from the rich summer grass for winter feeding and cow-dung cakes for winter fuel are more essential basic requirements in the Kars region than they are anywhere in eastern Anatolia.

[1] *Ayesha, the Maid of Kars*, Chapter III, p. 18.

Ani

An earth road, dusty and practicable only in summer, runs from Kars fifty kilometres eastwards to Ani, which overlooks the frontier with Soviet Armenia and the deep Arpa Çayi valley, the dividing line here. Ani was founded on this high plateau at the beginning of the ninth century A.D. on an old site which goes back to the second millennium B.C.[1] In the tenth century it became the capital city of Armenia and most of the splendid buildings and the double enclosing wall were built at that time. These walls, however, though heroically defended on more than one occasion, failed in the eleventh century to keep out a series of attackers, Georgian, Byzantine and Seljuk. The Kurds too had their moment of triumph here. After the Mongol sweep of the thirteenth century the city began its slow decline to its present abandoned state so that today the great thousand-year-old buildings stand out like decayed teeth in an old mouth.

There are still half a dozen churches standing within the walls. The greatest of these is the Cathedral, a rectangular building with a cruciform roof which once had a circular central drum and conical dome like the other church buildings of this period and region. But drum and dome have fallen. The outer walls are high and flat, with shallow blind arcades separated by tall slim pilasters. The stone facing, still almost complete, is of finely masoned ochre to dark-brown stone over the basic structure of lighter-coloured local stone. The stone-flagged interior is immensely impressive and the apse is seen today as a pure architectural concept, without the distraction of fresco painting and altar trappings, as at Santa Irene in Istanbul. The multiple construction of the four piers that sustained the dome, the pointed arches that rise from them, the semicircular apse with niches for the twelve Apostles

---

[1] *A.J.A.*, vol. 71, no. 2.

and the one narrow window, all these are in such perfect proportion and are so final a statement that one regrets the subsequent elaborations and vulgarisms imposed upon this design in the Christian world. This is surely one of the peaks of architectural achievement, the balanced and assured simplicity of this tenth-century masterpiece. I prefer not to think what it looked like when the interior was completely plastered and painted.

The Church of St. Gregory stands on the eastern rim of the plateau and overlooks the Arpa gorge. Here are the same flat exterior walls with tall blind arcades, separated here by beautifully slender double pilasters and topped with intricate stone carving. Much of the conical dome remains and there are traces of fresco painting.

About three hundred metres west of the Cathedral is the ruin of a twelfth-century mosque, with an unusual polygonal minaret, erected by Manuchar, the first Seljuk ruler of Ani. The roof was supported by six strong pillars of stone and the use of pink and black stone adds interest to this early and unique little mosque.

Further south, in the direction of the meeting of the two rivers, is a charming little chapel, also dedicated to St. Gregory the Illuminator, twelve-sided, with its twelve-arched drum and conical roof still standing. An extraordinary impression of height is given inside by the tall multiple columns supporting the drum, through whose twelve windows the light falls. This was a burial place of the Pahlavid kings of Ani, a convent church, and dates from the early eleventh century.

The well-built castle, with its rectangular decorated doorway, is at the extreme north-west corner of the city and is still impressive. There are other interesting relics of buildings and beautiful pieces of stone carving to be observed on the plateau. There are considerable remains of the tenth-century city wall. The slopes down to the two valleys of the Alaca and Arpa were once riddled with troglodyte dwellings cut out of the tufa rock and are said to house the souls of the dead. Lynch, with his tongue in his cheek, says, 'A stir and a hum, as of a teeming and busy populace, may be heard by night above the rustling of the Arpa Chai.'[1] I have not been there at night to test the truth of this. To the east of the city, down in the Arpa ravine and partly straddling the river, are the ruins of the extremely interesting monastery of Khosha Vank, difficult to visit. Lynch has some impressive photographs of it and claims to have found the tomb of King Ashot by the stream.

[1] op. cit., I, p. 386.

Ani

Permission must be obtained from the Vali of Kars for the visit to Ani and once arrived there the party is provided with a military escort for the walk round the old city. This is to make sure that no one strays too near the Soviet frontier, which is very near and about which the Russians are very sensitive. The earth outside their wire is kept freshly ploughed so that footmarks reveal any attempt to cross. An international flap is apt to develop if you leave your escort or behave in a suspicious way. Waving to Russian women working the fields beyond the Arpa is frowned upon and all such incidents cause embarrassment at the regular meetings between Turkish and Russian officers to discuss matters concerning the frontier.

At Digor, along a much better road from Kars than the one to Ani and about forty kilometres south-south-west of Ani, are more ruined Armenian churches of the same period. Here the style is rather different: more blind arches in the circular body of the church and a ninety-degree point to the twelve blind arches in the roof drum. A deeply ridged tiled cone meets the points of the arches. These churches are set against a wild mountain background. There are said to be underground temples here too but I have not been able to visit them.

To Artvin and the Black Sea

Two roads, both difficult, lead from Kars to Artvin and down to the Black Sea coast, through wonderful mountain country and along valleys where the ruins of little-known Georgian churches may be seen. It is also possible to go through Arpaçay and Çildir to Ardahan and on to the coast. This spectacular and difficult road runs between the extinct volcano Kısır Dağ and Lake Çildir (1,953 metres above sea level), with marvellous views of the lake, which is one of the sources of the Arpa River. The land here is under snow for eight months of the year. Lake Çildir is frozen over for half the year and can be safely crossed by sledge from December to April. This volcanic area was one of the main sources of the much prized obsidian and there are obsidian fields south-west of Lake Çildir. Near here too there are food collecting sites of the Upper Palaeolithic and Mesolithic Ages.[1] Neolithic cromlechs found on an island in the lake help to establish its importance as a habitation of early man.[2] Was the weather different then or was it easier to hunt animals for food in winter snow than in summer heat? Once the Black Sea coast road from Rize to the frontier at Hopa is complete, that will be the best way to get to Artvin and beyond into the mountains. Sidney Nowill tells me he recently took a 1300 c.c. saloon car over the difficult Yalniz Çam pass (2,650 metres) from Artvin to Ardahan. A rougher road from Artvin to Ardahan goes through the village of Şavşat, which has a ruined Georgian castle and a very old Georgian church, probably dating back to the fourth century. Ardahan, on the Ardahan River which becomes the Kur or Kura River and flows into Soviet Armenia and the Caspian Sea, has a castle which

[1] Ufuk Esin and Peter Benedict, 'Recent Developments in the Prehistory of Anatolia', *Current Anthropology*, 4.4.1963, pp. 339 ff.
[2] *A.J.A.*, Sevket Aziz Kansu, vol. 51(1947), p. 232.

was Armenian in origin but was re-fortified by Soliman the Magnificent early in the sixteenth century.

Artvin is a Georgian name and the town has also been called Çoruh. The pleasant, red-roofed hillside town, backed by its ancient ruined castle, is punctuated with poplars and early summer brings a glorious greenness to the mountains around. June and July are the best times to explore this part, when the forests of conifers, beech, alder, oak, chestnut, hornbeam and other trees are at their best and there is a wealth of flowers. Beehives are here slung into trees so that the bears can't get at the honey. Olives and pomegranates grow in the Çoruh valley and wheat and barley are the principal crops. Besides the usual sheep, cattle and horses, mules and angora goats are typical animals of the Artvin province.

The Çoruh river is navigable at Artvin by wooden boats that even use sail and the well-surfaced road to Borçka and Hopa runs through wonderful mountain scenery cut through by the Çoruh River on its way to cross the frontier and reach the sea at Batum. An exciting road.

From Artvin too a possible road through the mountains to Erzurum is spectacular, difficult and dangerous. From Borçka a road runs to Murgul, an industrial town which nestles in the mountains from which it digs its important copper. From Murgul a rougher road will take you on to the Black Sea coast south-west of Hopa if you prefer not to retrace your steps to Borçka.

South-west from Artvin run the Tatos Mountains, well described by D. C. Hills, who walked this part in order to climb the little-known Kaçkar Dağ (3,650 metres).[1] These mountains are the home of different varieties of rhododendron and azalea and crocuses and other alpine flowers. The rhododendrons and azaleas have a strange effect upon honey which was noted as long ago as the fourth century B.C. when Xenophon reported the strange effect eating the honey had on his soldiers marching back from Persia. I have mentioned earlier in this book how they vomited and suffered from diarrhoea and seemed to go mad if they'd eaten a lot. Even a little made them drunk and the effect was generally devastating. But they all recovered and after a few days felt no worse than if they'd taken a good purgative. So it might be as well to check the nature of any honey you eat in rhododendron or azalea country, though the inhabitants are unlikely to offer you what they call the *deli bal*, mad honey, but if they do, take it in small

[1] *My Travels in Turkey*, 1964.

quantities to limit its effect to mild intoxication of an alcoholic nature.

As you near the coast in these Pontic Mountains you pass through several belts of vegetation. The barren peaks rise from upland and often cloud-covered pastures where the Laz herdsmen take their flocks to graze in summer, living in the wooden *yaylas* which are to be found wherever transhumance is practised in the wooded uplands of Anatolia and the transported tent is not necessary. Below this line, on the rain-soaked northward-facing slopes and in the valleys, an explosion of growth occurs in summer which is well described by Lynch. 'Copious rainfall and abundant vegetation are characteristic of the northern peripheral mountains. . . . In summer months there is produced the likeness of a succession of forcing houses, the slopes and hollows being covered with a bewildering tangle of trees and creepers and scarcely passable undergrowth. From the branches are festooned the lichens, grey-white streamers like human hair; the crimson stools of a fungus shine out from the gloomy brakes, and the pointed pink petals of the Kolchian crocus clothe each respite of open ground.'[1] Robin Fedden has published beautiful colour photographs of the flora, people and peaks of this region, including the summit of Kaçkar Dağ, Laz herdsmen and the lovely yellow *rhododendron caucasicum* which grows high up near small glaciers.[2]

[1] op. cit., I, p. 432.
[2] 'In the Steps of the Argonauts', *Geographical Magazine*, August 1964.

The Pontic Coast

The coast road from Samsun eastwards enters our area at the little port of Terme, ancient Themiscyra, and from here on to Ordu there are lovely beaches, with the Black Sea at its bluest. Ünye, ancient Oenoe, is a pleasant little port once famous for boat building and with marvellous beaches, that of Çamlik the most attractive. Xenophon and what remained of his Ten Thousand finally embarked here for Greece. The eighteenth-century Government House in the town is an agreeable building and the excavation of prehistoric sites at Ünye reminds us that men have lived here for a very long time. Ten kilometres away there is the ancient castle of Çaleoğlu, near the village of Kaleköy, of Byzantine construction though according to tradition commanded by Mithridates of Pontus, who may well have had a fortress here. The castle is perched on a volcanic hill and at a high point within its walls is the entrance to a tunnel of four hundred steps down to water. There are Roman rock tombs nearby. The crater lake of Çambaşı, sixty kilometres almost due south of Ordu on a rough road, is said to be spectacular and full of trout, but I cannot vouch for this. All along this coast in early summer there is a wealth and a fragrance of blossoming fruit trees on green slopes backed by tremendous mountains. Early May is the most beautiful time, except for occasional mists and rain. From the sea the white houses with their red roofs and the slim white minarets of the villages are like freshly painted toys in the greenness. Fatsa, ancient Polemonium, is another harbour backed by hazel-nut plantations and a few kilometres beyond is the pretty village of Bolaman, in wonderful country and with a Byzantine church and castle, on whose walls a Turkish bey built a house which proved that he loved the sea. On across the headland and through Perşembe, and more hazel-nut plantations in a soft green landscape, to Ordu.

ORDU

Ordu, ancient Cotyora and an offshoot of Milesian Sinope, is a dull little town but well laid out and possessing a splendid new promenade along the sea. The sea is very shallow here and big ships anchor quite a way out to discharge cargo and passengers by boat to a jetty. Nut-packing factories are the thing to visit in Ordu. We went into a new factory where the beautiful machinery is all of wood, since contact with metal is thought to affect the flavour of the nuts. You can follow the nuts down from the great millstone crushers which remove the shells, past the sorting drums and driers and along conveyor belts to where girls sit in three shifts, continuously picking out bad nuts. We bought a kilo of nuts packed in a linen bag and they were the best I have ever tasted. The manager said these nuts were all for export, many of them to Britain.

GIRESUN

Giresun is thought to have been originally Pharnakeia, founded by Pharnakes, King of Pontus, in the second century B.C. If this was the place, it was called Kerasos when Lucullus came here during his campaign against Mithridates and he gave the name of the town to the cherry trees he found growing here and which he introduced to Rome. The name Kerasos became Giresun to the Turks, after giving the name for a delicious fruit to many European languages, as cherry, *cérise*, *ceirios* and so on.

The town consists chiefly of a long street rising uphill from the sea, with offshoots on either side. It is dominated by a castle on a high rock, with a pretty mosque half way up. The castle is Byzantine. Offshore is Büyük Ada, or Giresun Adası, Giresun Island, the ancient Aretias, which has ruins of a Byzantine monastery and of a temple said to have been dedicated by two Amazon queens to Ares, god of war. The Argonauts called here in their quest for the Golden Fleece.

Hazel-nuts and maize are the main products of the Giresun region but the town is famous for its sea food and for the sticky sweet known as *kadayif*. We watched *kadayif* being prepared on a great circular revolving heated tray. The people of Giresun are very friendly, and they were curious to know where we came from and happy to hear. They showed us copper being beaten into well-shaped bowls, hare and fox skins and one splendid wolf skin for which the man wanted one hundred and fifty liras. I wasn't sure how well it had been cured but I regret not buying it. We bought a length of seersucker cloth, also locally made. Wood is exported from here and men may be seen rolling great logs down the beach towards blue, yellow and red painted boats. A happy town, where the accent is on the active present, and its own kind of present, rather than on the crumbling past.

From Giresun the road eastwards clings to the sea past Kesap and then cuts inland through wooded hills before dropping down to Espiye and Tirebolu. Any place-name ending in -bolu is a relic of polis and Tirebolu is an ancient Tripolis, though no one would give it such a grand name today. Tirebolu was an outlet in ancient times for lead and silver mined at Argyria in its hinterland. Gümüşhane, more recently associated with silver, is not far to the south. The road passes other fishing harbours and goes on to Akçaabat, the last place of any importance before Trabzon and twelve kilometres short of that town. Here too there was an ancient town. The Comnenes had a castle here, the ruins of which, with a lighthouse tower, remain on a headland to the west of the town, and there are the remains of Byzantine churches in the town itself. Another castle, the Merkez Kale, also in the town, is associated with the Genoese. From here to Trabzon there are more lovely beaches.

TRABZON

For many visitors the first view of Trabzon is from the sea, for the ships of the Turkish line are still the pleasantest way of getting there, and this view explains the ancient name Trapezos, for the city was built on a little tableland, with a steep ascent from the sea and bounded by ravines. The western edge of the old city, still walled and turreted and rising sharply from a green valley, demonstrates the fortifiable nature of the place and explains why it was able to withstand so many enemies. It was founded about the sixth century B.C. by Greeks from Sinope, itself a colony of Miletus in south Turkey. It became part of Armenia, then of Pontus and of Galatian Cappadocia. The Romans made it a free city and the capital of Pontus Cappadocius. Hadrian gave it a new harbour (it has always needed breakwaters) and built a Temple of Apollo on the site later to be used for the Church of Hagia Sophia. It was sacked by the Goths in the third century A.D. but its fortifications were repaired by Justinian. Its most glorious period was the two and a half centuries from 1204, when the Comnenes who escaped from the ruthless Crusader seizure of Constantinople made it the capital of their brilliant little empire.[1] It was taken by Mehmet the Conqueror in 1461.

Trabzon today is an agreeable town, though cold and wet in winter. Its people are friendly and helpful and there are good hotels and restaurants. It makes an excellent base for the discovery of this unfrequented part of Turkey and can be reached by a daily air service from Istanbul and Ankara as well as by the weekly, comfortable and cheap ships of the Denizcilik Bankası, the Turkish Maritime Line. By road you may approach it either by the splendid drive we have been following along the Black Sea coast or by a good road from Erzurum, if you are coming up from the south. Since its foundation it has been a great port, not least of all because it was the head of an important trade route through Erzurum to Persia and further east. This is what attracted the Genoese and the Venetians to it in the Middle Ages.

The walled city remains, well defined and some years ago publicised by Rose Macaulay's *The Towers of Trebizond*, which should be read here. Trabzon contains a lower town, a middle town and, at the southern point of the fortifications, across the spur between the two valleys, the citadel. The most interesting buildings in Trabzon are the old Christian churches, taken over for Moslem worship and so preserved, though most of their decoration has gone, chipped away when not whitewashed over to avoid disturbing Moslem piety. You climb quickly up from the harbour to the Park Meydani, a big square and the centre for hotels and restaurants. *Döner* kebab, *tandır* dishes[2] and grilled Black Sea fish are specialities. The anchovies are very good.

Four hundred metres further on, along the Maraş Caddesi and on the southern side of the road, is the ninth-century Church of St. Anna, erected, as a worn inscription over the door states, in 884–5, during the reign of the Byzantine Emperor Basil I. Its main architectural interest is that it possesses a clerestory. Down a little street opposite this church, and to the north of the Maraş Caddesi, is another old church, of St. Basil, also constructed of material pillaged from Roman and earlier Byzantine buildings. Three hundred metres further on, and halfway between the two valleys, a street turns south through the wall and into the middle of the old city. Here, near the Vilayet, the

[1] See pp. 71–2.   [2] See p. 125.

administrative building of the province, is the Fatih Cami, the Mosque of the Conqueror, generally known as the Ortahisar Cami, or Mid-castle Mosque.

Before the Conqueror declared it a mosque this had been the most important church within the walls and known as the Panaghia Chrysokephalos, the Gold-topped Church of the Virgin, because of the polished copper lining of its dome. The recent opening-up of the original narthex and exonarthex, to the right as you enter, has revealed the shape of the building as a church, running roughly east–west. To suit the new orientation as a mosque a door, with its wooden porch, was opened in the north transept of the cruciform church and the *mihrab*, directed to Mecca, sited immediately opposite. The narthex was no longer needed and was closed up. Both *mihrab* and *mimber* are well designed but hardly compensate for the loss of mosaic and fresco decoration. Some mosaic pattern still remains in the apse and plaster may still conceal old painting. The wooden balcony in the north transept, facing the *mihrab*, has the effect of making the interior seem small and only by going to the west end can one form any notion of the noble proportions of the building. It seems that the earlier basilical plan of the church was altered to take a dome in the thirteenth century and it is not unnatural that Comnenes familiar with the architecture of Constantinople should think that such an imposing edifice should have a dome.

Continue westwards out of the old city and across the ravine and you come quickly to an open space with a very beautiful Ottoman mosque of the early sixteenth century, the Gülbahar Hatun Cami, known also as the Büyük Imaret, presumably because it once had (and may still have, I'm afraid I didn't enquire) a big *imaret* or kitchen for the distribution of food to the needy. It was founded by Gülbahar, a princess of the Dulkader dynasty and mother of Sultan Selim I. Selim's son, Soliman the Magnificent, was born at Trabzon. This mosque has a very exact and pleasing balance between its line of cupolas and the rather low dome, and the long columned portico with its sloping roof. The nearby tomb of Gülbahar (her name means springtime of roses) goes perfectly with the mosque.

There are other interesting buildings within and just outside the city walls. The Nakip Cami, to the north and in the western valley, now in a ruined condition, may have been the Church of St. Andrew, who is said to have brought Christianity to Trabzon, and it is probably

eleventh century. To the east of the citadel, up a long street from the
Church of St. Anne in the Maraş Caddesi, is the Yeni Cuma Cami,
the New Friday Mosque, so named because Mehmet the Conqueror
said his first Friday prayers here, in the Church of St. Eugenios, built
in the thirteenth century and then rebuilt, after a fire, in the fourteenth.
It is basilical in form, with three bays and a lovely dome with unusually
tall lights and railed interior balcony. It has been neatly whitewashed
and a quite pretty flower pattern has been painted over the windows
and elsewhere. The old muezzin is a veteran of the Balkan War and
adversely compared the Serbian treatment of Turkish villages with the
way the Turks have preserved old Christian buildings. There is some
truth in this and he was too nice for me to wish to attempt any qualification of his views. On the way down from this mosque you will
notice an attractive and slightly fantastic white-painted building
built early in the 1914–18 war, while the city was in Russian hands, to
welcome the Tsar of Russia, who never came. It is now a girls' college.
There are also baths, tombs and charming wooden houses to be seen,
and a splendid Ottoman caravanserai, the Taş Han, next to the Çarşı or
Market Mosque. There are no Seljuk buildings in Trabzon, which,
like Istanbul, passed directly from Byzantine to Ottoman hands.

By far the most interesting building in Trabzon is Aya Sofya,
Haghia Sophia or Santa Sophia, built in the thirteenth-century heyday
of Comnene Trebizond, to become under the Ottomans a mosque
and military storehouse. It is now preserved as a building of historical
importance and a museum. Well away from and to the west of the
town, it is situated on a hilltop near the sea, on the probable site of
Hadrian's Temple of Apollo, and its layout as a monastery church can
best be appreciated from the air. I found that the best view is from a
right-hand seat in the plane as it leaves Trabzon for Samsun and Ankara.

In 1959 the Turkish Government scheduled Aya Sofya as an ancient
monument. Work of restoration and preservation then went on more
rapidly for six summers under the direction of Professor and Mrs.
Talbot Rice, financed by the Russell Trust, with Mr. David Cornfield
in charge of cleaning and restoration. The paintings had suffered most
over the centuries, half of them destroyed and the others pitted to
take the plaster which eventually preserved them.[1] The church is
Byzantine in form, with unusual features, notably the sculptures which

[1] See *The Church of Haghia Sophia at Trebizond*, edited by D. Talbot Rice, 1968.
Also a very full review of this work by Anthony Bryer in *Apollo*, April 1969.

decorate the exterior and which remind one strongly of the ninth-century Armenian church on Aghtamar Island. There are Seljuk elements too, in the stalactite carving and ogival arches. The Comnenes not only brought with them Byzantine notions from Constantinople but had their contacts with Armenians, Mongol Ilhans of Persia and Seljuks. And they benefited from an influx of refugee craftsmen, Armenians from the Mongol destruction of Ani in 1239 and Seljuks from the Mongol slaughter at Köse Dağ near Eleşkirt in 1243. Columns and capitals were re-used from earlier buildings. The south front is the most spectacular, with panels of sculpture in high relief over the entrance, the Genesis frieze, Eden, the Creation of Eve, Adam and the Temptation of Eve. Eve, still in a state of innocence, is clothed here but after the expulsion from Eden both Adam and Eve are naked.[1] The west porch has Seljuk-type carvings upheld by fifth-century columns. The narthex here must have been a gem, with angled decorations in bright colours rising to a central boss with the symbols of the four Apostles round it.

The most complete pictures are of the miracles of the fishes and of the wine at Cana. On the arch of the south door of the narthex are Saints Sergius and Bacchus, surely in memory of Justinian's faith in them and of his church in their honour at Istanbul. Jacob's ladder is on the west wall of the north porch. Jacob lies dreaming in the left-hand corner, with red hair, bare knees and long red boots. His name is written above him. Then he struggles with an angel in a similar dress to his. There is a fragmentary Last Judgement in the west porch. The Talbot Rices are of the opinion that these paintings are the work of an individual and original artist, closer to Constantinople than to the painters of the Cappadocian monasteries of Göreme, and important in the history of art for the rich colour and naturalness of the work and for the spacious treatment of the conventional subjects. Near the south-west corner of the exterior of the church there is a sunken niche of semicircular arched form, a yard deep, over an opened tomb. At the back, suffering from damp but still clear, is a remarkable painting of two kings on horseback, looking very western European. Surely Comneni stressing their links with the west in this embattled enclave under Asiatic pressure. The fifteenth-century paintings in the fourteenth-century campanile are nothing like as masterly as those of the church.

Trabzon has not only its local dishes but its folk music and dancing.

[1] ibid., Plates 17 and 18.

It is famous for the *horon* music of the region, played on a fiddle held downwards.

The Kanita beach, *plaj* in modern Turkish, to the west of the town, is the popular swimming place and for picnics the choice is generally Soğuksu, Cold water, beautifully situated on a hillside seven kilometres south-west of the town, with a villa or *köşk* (the word which has given us kiosk), now a museum, where Ataturk spent three days in the heroic times of 1921. Outside the town, on the coast road eastwards, is the new University of Trabzon. This institution is planned to specialise in metallurgy and engineering, in line with the importance of mining in the hinterland of Trabzon and the future need of engineering in road-building and hydro-electric projects. The processing of tobacco is an important present-day industry.

RIZE

Rize, eighty kilometres east of Trabzon, has no deep-water harbour but a pier to which boats come from ships anchored off the coast. The beach east of this pier is covered with horse dung and is clearly the town stable during the summer months. To the west the beach has brightly coloured pebbles. Everything about Rize is bright; the neat red-tiled buildings of the town itself rise to three hills covered with gardens and orchards and dotted with lovely houses. The Ministry of Agriculture garden on the central hilltop should be visited not only for the pleasantness of the spot but for the all-round view it gives of farms, well-built farmhouses with circular chimneys of brick, tea terraces everywhere, palms, slender white minarets and then the un-broken forest of the background of mountains. There is tea cultivation right up to the tops of some of the nearer and lesser hills. Further to the south and east the land rises rapidly to the little-known heights of the Haros, Tatos and Kaçkar Mountains. On the mountain slopes nearer the town there are still relics of uncleared forest, then tea terraces and fruit trees, plum, apple, hazel, orange and tangerine. Forest thorns, with fearful two-inch spikes and a lovely white flower, have been trained into impenetrable hedges to protect gardens. The mountains supply a great variety of timber for the mills of Rize and there is good local basket-work and woodwork to be bought in the town. Rize has an important textile industry.

But Rize is now best known as the capital of Turkish tea production.

42. *Murgul: copper works*

43. *Rize*

44. *Giresun*

Tea has only recently become a popular drink in Turkey, chiefly because of the present high cost of coffee, one of the few permitted, though heavily taxed, imports since the Ataturk revolution. Russian experiment in the last decade of the nineteenth century established the tea plant in nearby Georgia, and since 1935 it has been grown in the Rize district, production rapidly increasing since 1945. Today's crop adequately meets Turkish requirements and a habit previously known only in the extreme east of Anatolia, under Georgian and Persian example, has spread through Turkey and the Turks today are as firm a tea-drinking nation as the Welsh. Not only is tea grown on big government estates but the Laz farmers and smallholders grow tea and bring the leaves for processing to the government factories along the coast. Tea has brought greater prosperity to the north-eastern coast of Turkey and one likes to think that it does less harm than tobacco. We visited a factory a few kilometres to the west of Rize where one is welcome to inspect the whole process, calling first of all at the office near the main gate. In early summer you will see tea growing there. They are glad to show visitors round and they have a kiosk where you may buy specially packed tea which is rather better than the ordinary Harman type generally sold. The machinery we saw was all either Indian or British and British advice is being taken on processing and blending. Over a thousand men are employed at this factory alone. When Turkish tea production reaches the level at which large-scale export is possible, some difficulty may well be found in competing with Indian tea in price, but the quality will be good.

East and west of Rize the green coastal hills are dotted with neat little houses, often with stepped paths leading up to them, each with a field or so, a tea plot and fruit trees. The mountains inland from the coast between Rize and Hopa, on the Russian frontier, become more and more luxuriantly treed, with mainly deciduous forest until you come to the upland conifers of the divide. The rare travellers in these mountains have enthused over the variety and size of the trees. Robin Fedden says, 'The forest was awe-inspiring. We had never seen such vast trees. Nourished by the coastal rains, beech, hornbeam, Spanish chestnut and spruce looked like giant ships under sail.'[1] Lynch measured a beech trunk and found it to be seventeen feet six inches (four metres thirty-five centimetres) round. He says, 'The under-growth was supplied by laurel and holly, and cascades leapt from the rocks.'[2]

[1] *Geographical Magazine*, August 1964, p. 313.   [2] op. cit., vol. I, p. 51.

Again he notes alder, lime, walnut, elm and ash, with holly, azalea and rhododendron ablaze with colour supplying the undergrowth.[1] Above the tree-line, on the high summer pastures of the Laz shepherds once the snow has retreated, one meets a profusion of Alpine flowers.

The lovely green coast continues from Rize to Hopa, past Çayeli nestling in its valley mouth and the little harbour of Ardeşen, another Georgian name. A little way inland and up valley from near Ardeşen are the curative hot springs of Çamlı-Hemşi. Then Fındıklı, named after the hazel-nut (*fındık*) with which it is surrounded. And everywhere tea plantations. Maize grows well here and in the autumn you will see golden heaps of grain ready for storing.

Short cuts to Murgul from the coast road are to be avoided. It is better to go on to Hopa, up to Borçka and thence to Göktaş and Murgul.

HOPA

I have found Hopa grim and undistinguished, with an end-of-the-world feeling about it and a sense of absolute estrangement from the activities going on beyond the nearby Russian frontier. You are allowed to drive to the frontier so long as you have your passports handy. Take them with you if you go off for a few hours from the ship. For the people of this area Batum was once the market centre and today they feel far from the bustle of trade. I was cheered to see boys playing cat-and-dog with a good stick and sharpened cattie, just as I played it as a boy in South Wales. The shops don't seem to open and there is hardly anything for sale here. From the bridge there is a good view of the huge mosque with its bright ugly windows, some fine old houses in seedy condition and a winding valley which has a north Italian air, wild enough to deter some and to entice others. From here a road, savage enough for anyone, through the mountains to Borçka, improves from Borçka to Artvin.

[1] ibid., vol. II, p. 239.

Trabzon to Erzurum

※✿❀✿※

Three kilometres along the coast road east of Trabzon a road turns south into a valley and on to an ancient caravan route for Maçka and Erzurum. The first few miles of the valley are very fertile, tobacco and rice are grown and hazel trees abound. Maize grows on the higher fields and in autumn you will see the yellow grain packed into baskets or earthenware containers under a shelter or covered with branches. The women here are unveiled and wear a wrapover skirt of bluish red with a white perpendicular stripe. This is Laz country and the people are fair and fresh complexioned, with longish noses.

SUMELA

At Maçka the sign Meriemana (Mother Mary), the type of sign used for places of historical interest, directs us south-eastwards up a steep wooded valley to the Sumela Monastery. There is good trout-fishing here. Twenty-three kilometres of earth road motorable in summer brings us to the foot of the rock face to which the Monastery of the Holy Virgin clings. A forestry guard near the foot of the stone steps keeps the key of this abandoned sanctuary. It was founded early in the sixth century on a narrow ledge of rock in a high cliff and built around a sacred cave, afterwards made into a little church. The oldest of the present buildings date from the Comnene Empire of Trebizond and the fact that Alexios III was crowned here in 1340 shows how important the place must have been to the Comnenes. The stone steps and a hostel within the walls were built in 1860 for the convenience of visitors. The buildings at the eastern end, where the ledge gets narrower, date from the seventeenth century. The central courtyard is surrounded by chapels and other monastic buildings and a room cut out of the rock was once the library. The monastery was abandoned in the general exodus of Greeks from this part after World War I and its paintings are rapidly falling into decay, since many of them have little protection against the ferocity of the elements here. The paintings on the side walls of the main church date from the fourteenth century, the time of Alexios III. Others are more recent.

At the foot of the cliff is a new monastery of nineteenth- and early twentieth-century construction. The main monastery is nearly fourteen hundred metres above sea level and is fastened on to a cliff which rises two hundred and fifty metres from the stream that rushes past its foot. Lynch took this valley as a short cut to Bayburt and Erzurum and says that from Sumela to Bayburt can be done in two days on horseback, crossing the range by the two thousand four hundred metre pass of Kazıklı Dağ, to the east of the Zigana.

There are other monasteries in these mountains, for those who have the time and interest to seek them out. From Küçük Konak, a village perched on the hillside fifteen kilometres up the main road from Macka, it is a day's excursion on foot to the Monastery of Vazelon, a fifth-century foundation known to the Turks as a nunnery. I know nothing of its history. And there are yet more monasteries in astonishing situations. The Turkish word *manastir* is close enough for your interest to be understood but these places are usually known by their individual names, and often a Turkish name, rather than under a general classification.

THE WAY BACK

The main road up from Maçka rises more steeply now and begins to climb out of the narrowing valley. There are still many houses, but they stand apart from each other, not in groups or villages. These people are not natural town-dwellers. For many miles up to the pass the road runs high along the ridge but I suspect that the old caravan route followed the stream until it was forced to climb, for, looking down, one can see beautiful humpbacked medieval bridges, lovely bent bows of stone flung across the torrent. Houses grow fewer and there are pines and we soon reach the undramatic and open Zigana Pass, at two thousand metres above sea level. This may have been the spot where Xenophon's advance guard saw the sea.

We now drop down through a sparse forest of mixed conifers, in which one kind of pine with an almost white trunk rises straight to a considerable height. The descent to Torul, previously Ardasa, is rapid. The mountains are now fearfully bare after the luxuriance of the northern slopes. A castle on a very high brown rock dominates the pass. We are in the Harşıt valley which runs to the sea near Tirebolu. As we near Gümüşhane the valley becomes more fertile and there are small farms with delightful Alpine-type houses, wooden built, two-storyed with pointed roofs, gable windows and wide eaves, plastered and white lime-washed, a style unique in Turkey. Gümüşhane too has a distinctly Alpine flavour, a pleasant town with good buildings. Wood is sawn here for the many uses to which it is put. It's a great place for apples and pears. The roadside town is quite new but the nearby Eski Gümüşhane has ruins of mosques, baths and churches. This was once a well-known summer resort and a centre of the silver trade. Hence the name Silver Caravanserai, for *gümüş* means silver. The new town could still be a good place for a quiet holiday. Fishing and shooting are good here and there are partridges galore.

From Gümüşhane the road passes orchards and then a government poplar farm with co-operative plantations, goes through Kale, frowned over by a tower on a high rock, crosses barren mountain country and the Pass of Vavuk (1,900 metres), drops down to a branch of the Çoruh River, rises again through rough bare hills and comes down to the main Çoruh River at Bayburt. This town, an important Turkish military, commercial and cultural centre ever since its occupation, embraces the river, and riverside houses have continuous balconies on wooden props over the water. Bayburt's most remarkable feature is the extraordinarily long castle which takes up the whole of the high ridge north of the town. Originally Armenian, repaired like so many others by Justinian, rebuilt by the Seljuks and strengthened by the Ottomans, it once controlled this important route and has long been garrisoned by the Turkish Army. A tunnel from the castle down to the river, to give access to water, is said to be still usable, but a tendency to claustrophobia has prevented my showing interest in it. The road now rises towards Maden along a tributary to the Çoruh which is a perfect trout stream. There are neat stone-built houses on all sides, many of them two-storeyed, and higher up almost every house has a little channel carrying water to a chute which once worked a little mill for grinding. There are no signs of use today and much evidence of a departed population. The road rises to the high Pass of Kop Dağ

(2,400 metres) and a splendid view of mountains in all directions. We are soon down at Aşkale and the Erzurum plain.

From Erzurum or Van you will leave this wild birthplace of so many of our western concepts by road, rail or air. Sea travellers will make for Trabzon or Iskenderun and will follow some of the most ancient sea-ways known to man.

Appendix

Eastern Turkey for the Alpinist Traveller
by Sidney E. P. Nowill

To the alpinist eastern Turkey offers new pastures: to the discerning traveller a wealth of remote and fascinating goals, set in a landscape of notable austerity and grandeur. The plateau landscapes are best seen in the early days of autumn when mountain ranges can be descried from immense distances, rising above the rim of the world with their snows sparkling faintly in the clear, planetary air. Viewed from a high pass like the Yalniz Çam, there is offered to the traveller an infinite recession —an ever more attentuated vision, of peaks extended to the limit of sight.

Climatically, eastern Turkey has a range that encompasses everything from the sub-arctic to the nearly tropical. Along the Black Sea on the mild rain-drenched littoral that extends from Trabzon to the Russian border, the tea gardens climb the foothills, and hardy Laz women with conical baskets on their backs gather the tender leaves, moving up and down the steep viridian hillsides with the effortless rhythm of their kind. Behind the tea gardens come the coast ranges, clothed with tropical rain forest. And beyond them, the great peaks of the Kaçkar Ranges (the 'Little Caucasus') which we shall consider later from the standpoint of the alpinist.

South of the Kaçkar extends the plateau, proper, which rises to over 6,000 feet (1,950 metres) at Erzurum. This is a barren, desolate land governed by an extreme continental climate, where the winter average mean can be as low as − 14 °C at places like Karaköse, and where the absolute minima can dip to − 37 °C. Life retreats then into small village huts, five feet high insulated by thick mud walls, where the livestock supply warmth and the sole fuel is animal dung.

Ararat stands watch over these lands, its 17,000 foot (5,165 metres) cone visible from many points and at impressive range, even, occasionally, from Lake Van. 1,720 metres above sea level, Lake Van is Turkey's largest lake; the lifeless bitter waters are ringed by substantial mountains, including Süphan Dağ. Until recently, with its officially designated height of 4,434 metres, Süphan Dağ seemed to be Turkey's second highest mountain. A recent survey however heartlessly eliminated 376 metres and demoted the summit to a mere 4,058 metres, which makes it lag behind at least two of the Cilo peaks.

South of Lake Van the crumpled landscape rises to its highest point (after Ararat) and to almost total orographical confusion; here are the Cilo/Sat ranges, Hesperides of the alpinist traveller, to which we shall devote the bulk of our survey. In the profound gulfs which separate Cilo and Sat, in those terraced valleys and gorges of the Rudbare Sin, the solar radiation and sheer reverberating heat of summer fully justify the label of 'tropical', and provide a severe trial to any traveller who embarks on this passage. We are, after all, only a couple of thousand feet above sea level here, and the latitude of $37\frac{1}{2}°$ N makes us almost level with the Karakoram. Here are the wildest mountain vistas between Switzerland and the Hindu Kush, landscapes which in their remoteness and savagery can offer a real challenge to the experienced alpinist traveller tending as he is now to be sated by the extension of Il Turismo to his chosen environment in other lands.

After a life of travel that has taken him to four continents and included the lost valleys of the Hadhramaut and the deserts and mountains of Iran and Jordan, the present writer still considers the lands between the Black Sea and the Cilo/Sat as unrivalled for their strangeness, and for a certain austere, bitter and timeless splendour.

Before offering detailed information about individual mountains or groups of peaks, it would be as well to give intending travellers and alpinists some hints which have general as opposed to specific validity.

LANGUAGE

The Turkish language is spoken throughout the area, and although the population may in some places tend to use Kurdish or Laz among themselves, it is unnecessary to possess any other tongue than Turkish. The presence of a Turkish-speaker in any climbing party, though not perhaps essential, is highly recommendable; it will minimise problems and enhance pleasure. The Anglo-Turkish Society in London can advise on how to attain basic adequacy and follow a simple course of groundwork conversation.

CLIMATE

This has already been referred to. Protection against solar radiation in the form of total filter creams is advised. Some degree of dehydration is common on eastern Turkish climbs, and fluid intake should be consistently high. Up to four litres a day may be necessary when pronounced activity and load-carrying is undertaken. Precipitation in the form of rain or snow is rare during the summer months, except occasionally on Ararat, and barometric pressures are stable. This makes height calculations with a Thommen altimeter relatively simple and exact when the temperature adjustments, according to the tables of CINA norms, are added into the Thommen readings. Considerable wind may be felt on high summits. This is particularly true on Ararat where extreme velocities are liable to be encountered. For this reason, however hot the sun, windproof clothing should always be carried on the summit leg of Ararat, and on all other summits of more than say 3,800 metres. Despite the Southern latitude night frost is the rule rather than the exception on bivouacs or camps above 3,000 metres.

EQUIPMENT

There is an advantage in opting for tents which can be brailed. Unless everyone is perpetually out climbing, the presence of a sewn-in groundsheet is a definite risk to a party using tentage exclusively of this type. In the event of sickness or even just the desire for a rest-day, non-brailable tents offer no refuge in daytime as they become red-hot and uninhabitable. (I have seen temperature of 120 °F or 49 °C inside a tent at 3,000 metres on Sat Dağ.) This means that each party should have at least one brailable tent.

Normal mountaineering equipment should be brought, including ice-axes and crampons. These will be needed for occasional passages in most areas. Normal cordage can be used and rappel rope is advised for parties pioneering or repeating the harder climbs in Kaçkar, Cilo or Sat, where a 'helmet' is a useful precaution.

Bleuet gas cylinders are not available in Turkey. Climbers should bring an adequate supply. Fuel for primuses may however be acquired in almost all places.

Repairs to equipment are very often possible, thanks to the genius for improvisation and the traditional desire to help travellers met with in eastern Turkey. (This does not apply to the Cilo/Sat where parties must be totally self-sufficient.) Replacement of lost or destroyed items is nowhere possible, not even in Istanbul or Ankara.

FOOD

Where possible, food should be brought in sufficient quantities to see a party through. Packet soups and instant milk are a must, as well as the main protein supplies. Ideally the latter should be in accelerated freeze-dried form. Availabilities in Turkey include oatmeal (Capa Marka brand) and excellent tinned tunny and sardines. Tea, salt, sugar, margerine and cheese are to be found in all towns and most villages. Fresh fruit is a problem in eastern Turkey, and not easily to be acquired. Breakfast cereals are unknown anywhere in Turkey. Tinned fruit is available, but of course presents a carrying and weight problem.

Restaurants in the main urban centres of the region we are considering, are cheap and usually provide tasty food. In the northern plateau segment of eastern Turkey the meat is particularly good and grills of really excellent quality are available at unbelievably low prices. The situation in this respect deteriorates as one travels south.

ROADS

The main roads vary from adequate to good. Four-wheel drive is not required and you can (with care) travel almost anywhere in an ordinary saloon car. At the time of writing the Rize/Hopa road is under construction and hard to follow in a small vehicle. The writer has recently taken a small 1300 c.c. saloon over the Yalniz Çam pass between Ardahan and Artvin. This route is considered to represent the extreme example of difficult driving in the area, but the scenery can only be described as stupendous.

SECURITY

With the exception of Sat Dağ, security is good in all areas. In northeastern Turkey one could indeed say that security is excellent. Crime seems to be rare. The prisons are virtually empty, and the whole region is under strong military surveillance and control. As one goes south security becomes only slightly less good, though it would be wiser to avoid night driving in the southern sector of eastern Turkey. The Cilo Mountains are more secure than Sat, where several acts of banditry have occurred in recent years, including one involving four members of the writer's 1966 party.

The region directly west of the Cilo/Sat is the least secure part of Turkey; but it is assumed that alpinist travellers reading these pages will not normally be moving around in this sector which is devoid of mountaineering interest. The fact is that dissident Kurds from Iraq can cross the frontier more or less at will in the remoter areas, with the result that the Turkish authorities sometimes have difficulty in policing the zones where contiguity with Iraq affords an easy get-away for marauders.

My advice to travellers under the general heading of 'security' includes the following: try as far as possible to spend the nights in towns or townships, and do not take it amiss if you are called on by the local police. In the Russian border zone camping or bivouacs are best avoided. One is perfectly safe, indeed more so than in Western Europe; but needless suspicions may be aroused in the minds of the local authorities. This zone has only very recently been demilitarised and opened to tourists, and the traveller should obey carefully any directions he may receive from the civil or military personnel of the area.

PERMITS

No permits are required for mountain climbing or travel in eastern Turkey. It is a definite mistake to ask for a permit. People who have done this tend subsequently to be arrested or interrogated. Even though one is always released it must be disconcerting to be rounded up. The sensible approach is to motor to one's destination town and there call on the chief local official (either the provincial governor or Vali, or else the sub-prefect or Kaymakam), report one's intentions, and ask for help in providing trusted muleteers or guides. Such action at once establishes one's bona fides, and even if the muleteer is expected to deliver a full report on your doings immediately after his return, this will not trouble any genuine climbing group, and is a small price to pay for the help and blessing of the authorities. In the event of an accident or emergency it is as well that the local officialdom should know of one's whereabouts and likely field of endeavour. This makes them more ready to send out help if required.

Appendix on Eastern Turkey

A necessary part of travel in the area. Owing to the fact that there are
(fortunately) no climbing huts or other facilities, the establishment of
a base camp, or subsequent camps, demands the help of animal transport. This will normally be in the shape of donkeys, but may in some
areas take the form of ponies or mules. As a rough guide (1969 prices)
T.L. 25.00 per animal per day, with an indeterminate but relatively
small amount thrown in for each man-day, is the normal charge. A
party of four spending a fortnight in the mountains is unlikely, unless
rather spartan, to have less than about a quarter of a ton to be lifted.
It will require about four average donkeys to do this. Although the
muleteer guide will bring his own food, he will welcome a bowl of
soup in the evening; he will not however expect to be kitted out.

KAÇKAR MOUNTAINS
Though small in compass the Kaçkar peaks offer to the western alpinist
one of the three finest arenas for serious climbing in all of Turkey.
The other (and far more extensive) areas are the Cilo/Sat and the Ala
Dağ. The approaches to Kaçkar from the north lie through the enormous rain forests bordering the Black Sea, up the lush valley of
Kavron, and past the hot mineral water springs of Ilica. Because of the
annual rainfall exceeding 2,500 mm. (100 inches), these mountains
carry glaciers.

The area has been little visited by mountain climbers and the biblio-
graphy is sparse. Among the few references is *Alpine Journal* 46 282
(Rickmers). A glaciological expedition published its findings in *La
Revue de la Faculté des Sciences de l'Université d'Istanbul*, Series B Volume
XIV, but the sketch map in this report is said to be inaccurate (see
Alpine Journal 1964 (1) pp. 129–132 (Fedden), on which most of the
following notes are based).

All the Kaçkar peaks have alternative access via their dry southern
walking approaches; but from the north they offer both rock climbing
and snow and ice routes, comparable with good second-class alpine
peaks of 3,200/2,500 metres. The rock is mainly granitic and of excellent
quality on the faces.

Twenty-five kilometres S.W. of Kaçkar lies a separate group commanded by the Vercinin Tepe (3,711 metres).

Weather conditions are strange and troubling. During the summer, when most parties will be visiting the area, the proximity of the Black Sea brings almost perpetual rain and drizzle. This vaporous and misty zone extends to 2,700–3,000 metres in height. Above the cloud zone the peaks lift themselves into sparkling sunlight. One climbs in radiant conditions, only to return to a dripping camp in the evening. In the autumn the weather is often more stable; late October or even November can bring fine days, and the range can then be viewed in all its glory even from the coast. For the climber, however, the shortness of daylight hours and the risk of serious, as opposed to merely trouble-some, perturbations in the weather must make these months of autumn a somewhat risky season. On a November day of altogether exceptional clarity the writer was once lucky enough to see the whole range of the Caucasus effulgent in early morning sun, just over the rim of the planet, across the almost unbelievable gap separating it from the hills near Hopa. How much grander would it appear to the alpinist bestriding the Kaçkar Dağ at 3,937 metres!

Kaçkar Dağ can be climbed by the North Glacier and the N..E ridge; or else by the West Glacier and the S.W. ridge. Grading thought to be around P.D. in each case.

Kaçkar Tepe (3,605 metres) is the highest summit of the N.E. group of peaks, also known as the Altı Parmak (Six Fingers). Excellent rock climbing can be had on the six granite buttresses to a standard of III/IV or higher, according to the routes taken.

Aiguille Point (3,450 metres) lies N.E. of Kaçkar Dağ and was first climbed in 1963 by Fedden's party. Grading about III/IV.

The N.W. walls of Kaçkar Dağ still await their conquerors and many new routes remain to be done.

The fauna of the region include bears, ibex and chamois. And the area is noted for the presence of the Snow Cock (*Tetraogallus Caspius*). As one would expect, the flora is lush and impressive. In the forest belt are Rhododendrum Ponticum and the Pontic Lily. Higher up, near the snow-line, sheets of yellow azalea. Altogether a rewarding playground if one can rise above the weather factor!

MUNZUR MOUNTAINS

These lie south of Erzincan, between Erzincan and Tunceli, and just qualify for inclusion in this survey although they form part of the most westerly sector of eastern Turkey. The Munzur group is the least known all of the major mountain ranges in Turkey. The Austrian party which visited the area in 1964 was probably the first serious climbing party ever to set up camp there. They claim to have ascended sixteen virgin peaks as well as seven summits already cairned. Most of these mountains rise to between 3,000 and 3,400 metres; they have been described to the writer by Latif Osman Çikigil, President of the Turkish Mountaineering Federation, as having great charm and seclusion and as being well worth a visit by less ambitious climbing parties.

Nothing appears to have been published about the 1964 Austrian party, but the photographs taken show an interesting area with attractive northern faces offering medium-length climbs on rather friable rock—described in the typewritten account as being of mesozoic limestone. These mountains are clearly not in the same league as the Cilo/Sat or the Ala Dağ; but have the attraction of a little-trodden landscape, remote and yet not too difficult of access. The sketch map of the 1964 Austrian party (Sektion Wien des O.A.V.) intriguingly enough pinpoints nine peaks unclimbed by the Austrians, and presumably still virgin.

ARARAT (5,165 metres)

Traditional site of the landing of the Ark, Ararat is one of the most imposing mountains in the world. The single unbroken slope of 4,400 metres (say 14,500 feet) that sweeps up from the Araxes valley to the summit pyramid, is described by a French authority on the mountain as the greatest single unbroken slope in the world. Whether this is so or not, there is no doubt that Ararat viewed from any side offers an overwhelming impression of majesty and size. My favourite remembered view is from far away in Iran dating from an occasion when once we bivouacked on the craggy steppes beyond Maku, and rose to breakfast in full view of that soaring cone, now steeper and taller in appearance than when seen the previous day in Turkey, because foreshortening had then denied to the uppermost slopes the full power of their skyward thrust.

The standard way to climb Ararat is to set out with animals from Doğu Beyazit and establish camps at roughly 3,000 and 4,000 metres, leaving 1,150 metres or so for the final day. The climb presents no technical difficulty, but demands a considerable effort. Some prior acclimatisation to the height is recommended. The extensively glaciated summit plateau is relatively benign in that crevasse risks are not serious, and the gradients not particularly steep. Local mythology makes much of the 'Zone of the Spiders', the 'Zone of the Bears' and the 'Zone of the Snakes'. All exist, but none are troublesome. Somewhat more serious are the unstable boulders and treacherous moraine slopes. Most serious is the wind.

I remember a morning in '69 descending the east face after a bivouac on the ice (in 21° of frost at 4,500 metres); hurricane gusts kept dislodging rocks above our line of traverse with the result that we became more agile than our state of fatigue could have led us to believe possible!

Other approaches to Ararat can be made setting out from Iğdir. The easiest of these, and it is very easy, is the east face via the Mih Tepe. More impressive is the approach via the avalanche-swept Ahuri Chasm. Here hanging glaciers perch precariously above the gorge, scene of a terrible natural cataclysm in the last century; and sulphurous emanations survive to recall the disaster that overwhelmed the village and monastery of Adhora. The locals here have renamed this valley the Cehennem Dere, or Vale of Hell. No direct route here has yet been made, and any party attempting it should study carefully the risks of their intended path being exposed to falls of seracs.

Long tongues of glacier descend low from the summit into the more sheltered valleys of Ararat, particularly on the north, and the western face is surmounted by a fine barrier of ice walls.

While July and August offer the easiest approach on snow-free terrain for establishing camps, the month of June gives the best weather. The Mih Tepe route suffers from the basic disadvantage that the locally (i.e. Iğdir) accredited 'guide' seems unable to secure pack animals with pack saddles. Better really to seek the help of the authorities in Doğubeyazit and hire a couple of experienced donkeymen for the southern approach, or else try the ascent via the west face (which has seldom been visited by any party).

Water on Ararat is liable to be a problem. During the best climbing month of June the crossing of glacier-melt torrents can present difficulty during the afternoons. But in the early morning there may be no water at all. On any but the standard route from the south, with its recognised camp positions, some thought must be devoted to the siting of one's base, so that water may always be available and yet not in such quantities as to cause difficulty in crossing it.

One may sum up by saying that Ararat is in no sense a mountaineer's peak; but for the mountain wayfarer, the ascent of this giant orographical mass with its all-encompassing view from the summit must surely afford the most notable satisfaction procurable in the Turkish Highlands, of which it is undeniably the greatest single feature.

THE CILO/SAT

Here is the great playground. Habitat of bears and tribesmen. Severe, remote and taxing. Country of dolomitic peaks and glaciers juxtaposed with tropical valleys. Movement in these regions calls for experience in the traveller, careful planning and a good deal of physical toughness. Until very recently (1965) the Cilo/Sat was a closed area. In the 64 years between Maunsell's visit and the three British parties of 1965 (in order of date: Nowill, Fedden and Jackson), only 8 foreign groups appear to have visited the region—an average of one expedition every eight years. Since then the rush has started, and the Turkish Government has now declared the area to be a national park. We must therefore expect roads to be built and tracks to be improved, with the result that the aura of inaccessibility and the flavour of exploration which it was still possible to experience in '65 and '66 will begin to fade as the $2\frac{1}{2}$ day march in to Bay Lake from Yuksekova settles down to a single day's journey from Semdinli.

At the end of this conspectus of eastern Turkish mountains the writer offers a bibliography and list of visits to the Cilo/Sat which is thought to be complete and which is hitherto unpublished. Serious travellers may wish to browse around among this material, most of which is available in the Library of the Alpine Club in London. ('A.J.' stands for *Alpine Journal*.)

Parties interested purely in mountaineering and wishing to read the best general survey of the area with a view to planning a specific climbing programme on predetermined grades of difficulty cannot do better than refer to Douglas Scott's excellent article in *Alpine Climbing* (The Bulletin of the Alpine Climbing Group 1969) compiled with the help of Maciej Popko from Warsaw. This authoritative survey will be a blessing to future expeditions and contains two sketch maps based on Dr. Hans Bobek (1938), revised by R. E. Holmes, F.R.G.S. The only emendation we would make to these maps is to change the heights given for Bay Lake and Gevaruk Lake from 2,750 metres and 2,850 metres, to 2,950 metres and 2,920 metres respectively. The 1938 Bobek lake height measurements must be wrong (or else the height of Ciae Hendevade must be approximately 200 metres too low).

For background reading and to imbibe the general flavour of travel in the Cilo/Sat, the less technical reader should refer to *My Travels in Turkey*, George Allen and Unwin 1964 (Dennis Hill), or to the article in the April 1966 *Blackwood's Magazine*.

The main peculiarity of the Cilo/Sat is attributable to the climate. In the winter the snowfall in the mountains seems to vary between nine and ten metres. Even down in Yuksekova it is liable to snow three metres, and people sometimes have to tunnel between the houses. As late as early June you can still see from four to six metre drifts in the mountains. A little further north in the Hakkari Province—at Başkale for example, which is Turkey's highest town, more than 2,400 metres above sea level—there is practically no snowfall. You have here a classic rain-shadow (or snow-shadow) phenomenon, whereby all precipitation is squeezed, through cooling and contraction, out of the northward-moving masses of warm, humid air on to the 4,000 metre barrier of the Cilo/Sat mountains. It is only the unusual winter snowfall that can explain the presence of glaciers in so southern a latitude at the relatively modest heights of 2,800 to 3,300 metres. And it is this juxta-position of subtropicality and glaciation which gives to the Cilo/Sat their unique atmosphere. The glaciers are now in regression, and photographs taken in 1945 by Uyanik show a substantial retreat compared to 1965. But the Mia Vara amphitheatre and the Erbis cirque, respectively on the N.W. and N.E. flanks of Resko, still flaunt a panoply of genuine ice (as opposed to Neve).

In the extraordinarily dry desert air of these regions, and under the fierce solar radiation of summer, the mountain snows remain compacted and hard throughout the day, tending to sublime rather than to melt. But unlike the Aladağ or even Ararat the Cilo/Sat are plentifully watered, and the finding of drinking supplies presents no problem. The flora is almost uniquely opulent. Sheets of giant perfumed colchicums at Erbis, and equally impressive growths of gentians and primulas at the Gevaruk Lake, form the most arresting of my alpine flower memories.

The fauna of these mountains is suitably wild. The bear population is, alas, on the wane, but still numerous enough to afford at least a few sightings to parties travelling in Cilo. Much more seldom met with are the shy ibexes and the rare moufflon and lynx. Even flies are in keeping with their surroundings and in some instances at least eight times the normal size. They can be a severe trial on occasion.

The nomadic Kurdish tribesfolk, who make their summer homes with their flocks amid the higher valleys, tend to suffer from trachoma, and medicines are eagerly sought from climbing parties. It is as well to know this and come suitably supplied although anyone who has travelled in remote areas will expect to be asked for assistance in curing all manner of complaints.

Cilo and Sat are really two separate regions forming part of the same chain or complex of mountains in the Hakkari Province of Turkey; but they differ quite considerably in character. The line of division between the two groups of peaks is the deep gulf of the Rudbare Sin.

The peaks of Sat Dağ are thinner, more delicate and possibly more complex. The area is studded with lakes of which Bay Göl (Bay Lake) is the supreme example for the beauty of its setting and the splendour of the peaks surrounding it.

Cilo Dağ has more formidable walls and higher mountains, including at least two four-thousanders (Resko or Gelyas, 4,168 metres, and Suppa Durak, 4,060 metres).

For readers who may be unable to journey to the Cilo/Sat, or acquire any of the recommended reading material, I will end this account of eastern Turkish mountains by quoting two brief passages, one from a lecture given at Robert College in 1969, and the other from an article in *Blackwood's Magazine* published in 1966—a couple of vignettes which recall the sights, sounds and scents, and perhaps convey something of the flavour of travel in these mountains:

Sat Dağ: Camp at Bay Lake in June 1966
'What I will ask you to imagine is a great amphitheatre, with rock walls going up, in places, for almost 3,000 feet (900 metres); a cirque of steep snowfields and glaciers coming down to a green lake studded with ice floes. Some of this can be divined from the photographs. But the sounds and texture of life at 2,950 metres above sea-level in such surroundings and so extraordinarily sundered from all human contact can only really be *experienced*. One woke in the morning around 3.15 a.m. to the liquid trill, the four-note call of the giant partridge. The occasional rumble of snow and ice avalanches across the lake would punctuate the day. And every now and then the crash of a rock fall from the West side of the cirque gave a frisson to our camp. Mostly we would be out climbing, exploring, visiting other lakes and valleys, on 10 and even 14 hour days; but if in camp our lives were regulated by the rotation of the planet. The first sun would hit us at 7.30 a.m. (four hours after sunrise); and from then until five to three we were in

the burning glass rays and intense radiation of tropical light. The tents became red-hot and uninhabitable unless brailed; when brailed they were assaulted by clouds of giant flies. But at five to three the sun dipped behind the western walls and a sudden chill invaded the arena. By five p.m. we would be preparing for dinner and bed, and watching the lake start to freeze in front of us. Later on a brilliant moon would hang above spiky peaks, still orange in a light that had long since left us. People would sit around in duvet jackets, enjoying an evening drink and discussing the incidents of the day. At night the constellations blazed with unimaginable brilliance.

'Such was life at Bay Lake for the alpinist/traveller, a remote and hard-to-attain Hesperides—a place where some of us lived for a time completely free of every worldly link, self-reliant and untrammelled by any human agency or service, something which is healthful and cleansing to achieve, if only once in a lifetime.'

Cilo Dağ: Evening near a nomad settlement (or Zoma) (From 'Hakkari—1965', *Blackwood's Magazine*, April 1966)

'The day drew to its close under lowering, thundery skies. As we ate our supper in the dusk, the blue smoke from the Kurdish lines curled up into the evening and the camp fires from a hundred goat-hair tents pricked the gloom. Dogs bayed and the flocks gave occasional tongue. But gradually the small sounds from the *Zoma* became ever more muted. A faint acrid smell from the burning of dried dung floated over our camp. Then all was silence under the stars. Down in the valley, the steady note, attenuated by distance, of the glacier torrent, supplied only a faint undertone. Slowly, as we withdrew into sleep, it faded away.'

HISTORY AND BIBLIOGRAPHY OF THE CILO/SAT

1901 F. R. Maunsell (*Geographical Journal*, Vol. XVIII, p. 121, Map P 248).

1909 B. Dickson (*Geographical Journal*, 1910, p. 357).

1937 Dr. H. Bobek (*Petermanns Geographische Mitteilurger*, Vol. 84, 1938, pp. 152–62, 215–28). *Die Alpen*, 1939, No. 7, pp. 254–61 (H. Kuntscher). This was a major geological and cartographical expedition during which several high peaks were climbed.

1945 M. Uyanik and party.

1948 L. O. Çikigil and party.

1955–62 Dennis Hill made numerous journeys in Turkey. *My Travels in Turkey* (including Cilo Dağ and Sat), George Allen and Unwin, 1964.

1954? H. Bogel and F. Henkel (*Jahrbuch des Deutschen Alpenvereins*, 1954)

M. Blumenthal, *Die Alpen*, 1954, p. 223.

1956 Austrian expedition—very active (*Die Alpen*, 1966, p. 231). (See also *Österreichische Alpenzeitung*, No. 11, p. 1599. November 1956.)

1957 British expedition (see *Scottish Mountaineering Club Journal*, 1958, pp. 235–44).

1958 Austrian expedition (see *Österreichische Touristenzeitung*, Folge 3, March 1959, p. 25, and *Österreichische Alpenzeitung*, No. 1308, pp. 175–9).

1962 München Expedition (Berggeist section), B. Maidl, R. Steuer, (*Jahrbuch des Deutschen Alpenvereins*, 1963), expedition to the Sat (*Die Alpen*, 1966, p. 231).

1965 This was the first year of more numerous British expeditions. S. E. P. Nowill and party (A.J., No. 311, November 1965, p. 313). R. Fedden and party (see A.J., No. 312, May 1966, and *Geographical Magazine*, December 1965).

Monica Jackson and Party (*Turkish Time Machine* by Monica Jackson, Hodder and Stoughton).

1966 (*a*) Italian expedition (see *Alpinismus* 8, 1967, p. 44).

(*b*) Dux Schnieder (see *Die Alpen*, 1966, p. 231).

(*c*) S. E. P. Nowill and party to Sat Dağ (A.J., No. 314, May 1967, pp. 117–21).

(*d*) See also Nowill article in *Blackwood's Magazine*, April 1966, pp. 313–328, 'Hakkari 1965',

(*e*) and Speakman's article in *Blackwood's Magazine*, December 1966, pp. 509–519, 'Beyond the Great Zap'.

(*f*) Nottingham Climbers' club leads a 30-strong Youth Club/ Schoolboy expedition to Cilo Dag (see A.J., No. 314, May 1967, pp. 129–131).

(*g*) Austrian Expedition (*Bergkamerad*, February 1967, pp. 231–3).

1967 (*a*) J. Cheesman and party (Buxton).

(*b*) B. Royal and party (Nottingham/Staffs.).

(*c*) Polish expedition (see *Alpinismus* 3, 1968, p. 53).

(*d*) München expedition (see *Alpinismus* 3, 1968, p. 53).
(See also general account in this edition by the Turkish traveller Muvaffak Uyanik.)

(*e*) 1967 *Journal of the Association of British Members of the Swiss Alpine Club*, pp. 23–31.

(*f*) University of Birmingham expedition (see *Stoates*, No. 10, 1968, pp. 14–18).

(*g*) French/Swiss Expedition (*Die Alpen* 4, 1968, pp. 244–50).

(*h*) *Ladies' Alpine Club Journal*, 1967, pp. 3–12.

1968 (*a*) Polish Expedition (Maciej Popko, Warszawa 86, Ul, Podlesna 52/108, Poland).

(*b*) Nottingham Expedition (B. Royal, c/o C.C.P.R., St. Anne's Chambers, St. Anne's Road, Nottingham).

(*c*) German expedition (Hans Thoma, *Alpinismus*, November/December 1968).

1969 Alpine Climbing Group Bulletin, 1969—Supplement on Cilo Dağ and Sat Dağ.

La Montagne et Alpinisme, No. 73, Juin 1969, pp. 90–96, 'Les Montagnes de Turquie' by Nowill.

Bibliography

Abbreviations: Camb. Anc. Hist. for *Cambridge Ancient History*; Fasc. for Fascicle

Akurgal, Ekrem: *The Art of the Hittites*, Thames and Hudson, 1962.

Allen, W. E. D.: *History of the Georgian People*, Kegan Paul, 1932.

Anatolian Studies: Journal of the British Institute of Archaeology at Ankara.

And, Metin: *A History of Theatre and Popular Entertainment in Turkey*, Forum Press, Ankara, 1963–4.

Arfa, Hassan: *The Kurds*, Oxford University Press, 1966.

Aslanapa, Oktay: *Turkish Arts*, Doğan Kardeş Press, Istanbul, 1961.

Badger, G. P.: *The Nestorians and their Rituals*, London, 1852.

Barnett, R. D.: *Phrygia and the Peoples of Anatolia in the Iron Age*, Camb. Anc. Hist. Fasc. 56, 1967.

Barthold, W.: *Turkestan down to the Mongol Invasion*, translated from the Russian by W. Barthold and H. A. R. Gibb, Luzac, 1958.

Braidwood, R. J.: *The Near East and the Foundation for Civilisation*, Third Printing, Eugene, Oregon, 1962.

Bryer, A.: 'Edward I and the Mongols', *History Today*, October 1964.

Çambel, Halet, and Braidwood, R. J.: 'Report on the Çayönü Excavations', *American Journal of Archaeology*, Vol. 73, No. 2, April 1969.

Catalogue of the Arts Council Exhibition of Hittite Art, London, 1964.

Catholic Encyclopedia, Robert Appleton Co., New York, 1907–14.

Çelebi, Evliya: *Seyahat Name*.

Charanis, P.: *The Armenians in the Byzantine Empire*, Livraria Bertrand, Lisbon, 1963.

Cook, J. M.: *The Greek in Ionia and the East*, Thames and Hudson, 1962.

Bibliography

Creswell, K. A. C.: *The Muslim Architecture of Egypt*, Oxford University Press, 1959.

Crossland, R. A.: *Immigrants from the North* (for early languages in Anatolia), Camb. Anc. Hist. Fasc. 60, 1967.

Dictionnaire d'Archéologie Chrétienne, Letouzey and Ané, Paris, 1907.

Encyclopaedia of Islam: new edition currently appearing in fascicles.

Erdmann, Kurt: *Der Türkische Teppich des 15 Jahrhunderts*, Istanbul University Faculty of Letters Publication No. 715, undated.

Esin, Ufuk, and Benedict, Peter: 'Recent Developments in the Pre-history of Anatolia', *Current Anthropology*, 1963.

Fedden, R.: 'In the Steps of the Argonauts', *Geographical Magazine*, August 1964.

Forster, E. M.: *Alexandria: a History and Guide*, Whitehead Morris, Alexandria, 1938.

Gadd, C. J.: 'The Harran Inscriptions of Nabonidus', *Anatolian Studies*, Vol. VIII, 1958.

Garrod, D. A. E., and Clark, J. G. D.: *Primitive Man in Egypt, Western Asia and Europe*, Camb. Anc. Hist. Fasc. 30, 1965.

Gibbon, Edward: *Decline and Fall of the Roman Empire*.

Gough, Michael: *The Early Christians*, Thames and Hudson, 1961.

Gurney, O. R.: *The Hittites*, Pelican Books, 1964; *Anatolia c. 1750–1600 B.C.*, Camb. Anc. Hist. Fasc. II, 1965; *Anatolia c. 1600–1380 B.C.*, Camb. Anc. Hist. Fasc. 44, 1966.

Hill, D., and Grabar, O.: *Islamic Architecture and its Decoration*, Faber and Faber, 1964.

Hills, D. C.: *My Travels in Turkey*, Allen and Unwin, 1964.

Hogarth, D. G.: *Accidents of an Antiquary's Life*, Macmillan, 1910; *The Wandering Scholar*, Oxford University Press, 1925.

Jones, A. H. M.: *Cities of the Eastern Roman Empire*, Oxford University Press, 1937.

Kansu, Sevket Aziz: 'Stone Age Cultures in Turkey', *American Journal of Archaeology*, No. 51, 1947.

Lambert, W. G., and Gurney, O. R.: 'The Sultantepe Tablets', *Anatolian Studies*, Vol. IV, 1954.

Lawrence, T. E.: *Oriental Assembly*, Williams and Norgate, 1939.

Lloyd, Seton: *Early Highland Peoples of Anatolia*, Thames and Hudson, 1967; 'The Sin-Temples of Harran', *Listener*, April 24, 1952.

Lynch, H. F. B.: *Armenia*. Reprint by Khayats, Beirut, 1967.

Mellaart, J.: *Earliest Civilisations of the Near East*, Thames and Hudson,

Bibliography

1965; *Anatolia c. 4000–2300 B.C.*, Camb. Anc. Hist. Fasc. 8, 1965; *Anatolia Before c. 4000 B.C. and 2300–1750 B.C.*, Camb. Anc. Hist. Fasc. 20, 1967.

Mellink, M. J.: *Archaeology in Asia Minor*. Digests in *American Journal of Archaeology*.

Mnatsakanyan, A.: 'Treasures from an Armenian Lake', *Illustrated London News*, Arch. Sect. 2265, April 15, 1967.

Morier, James: *Ayesha, Maid of Kars*, Goubaud and Son, 1837; *A Journey through Persia, Armenia and Asia Minor to Constantinople*, Longman, Hurst, Rees, Orme and Brown, 1812; *A Second Journey through Persia, Armenia and Asia Minor*, Longman etc. 1818.

New Catholic Encyclopedia: McGraw-Hill, Washington, 1967.

Oxford Dictionary of the Christian Church: ed. Cross, O.U.P., 1957.

Piotrovskii, B. B.: *Urartu*, Evelyn, Adams and Mackay, 1967.

Pliny the Elder: *Natural History*.

Pliny the Younger: *Letters*, translated by B. Radice, Penguin Classics, 1963.

Ramsay, Sir William: 'The Intermixture of Races in Asia Minor', *Proceedings of the British Academy*, Vol. VII, 1917.

Rice, D. Talbot: *Art of the Byzantine Era*, Thames and Hudson, 1963; (editor) *The Church of Haghia Sophia at Trebizond*, Edinburgh, 1968.

Rice, T. Talbot: *The Seljuks*, Thames and Hudson, 1961.

Sanat Tarih Yıllığı 1964–5: University of Istanbul Institute of Fine Arts.

Segal, J. B.: 'Pagan Syriac Monuments in the Vilayet of Urfa', *Anatolian Studies*, Vol. III, 1953.

Stark, Freya: *Rome on the Euphrates*, John Murray, 1966; *Riding to the Tigris*, John Murray, 1959.

Strabo: *Geographica*.

Uyanik, Muvaffak, and Özdoğan, Mehmet: 'Stone Age Cultures in Turkey', *Belleten*, Ankara, 1968.

Warkworth, Lord: *Notes from a Diary in Asiatic Turkey*, Arnold, 1898.

Wheeler, Sir Mortimer: *Rome Beyond the Imperial Frontiers*, Pelican Books, 1955.

Williams, Gwyn: *Turkey: a Traveller's Guide and History*, Faber and Faber, 1967, second impression 1970.

Wright and Godus: Distribution and Utility of Obsidian from Lake Van Sources between 7500 and 3500 B.C., *American Journal of Archaeology*, Vol. 73, No. 1, 1969.

Bibliography

Xenophon: *The Persian Expedition*, translated by Rex Warner, Penguin Classics, 1967.

Yetkin, Özgüc, Sümer, Ülken, Cağatay and Karamağaralı: *Turkish Architecture*, translated by Ahmet Edip Uysal, Ankara University Press, 1965.

Index

The order of the Turkish alphabet is followed; C before Ç, O before Ö, S before Ş, U before Ü.

Abraham at Urfa, 166–7
Adilcevaz, 120–1; statue from, 104
Aghtamar Island, 115–18; church on, 116–17; relief sculptures on church at, 116–17
Ağrı (Karaköse), 202–3
Ağrı Dağ, *see* Ararat
Ahlat, 122–3; Seljuk cemetery at, 122–3
Akkoyunlu, the, 86
akritai, 88
Alexander the Great, 58–9
Alp Arslan, 73–4
Altınova, 153
Altıntepe, 187–9
Amida (Diyarbakır), 155
anchovies at Trabzon, 220
Ani, 211–13
animals, 31
Antep, *see* Gaziantep
Antiochos I, 180
apples of Malatya, 181–2
Arabs, the, 87
Arap Baba, tomb of, 149–50
Ararat (Ağrı Dağ) 202–5, 238–40; James Morier on, 203–4
Aras River (Araxes), 201
Ardahan, 214
Ardeşen, 226
Armenians, the 51–8; in Byzantium, 71
Artuks (Urtukids, Ortakids), the, 84–6
Artvin, 214–15

Artvin province, flora and fauna of, 215–16
Assyrian attacks on Urartu, 44–5
Aznavur, fortress of, at Patnos, 120

Bağtepe (Halenzie), 139–40
Balawat, record of Hittites at, 43
Baliki tribe, the, 121
bandits, 27
bastırma, 199
Başkale, 129, 241
Batman, 142
Battal Gazi, 184
Bayburt, 229
Beşiri, 142
Beys and Emirs, 86
Bingöl, 145
Bingöl Kale, the peak of, 146
Bingöl Massif, flowers of the, 145; trout in the, 145
Birecik, 176
Bir Yacub (Jacob's Well) at Harran, 171
Bitlis, 132–4
Bolaman, 217
boustrophedon, 40
bride-seekers, 202
Bulanık, 145
Byzantines, the, 70–3

camping, 24
Caracalla, 172

Index

Carreg Cennen Castle, 109
Carrhae, the Battle of, 70, 172
cat-and-dog played at Hopa, 226
cats of Divriği, 190–1, of Van; 27
Caucasus Mountains, legends about the, 121
Cavuştepe, Urartian citadel of, 128
chicory flowers, 119–20
Cilo and Sat Mountains, 235, 240–3
Cimmerian incursion, the, 48
Cimmerians, the, at Toprak Kale, 110
climate, 29–30; of eastern Anatolia, 233
climbing, 26, 233–42
Colchis, 69
Commagene, 59
Comnenes, the, 72; at Sumela, 227–8; at Trebizond, 223
Constantinople sacked by Crusaders, 79
Crassus at Harran (Carrhae), 172
Croydon, bell cast at, 195
Crusade, the First, 79; the Second, 79; the Third, 79
Crusaders, the, 79

Çaldıran, the Battle of, 88; weather prophet at, 119
Çambaşı, Lake, 217
Çamli-Hemşi, 226
Çatal Hüyük, 19
Çayönü, excavations at, 36
Çetinkaya, 191
Çildir, Lake, 214
Çobandede, curative pool at, 202; thief-catcher of, 202
Çobandede Bridge, 201–2
Çölemerik (Hakkari), 130
Çoruh River, 229

Danishmends, the, 74, 84
deli bal (mad honey), 215–16
Der Zafaran Monastery, 161
Digor, 213
Divriği, 190–1
Diyarbakır, 155–9; Ataturk's kiosk at, 156; the Deliler Han at, 157; food at, 159; industries of, 159; mosques and minarets, 158–9; the museum, 158; the Ulu Cami, 157; the walls, 155–7; the Zinciriye Medrese (museum), 157–8
Doğubeyazit, 26, 205–7; smuggled tea at, 206–7

early Christianity in Asia Minor, 69
Edessa, 164 and n. 1
Elazığ, 147–8; the grapes of, 148; the museum, 147
Elbistan, 185
Eleşkirt, 202
epic of Amir Danishmend, 84
Erebuni, Hittite palace at, 43–4
Ergani, 154
Erzincan, 186–7
Erzurum, 193–200; architecture of, 194–7; crafts of, 194–5; the frozen cat, 194; James Morier on, 199–200; University of, 198–9
Eski Malatya, see Malatya
Eski Pertek, 153
Etruria, 189
Evliya Çelebi at Divriği, 190; at Erzincan, 187; at Erzurum, 194; at Malatya, 181

Fedden, Robin, on the Pontic Forests, 225
Fertile Crescent, the, 18, 33
fishing, 25–6
flora and fauna of Artvin province, 215–6; of Hakkari, 241

Galatians, the, 59–60
Gaziantep, food, fruit, weaving, products, 178
Genghiz Khan, 80, 84
Georgian architecture, 82; language, 81
Georgians, the, 81–2
Gevaruk, Lake, 241
Gilgamesh, 41, 168
Giresun, 218–19
glaciers, 241
Greek fire, 87
Gregory the Illuminator, Saint, 53–4; at Erzincan, 187

Index

Gümüşhane, 229
Güzelsu, 128

Hacılar, 19
Haci Muhittin, 131
Hakkari, 127; flora and fauna, 130; the town, 130–1
Halaf culture, 35
han at Malatya, 184
Harput, 148–50; Artuk and Akkoyun buildings at, 148; the castle, 149; Meryem Ana Church at, 148; tomb of Arap Baba at, 149–50
Harran, 170–5; the Temple of Sin at, 171; T. E. Lawrence at, 170 n. 2, 174
Harşıt Valley, the, 229
Hasankayf, 162
Hattian culture, 38
Hazar Gölü, 154
hazel plantations, 226; nuts, 218
hellenisation, 58–9
heroic poetry, 88
Hila Caves, rock drawings at the, 154
Hittite sculpture at Ivriz and Malatya, 18
Hittites, the 39–42; the art of the, 40–1
Holbein carpets, 77
honey, 215–16
Hopa, 226
Horasan, 202
Hoşap Castle, 128–9

Ibn Tulun, 92
Ibrahim Hakki, 140–1
iğde (oleaster), 118
Ilhans, the Persian, 80
Ishak Paşa Saray, 205–6
Ivriz, rock sculpture at, 18

Jacob and Rachel at Harran, 171
John Curcuas, 87
Julian, the Emperor, at Harran, 172

Kaçkar Dağ, 29, 215–16, 231, 236–7
kadayif, 218
Kalecik, 119; reception at, 112

Karaköse (Ağrı), 202–3
Karakoyunlu, the, 86
Karaz, early Bronze Age site at, 37
Karkemiş, 176–7
Karliova, 146
Kars, 208–10
Kazıklı Dağ, Pass of, 228
Keban, 151
Keban Dam, the, 151–3
Keban Dam area, Bronze Age houses in the, 37
Kefkalesi (Adilcevaz), 120–1
Keman, 191
Keykubad I, 75
Kiliç Arslan II, 74
Kop Dağ Pass, 229
kopuz, 78
Korucutepe, 153
Kotur valley, the, 114
Kose Dağ, 201–2
Köprüköy, 201–2
Kurdish, the dialects of, 61
Kurdish crafts, 139; dress, 130–1; singer, 136
Kurds, the, 61–5, 88
Kurtalan, 142
Kültepe, Assyrian merchants at, 38–9
Küpkıran, 203

Lawrence, T. E., at Harran, 170 n. 2, 174
Laz, the, 83, 227; language, 83
Laz, herdsmen, 216
Lynch, H. F. B., at Ani, 212; on Ararat, 204; on Erzurum, 195; on Kars, 209; on the Pontic Forests, 225–6; on Pontic vegetation, 216

Macaulay, Rose, *The Towers of Trebizond*, 220
Maçka, 227
Maden, 154, 229; copper and chromium mining at, 154–5
Malatya, 179, 181–4; crafts, 181; Eski Malatya, 182–4; Lion Gate of Eski Malatya, 18
Maraş, 179

Index

Marco Polo at Erzincan, 187
Mardin, 160–2; the Citadel, 160–1; the mosques of, 161
medrese, the, 93
Midyat, 162
minaret, the, 91–3
minerals, 31–2
Mitanni, the Kingdom of, 39
Mithraism, 51
Mithridates VI of Pontus, 68
Mongols, the, 80–1
Morier, James, on Ararat, 203–4; on Erzurum, 195 n. 2, 199–200; on Kars, 209–10; on the Yazidis, 62
Moslem architecture, 90–3
Mossynoici, curious customs of the, 50
motoring, 23–5
Munzur Dağlar, 186–7, 237–8
Muradiye, Castle of, 119
Musasir, Assyrian attack on, 44–5
Muş and its province, 144

Nabonidus at Harran, 173
Neolithic cultures, 19, 34
Nergal and Ereshkigal, 169
Nestorian church, 129–30
Nestorians, the, 66–7
ney, 78
Nicephoros Phocas, 87
Nimrut Dağ (Adiyaman), 179–80
Nimrut Dağ near Tatvan, 124–5
Nizip, 176

obsidian, 34
olive cultivation, 176
Ordu, 218
otlupeynir (herb cheese), 101–2
Ottomans, the (Osmanli), 87–9
Ovacık, 186
ozan, 78

Öğrenburc, 112–14
Özalp, 113

Palaeolithic Man, 33–4
Pasinler, 201
Persian Royal Road, the, 51

Persians, the, 48–51
Perşembe, 217
Peryplus, the, 69
Peter the Hermit, 79
Phrygians, the, 47–8
Poem of the Righteous Sufferer, the, 169
Pontic Mountains, 30, 216
Pulur, Bronze Age houses at, 37, 153

Rebecca at Harran, 171
Rize, 224–5
Romans, the, 67–70
Russian frontier, the, 25
Russians, the, at Kars, 208–10

Sabian worship at Urfa, 167
salt at Van, 102
Sarıkamiş, 208
Sat Dağ, 234; flora and fauna on, 237
sea routes to Turkey, 24
Seleucids, the, 58–9
Seljuk architecture, 75–9, 93; carpet-weaving, 77; *han*, 78–9; wood-carving, 77–8
Seljuks, the, 73–9
Sevan, Lake, 42
Sèvres, the Treaty of, 63
Shanidar, 34
shooting, 26
Siirt, 138–9
Silvan (Miyafarikin), 143
Siyah Kalem, 81
smuggling, 177
spring water, 131
Sultantepe, 168–9
Sumatar, 170
Sumela Monastery, 227–8
Sümbül Dağ, 130
Süphan Dağ, 29, 118–20, 232

Tahir and Tahir Pass, 202
Tahtaci, the, 50
Tamburlaine (Timur Lenk), 87
tandır, 125 and n. 1
Tatos Mountains, 215
Tatvan, 124–6
tea production, 224–5

Index

Tektek Dağ, 174
Tillo, 139–41
Timur Lenk (Tamburlaine), 81
Tirebolu, 219
Toprak Kale, 108–11; flowers at, 111; underground palace at, 108–9
Trabzon, 219–24; Church of Santa Sophia, 222–3; Soliman the Magnificent born at, 221; University of, 224
Trebizond, 71–2; Geoffrey of Langley at, 72
trout, 191, 217, 227, 229; fishing at Çatak, 118
tuğra, the, 78
Turkish ambassadors to Byzantium, 71; baths at Pasinler, 201
turpentine nut tree (butum) (pistacia terebinthas), 141

ulu cami, 91
Urartian objects from Altıntepe, 188
Urartians, the, 42–7
Urartu, the architecture of, 44–5; the art of, 46–7
Urfa, 163–8; the architecture of, 165; a curious restaurant at, 167; the sacred fish pools of, 165–6

Ünye, 217

Van, accommodation and food in, 101–2; ancient irrigation at, 31; approach to, 99–100; education in, 102–3; Eski Van, the old city, 101, 108; history of, 100–1; market quarter of, 102; the museum, 103–4
Van, Lake, 29, 104–5, 232; fish in, 105; swimming in, 104–5
Van Kalesi, rock chambers at, 107
Varag, the Monastery of, 127
Varto, 145
Vavuk Pass, the, 229
Vazelon, the Monastery of, 228

Walter the Penniless, 74, 79
Warkworth, Lord, at Doğubeyazit, 205; at Kars, 209

Xenophon, 228; and the March of the Ten Thousand, 48–50; on beer, 201; on honey, 215

Yazidis, the, 62
Yedi Kilise, 127

Zab River, the, 129–30
Zigana Pass, the, 228